Living History

On the Front Lines for Israel and the Jews, 2003–2015

Phyllis Chesler

Copyright © Phyllis Chesler
Jerusalem 2015/5775

All rights reserved. No part of this publication may be translated, reproduced, stored in a retrieval system or transmitted, in any form or by any means, electronic, mechanical, photocopying, recording or otherwise, without express written permission from the publishers.

Cover Design: Leah Ben Avraham/Noonim Graphics
Typesetting: Irit Nachum
Author photograph on back cover: Joan L. Roth

ISBN: 978-965-229-854-6

1 3 5 7 9 8 6 4 2

Gefen Publishing House Ltd.
6 Hatzvi Street
Jerusalem 94386, Israel
972-2-538-0247
orders@gefenpublishing.com

Gefen Books
11 Edison Place
Springfield, NJ 07081
516-593-1234
orders@gefenpublishing.com

www.gefenpublishing.com

Printed in Israel

Send for our free catalog

Library of Congress Control Number: 2015942356

Table of Contents

Acknowledgements	ix
Introduction	1
1. The Anti-Semitic Intelligentsia (8/21/03)	7
2. The Brownshirts of Our Time (11/19/03)	11
3. Jews on the Precipice (5/19/04)	16
4. Listener-Sponsored Hate Radio on the Left Coast (6/18/04)	21
5. The Race Against Lies (8/11/04)	27
6. Duke's Terror Conference (October 2004)	33
7. Murder, Lies, and Videotape (11/1/05)	38
8. The Lamentable Case of Joan Scott (2/21/06)	43
9. Academic Goon Squad (6/16/06)	50
10. Manifesto for Survival (12/13/06)	55
11. Celluloid Fantasies (2/14/07)	60
12. Standing Up For the Truth Should Not Make You a Hero (10/24/07)	63
13. *Ms.* Magazine Fails the Cause of Freedom (1/15/08)	68
14. Obama Is Our First Muslim Presidential Contender (2/26/08)	72

15. Stop the Israel Bashing In the Media and the Jews Will No Longer Be Hated (5/21/08–5/22/08)   75
16. Staged Palestinian Hoaxes in the First Lebanon War (5/23/08)   77
17. A Day in the Life of the *New York Islamic Times* (6/23/08)   79
18. A Young Jew Is Savagely Beaten In Paris (6/24/08)   83
19. A Must-See Pro-Israel Film (11/5/08)   85
20. The Palestinian Con: Paying Off the Thugs (11/25/08)   88
21. Madoff the Jew: The Media's Hypocritical Obsession with the Fraudster's Faith (12/23/08)   90
22. Israel's Quiet Nightmare (1/6/09)   92
23. British Lies (1/26/09)   96
24. Jews: To the Muslim Gas Chamber (1/30/09)   101
25. Jewish Students Cornered, Humiliated, Cursed At York University (2/16/09)   106
26. Israeli Tennis Team under Guard in Sweden: Anti-Semitism and the Politicization of Sports (3/8/09)   109
27. Our Eternal Struggle (3/25/09)   111
28. Pierre Rehov: The Lion in Exile (4/1/09)   115
29. From Treblinka to Glen Cove, Long Island (4/6/09)   121
30. The Legacy of Islamic Anti-Semitism. A Book Review (4/10/09)   124
31. The Blood Libels at National Geographic Magazine (5/18/09)   127
32. Homegrown Islamic Jihad in the Bronx (5/21/09)   132
33. End the Illegal Occupation of Jerusalem (6/17/09)   135
34. Vienna, My City Of Dreams/Nightmares (12/14/09)   139

35. Artists4Israel 2 the Rescue (1/7/10) — 142
36. *Lancet* Study Blames Palestinian Wife-Beating on Israel (1/24/10) — 146
37. Israel's Rebirth "A Boring Story" to U.S. Jews: An Interview with American Zionist Hero Dr. David Gutmann (3/29/10) — 152
38. Jews Confront the Abyss: "The Absence of Outrage Is Outrageous" (4/13/10) — 156
39. The Palestinians Already Have Two States: The Truth According to Khaled Abu Toameh (4/15/10) — 161
40. Jews Not Wanted on Campus If They Support Israel—Not Even at Brandeis (5/3/10) — 165
41. Turkey Attacks Israel: Does The Old Ottoman Empire Want to Lead the Caliphate? (5/31/10) — 169
42. Alice Walker: Stop Telling Lies about Israel (6/6/10) — 173
43. An Avalanche of Anti-Israel Propaganda (7/6/10) — 176
44. Just Out: *Time* Magazine's Latest Blood Libel about Israel (9/4/10) — 178
45. A New Kind of Theater: Actors Against Israel (9/15/10) — 182
46. Will the World Learn the Lessons of the Holocaust in Time? (10/4/10) — 185
47. Darkest Anti-Semitism in Holland (10/12/10) — 188
48. Anti-Semitism Cannot Be Equated with Islamophobia (10/19/10) — 192
49. Israel's PR War Needs Stuxnet (12/13/10) — 195
50. Is It Not Torture When the Prisoner Is a Jew? (12/22/10) — 197
51. Peretz-the-Leftist Defames Pollard as "Repellent Viper" (1/3/11) — 201

52. Israeli Apartheid Week: Political Theater at Its Worst (3/8/11) — 205
53. The "Palestinianization" of Lesbian Activism (3/22/11) — 209
54. The Goldstone Recantation (4/4/11) — 212
55. The Communist University of New York Honors Anti-Zionist Celebrity Playwright Tony Kushner (May 2011) — 215
56. Equating Anti-Semitism with "Islamophobia" (5/31/11) — 220
57. Islam and Anti-Semitism at Yale (6/13/11) — 223
58. Unmasked: Judeophobia. A Film Review (10/19/11) — 227
59. There Never Was a "Palestinian" People. Read Hadriani Relandi (12/12/11) — 231
60. Up Against a Faux-istinian Culture of Human Sacrifice (11/19/12) — 235
61. *The Grand Deception*: A Film Review (06/20/13) — 238
62. UNICEF's Blood Libel against Israel (6/20/13) — 241
63. Christmas in Londonistan (12/24/13) — 244
64. Buried by the *Times* (12/29/13) — 246
65. *J Street Challenge*: Truth Trumps Lies (2/18/14) — 250
66. Hijacking Feminism to Attack Israel at Women's Studies Association Conference (6/6/14) — 254
67. White House's "Condolences" for Murdered Israeli Teens Are Not Enough (6/30/14) — 258
68. An American-Jewish Hero in Israel (7/4/14) — 261
69. A Letter to My People (7/21/14) — 265
70. Condemnation of Israel Persists Even as UN Official Admits Hamas Wages War from UN Buildings (7/31/14) — 267

71. West Bank Feminist Academics Condemn Israel (!)
    for Promoting Rape, Sexism, and Genocide
    (8/7/2014)   270
72. *The Lancet* Specialty: Anti-Zionism, not Scientific
    Medicine (8/4/14–8/5/14)   273
73. Gaza in Manhattan: Individual Jews Held Guilty
    and Attacked (8/26/14)   277
74. Body and Soul: The State of the Jewish Nation.
    A Film Review (10/13/14)   280
75. Opera v. Truth: *The Death of Klinghoffer*
    (10/19/14–10/24/14)   284
76. Je Suis *Charlie Hebdo* Aussi (1/8/15)   293
77. #Je Suis Juif (I am a Jew) (1/9/15)   296
78. What the West Must Do in order to Survive
    (1/13/15)   299
79. Everything Has Been Turned on Its Head
    (1/15/15)   302
80. Jihad by Civilian (1/21/15)   308
81. Portugal Extends Olive Branch to Jews Violently
    Expelled in 1536 (1/23/15)   311
82. *New York Times* Lethal Anti-Israel Journalism
    Strikes Again (1/26/15)   314
83. France Implores Jews Not to Leave, Offers Military
    Protection (1/28/15)   317
84. Obama's Boys Campaign from Tel Aviv – Ted Cruz
    Responds (1/30/15)   322
85. Sadistic Death Pornography Coming to a Theater
    Near You (2/4/15)   327
86. Netanyahu's Speech Unites Congress—
    and Diminishes Obama (3/3/15)   330

Acknowledgements

I wish to thank the entire team at Gefen for their enthusiasm and efficiency: Ilan Greenfield, Lynn Douek, Marion Rosen, Casriel Silver, Andy Kohlenberg and above all, Murray Greenfield, who founded Gefen Publishing House.

I deeply appreciate the work of my agents Jane Dystel and Miriam Goderich, who helped me with the contracts that led to both the 2015 Gefen edition of *The New Anti-Semitism* and to *Living History. On The Front Lines for Israel and the Jews 2003-2015*.

My research and editorial assistant, Jennifer C. Werner has been an incredible asset in copy-editing and proofing both these works and I am in her debt. Unbelievably, we met through Craigslist—truly a destined miracle.

I am grateful for the invaluable funding and intellectual support of Dr. Daniel Pipes of the Middle East Forum; Cornelia Foster Wood's loyal funding and loving friendship; and donations made by appreciative readers, especially: Aquarius Consulting (Barbara Chasen and Raphael Rubenstein), Stephen Cohen, Lillian Glowinsky, Bruce and Susan Heitler, Dr. Lynne Hennecke, and Abigail Martin.

I am proud to be working at the same time as the very best pro-Israel and anti-terrorism advocates are also on the job; it is a privilege to serve with them. You will find some of their names or the names of their websites in the Selected Internet

Resource section of *The New Anti-Semitism*. Of special note: Yigal Carmon (Middle East Media Research Institute), Omri Ceren (The Israel Project), Commander J.J. Dyer of the *Optimistic Conservative*, Steven Emerson (Investigative Project on Terrorism), Carolyn Glick, Dr. Mordechai Kedar, Dr. Richard Landes, Itamar Marcus (Palestinian Media Watch), Lauri Regan, Esq., Dr. Charles Small, the founder of the Institute for the Study of Global Antisemitism and Policy (ISGAP) and Gerald Steinberg (NGO Monitor).

I am indebted to all the websites and newspapers where my work has appeared: *Breitbart, FrontPage Magazine, Hadassah Magazine*, Institute for the Study of Global Antisemitism and Policy (ISGAP), *Israel National News, Jerusalem Post*, the *Jewish Press, National Post, NewsReal Blog, New York Post, PJ Media, Times of Israel*, and *World Jewish Digest*.

I have been moved and honored by the reviews of the new edition of *The New Anti-Semitism* which were recently written by Fern Sidman, Lori Lowenthal Marcus, Jerry Gordon, Rochel Sylvetsky, and Stewart Ain.

Finally, I must thank: Susan L. Bender, Esq., who has been the "wind beneath my sails" in so many ways, both financially and otherwise; Merle Hoffman, who has been a true friend, intellectual sounding board, and gracious country hostess; and my darling son Ariel, daughter-in-law, Shannon (Shanie), and my granddaughters Lily (Aviva Chaya) and Kate (Miri Shoshanna), who root me to earth and make me smile even as I troll "the dark side."

INTRODUCTION

"Now, we are all Israelis" was my immediate and instinctive response to 9/11.

I had been tracking the propaganda war against Israel since the early 1970s and, more recently, the "slow motion Holocaust" that took place in Israel from the moment the carefully planned Al-Aqsa Intifada was unleashed—a Holocaust that remained invisible to most of the world.

In 2001/2002, while Israeli civilians were being blown up in cafes, nightclubs, hotels, buses, and supermarkets, I stopped everything else and began writing around the clock, day after day, even as I was still researching the topic. I documented the Arab Muslim attacks against Jews in Israel from the beginning of the 20th century (when there was no alleged Israeli "occupation" of disputed lands), and the Muslim attacks against the West from 1979 on (when Khomeini came to power).

Given historical reality, I could not bear how the Western media and professoriate covered the bloody Intifada against the Jews. They distorted both facts and context in grotesque ways. Even Orwell would be stunned by the linguistic reversal of reality and the scapegoating of Israel for the very crimes being committed by Arab Islamists.

I published the first edition of *The New Anti-Semitism* in 2003.

It was as if I had not spoken.

Please understand: My previous books had garnered front page reviews in the mainstream media and my face had graced mainstream magazine covers. For the first time in my career, the increasingly left-liberal media was not interested in reviewing my work or in interviewing me. My single interview on CNN was an attack—which I easily fielded. I will never forget that a camera man came out from behind his camera "to shake my hand."

Why was I surprised? After all, I was holding the Western intelligentsia, including the media, responsible for making common cause with Jew-haters, America-haters, and with the most barbaric and misogynist of totalitarian movements. How foolish of me to think that those whom I had exposed would give me a fair hearing.

For the last twenty years of the 20th century, and even more dramatically in the 21st century, Western academic feminists became increasingly Stalinized and Palestinianized. My ideological sisters and daughters were more obsessed with the alleged "occupation" of a country that had never existed—Palestine—than they were with the real occupation of women's bodies globally. They dared not focus on the occupation of Muslim and infidel women's bodies in rapidly, radicalized Muslim countries lest they be shunned as racists and Islamophobes.

Those in the West who benefited from free speech, women's rights, human rights, gay rights, and freedom of religion were defending or at least refusing to criticize the utter absence of such rights in the Muslim world. Instead, and quite bizarrely, academics and journalists had decided that Israel was the worst possible nation on earth and that if Israel were boycotted, or abolished, that gender and racial justice would prevail and the world would be at peace.

By telling the truth, I had become "politically incorrect." Amazingly (but only to me), my ideas were embraced by Christian, Jewish, and Hindu conservatives, Zionists, Muslim dissidents and feminists, and by ex-Muslim anti-Islamists.

I delivered lectures about anti-Semitism/anti-Zionism when I was asked to do so, but I found myself disinvited by the Anti-Defamation League because they viewed me as the "enemy competition." Really, who could make this up?

I was not invited to speak at most liberal synagogues, Jewish Museums, large Jewish organizations, neither privately nor publicly, nor by the many places that had previously welcomed me. This included feminist organizations and groups that I myself had co-founded.

Like a handful of blessed others, I was seen as "too Jewish," "too conservative," an "Islamophobe," and, ironically, as a traitor to the cause of women's freedom.

Sometimes, when I spoke on campus about Israel and anti-Semitism and about Islamic gender and religious apartheid, I required bodyguards.

With some important exceptions, I lost most of my intellectual and feminist friends.

I made new friends and allies.

Whatever disappointments, discomforts, or insults that I may have endured, they paled in comparison to the imprisonment, torture, and murder of my anti-Jihadist counterparts in Europe, North and South America, and in the Muslim world. Unlike some high profile European anti-Islamists, I was not sued for what I said, nor were attempts made on my life.

The subject would not let me go. World events demanded that I continue and expand my work on anti-Semitism. Like Christians, Hindus, and others, the Jews are considered infidels (*kuffars*)—sub-human; Jews are also the most potent and most despised symbol of the entire Judeo-Christian Western post-Enlightenment enterprise.

A Jewish Israel in the heart of the Arab Muslim Middle East makes Muslims crazy—after all, they ejected all 850,000 of their Jews who had lived among them as second- and third-class citizens for millennia. Except for Israel, the Middle East is "*Judenrein*." Persecuted Arab and south Asian Christians are now in flight from an increasingly hostile Muslim world.

Many have said, "It begins with the Jews but it never ends with us." However, if the world refuses to acknowledge and refuses to condemn and abolish the kind of hate propaganda, which inevitably leads to genocide, that world will soon inherit the whirlwind.

And so it has. Europe's willingness to demonize and sacrifice Jewish Israel as a way of appeasing its own hostile "Muslim Street" has not rendered Europe safe. On the contrary. Who can forget the kidnapping and beheading of Western aid workers and journalists in Muslim countries, the Madrid train bombing, the assassination of Theo Van Gogh in Amsterdam, the London subway bombing, the torture-murder of Ilan Halimi, a Jew, in Paris, the murder of four Jews in the Jewish Museum of Belgium, or the massacre of *Charlie Hebdo* journalists and of four Jews shopping for the Sabbath in a kosher supermarket in Paris?

From 2003 through the end of 2014, I wrote more than 200,000 words about anti-Semitism/anti-Zionism. I have selected the most important, most representative, or most unique pieces in this approximately 63,000-word volume.

In some cases, I may have written 4-5 articles about a developing story. Here, I have condensed that into one article. I dropped many articles about important events; I have kept those that went viral or those that deserved a larger readership but got lost instead.

I have included certain kinds of "signature" articles; for example, the betrayal of the Jews and of Western civilization by academics and intellectuals and the infiltration of both popular and high culture by a false and lethal Palestinian narrative.

Re-reading my work humbled me. I realized the extent to which I had repeated my analysis. In cyberspace, one never knows whether a reader has read one's previous works or not and repetition is inevitable and mandatory. Such repetition is not appropriate for a book.

I have also strengthened my language. No longer do I write about "suicide bombers." The word "suicide" immediately inclines us to view someone, even a killer, compassionately—they must have been suffering. Instead, I write about "human homicide bombs." I am increasingly clear about the importance of the propaganda war against the Jews, Israel, and the West—a war that has been led by Westerners who were funded by Arabs, Iranians, and left-wing philanthropists such as George Soros.

I hope that this book will arm students on campus, professors who have an independent mind, future historians, and religious and government leaders.

I want you to remember these events and to never forget them.

These pieces first appeared at *Breitbart*, *FrontPage Magazine*, *Hadassah Magazine*, Institute for the Study of Global Antisemitism and Policy (ISGAP), *Israel National News*, *Jerusalem Post*, the *Jewish Press*, *National Post*, *NewsReal Blog*, *New York Post*, *PJ Media*, *Times of Israel*, and *World Jewish Digest*.

1 THE ANTI-SEMITIC INTELLIGENTSIA

*T*he hit Swedish film *Lilya 4-ever* is a relentless and lyrical work about female sexual slavery. Professor Donna Hughes, who recently testified before the U.S. Senate Foreign Relations Committee about global trafficking, compared the film to Harriet Beecher Stowe's *Uncle Tom's Cabin*. The film depicts the Russian teenager Lilya's abandonment and betrayal by her mother, leaving her vulnerable to a sweet-talking pimp who traffics her into hell and death in Sweden. The film has been shown in many countries where trafficking and brothels flourish. As an artist, the film's director, Lukas Moodysson, empathizes with suffering and distinguishes the victim from the victimizer.

Moodysson refused to allow the film to be shown in Israel. According to Leah Gruenpeter and Nissan Ben Ami of Machon Toda`a (an Israeli Awareness Center), Moodysson "personally bought back the distribution rights for Israel" and would not allow its showing at their upcoming conference opposing such trafficking in Israel. For a decade, Gruenpeter and Ben Ami have been trying to rescue the "Lilyas" in Israel (there are 3,000 a year, mainly from Eastern Europe) who sexually service Israelis: Jews, Arab Muslims, Christians, and tourists. Gruenpeter and Ben Ami are now expanding their fight on behalf of trafficking victims by opposing legislation that would legalize such sexual exploitation.

Moodysson's personal boycott is outrageous but hardly unique. European and North American intellectuals and artists have been systematically excluding and condemning their Israeli counterparts for the so-called crimes of Israel (the Jew among nation-states).

In the last two years, Western academics have called for boycotts and the de-funding of Israeli academics. They have disinvited Israeli scholars, fired Israeli academics, rejected university applications from Israeli students, refused to stage exhibits by Israeli artists or sell textbooks to Israeli universities, written inflammatory and defamatory editorials in prestigious journals condemning Israel for massacres that never occurred, refused to sell Israeli scientists materials that would aid in Israeli research to help Palestinian children, and refused to sell gas kits to Israel that would enable doctors to quickly identify gas and counteract a gas attack against civilians.

In a sense, this singling out of individual intellectuals for punishment is morally similar to what human homicide bombs do when they single out Israeli or American civilians for death.

Such obsessive anti-Zionist positions by intellectuals are examples of Jew-hating. Why? Western intellectuals have not even-handedly condemned academics from China (the Occupier of Tibet), North Korea (which possesses weapons of mass destruction), Rwanda (with its grievous record of genocide), Holland (whose peacekeeping soldiers in Bosnia allowed 8,000 Muslims to be massacred in Srebrenica), or Jordan (which in one month, September of 1970, killed more Palestinians than Israel has killed in 55 years of self-defensive wars).

Western intellectuals have not condemned their counterparts in Arab and Muslim countries who have, for millennia, persecuted Buddhists, Hindus, Jews, and Christians; repressed, jailed, tortured, and murdered Muslim intellectuals; and savagely subordinated women within a system of gender apartheid. For the last 50 years, Arab and Muslim leaders and groups have systematically funded and carried out massacres and human homicide bombings of civilians.

Israel has endured genocidally murderous attacks almost every month, sometimes every week, for the last three years and is engaged in a battle for its survival. Nevertheless, both Muslim propagandists and Western intellectuals present Israeli self-defensive strategies as "worse than the Nazis," as "genocidal" and "racist." Orwell himself might weep over the non-stop Big Lies, the distortions and reversals of reality by linguistic and photographic means. As Camus wrote, "To misname things is to add misery to the world." Western intellectuals are indeed adding to the world's misery.

Gruenpeter and Ben Ami told me that Moodysson's refusal to allow his movie to be screened in Israel only prevents raising awareness among the Israeli population and denies hope to the trafficked women that his movie was supposed to help. Clearly, Moodysson is willing to sacrifice the trafficked women in Israel in order to cut a politically correct figure among the anti-Semitic intelligentsia.

Our Israeli heroes, Gruenpeter and Ben Ami, persisted.

They found me and they also found Swedish journalist, Louise Eek, who exposed Moodysson in the pages of a leading Swedish newspaper (*Aftonbladet*). Moodysson emailed me, said he knew my work, and how dare I tell him what to do.

However, Moodysson *changed his mind*, because in Gruenpeter and Ben Ami's words "he is very careful of his reputation," not because he understands the difference between innocent Israeli civilians and the human homicide bombers who have been murdering them. It is their understanding that Moodysson still wants it to be announced at the Israeli showing that he opposes Israeli policies. The film can only be shown once, and then only through the Swedish Embassy.

It is important to expose Jew-hatred and to call it by its right name. Some people might not change their minds but they might change their actions if they know they are being watched.

(8/21/03)

2 THE BROWNSHIRTS OF OUR TIME

On Saturday evening, November 8, 2003, I addressed a women's "networking" conference of mainly African-American and Hispanic-American womanists and feminists at Barnard College. The conference was sponsored by WERISE (Women Empowered through Revolutionary Ideas Supporting Enterprise), which was described as a grassroots, multi-cultural, multi-generational, and multi-disciplinary organization for women in the arts. The women ranged in age from 20 to 65 and were dressed in corporate business suits, colorful African and ethnic attire, and youthful jeans.

I doubt that the organizers of this conference knew anything of my background, but they were more than welcoming. They had class and soul. For example, when I'd explained that I was in the midst of a major move to Manhattan and a book tour, one organizer said, "We understand what it's like when a woman is jammed up doing too much. We'll love you anyway. You can let us know at the last minute." She was so upbeat and understanding that I decided I'd come no matter what.

A few days before the conference one of the organizers asked me about my most recent book and I told her it was *The New Anti-Semitism*. I explained that Jew-hatred was a form of racism—only it was not being treated as such by anti-racist "politically correct" people. The organizer did not voice her disagreement nor did she say that the subject wouldn't play well to her constituency. She only said that they needed me to explain the ways in which women sabotage each other, so that women could understand and overcome them in order to come together. They wanted me to talk about my book *Woman's Inhumanity to Woman*. "Your speech will precede our big Unity panel," she said.

I had been asked to talk about what women can do, psychologically and ethically, to enable sisterhood and to work in productive, even radical ways. As I spoke, the women in the audience sighed, cheered, applauded, nodded in agreement, laughed, groaned, nudged each other—it was a half hour of good vibes.

And then my first questioner blew it all to hell. I could not see who was speaking. A disembodied voice demanded to know where I stood on the question of the women of Palestine. Her tone was forceful, hostile, relentless, and prepared. I could have said that I am deeply concerned with the women of Palestine, but I did not.

Instead, I took a deep breath and said that I did not respect people who hijacked airplanes or hijacked conferences, or who, at this very moment, were trying to hijack *this* lecture. I pointed out that the subject of my talk was not Israel or Palestine. I did not want us to lose our focus. She grew even more hostile and demanding. She said, "Tell this audience what you said on WBAI. I heard you on that program." Clearly, she wanted to "unmask" me before this audience as a Jew-lover and an Israel-defender.

I took the question head-on. I said if she was really asking about apartheid, I'd talk about it. I said that contrary to myth and propaganda, Israel is not an apartheid state. The largest practitioner of apartheid in the world is Islam, which practices both gender and religious apartheid. Palestinian women—and all women who live under Islam—are oppressed by "honor" killings, daughter-beatings, forced veiling, segregation, being stoned to death for alleged adultery, and suffer from female genital mutilation, polygamy, and sexual slavery.

I told them that Islam also practices religious apartheid. All non-Muslims (Christians, Jews, Hindus, Buddhists, Bahá'í, Zoroastrians, animists, etc.) have historically been treated as sub-humans and must either convert to Islam or be mercilessly taxed, beaten, jailed, murdered, or exiled. Today, the entire Middle East is *Judenrein*; there are no Jews in 22 Arab countries. Between 1948 and 1956, 850,000 Arab Jews were forced to flee Muslim countries. They can only live in Israel, the only Middle Eastern country where Jews are welcome.

I told the truth. They had not heard it before. The audience collectively gasped. Then, people went a little crazy.

Someone muttered darkly, coarsely, in a near-growl, "What about the checkpoints? What about the fence?" As if checkpoints and fences are the same as being killed by your brother or father or, most recently in Ramallah in the Rofayda Qaoud case, by your mother (!) for the crime of having been raped—in the Qaoud case, raped and impregnated by your mother's two sons. I asked the audience if they thought that being detained at a checkpoint was really the same as having your clitoris sliced off, the same as being stoned to death for alleged adultery. The only response I got was from the first questioner who demanded that I denounce Ariel Sharon—but not Yasser Arafat—as a murderer.

I refused to do so.

The lightning rod of "Palestine" was enough to turn a very friendly audience quite hostile and a bit unhinged. Two or three women proceeded to ask aggressive questions in which they accused me of somehow disrespecting poor women in my remarks.

As I was trying to leave, one woman, who said her name was "Lupe" (she was dressed in a button-festooned serape, and had a cross tattooed between her eyebrows), loped after me and demanded that I deal with the Palestine question. She kept trying to get at me physically. One of the organizers kept putting her own body between Lupe and me. Lupe behaved like a trained operative; her rage was empowered by her politics.

The questioner had at least one, and possibly two, henchwoman with her. Clearly, they wanted to "get" the pro-Israel white Jew.

A young African-American woman stopped me to say that I'd "hurt" her by how I had "disrespected" a "brown" woman. "What brown woman?" I asked. "Your first questioner was a brown woman," she said, "and so are Palestinian women." I said, "Jewish women, especially in Israel also come in many colors including brown and black." She stopped me and said, "But you're a white Jew"—as if this was proof of a crime.

The three young African-American women who had invited me were *very* supportive: they hugged me and thanked me for coming and looked rather embarrassed about what had happened.

What's important is this: Not one of them tried to stop what was happening, no one stood up and said, "Something good has just turned ugly and we must not permit this to happen." Thus, the "good" people did nothing to disperse the hostility. Perhaps they were unprepared or agreed with the view of Israel as an apartheid state. Perhaps they simply lacked the courage to stand up to the extremists in their midst.

Clearly, my speech had touched hearts and minds; there was room for common ground and for civilized discourse, but once the word "Palestine" was uttered—"Palestine," the symbol for all downtrodden groups of color that are "resisting" the racist-imperialist American and Zionist Empires—everyone responded on cue, as if brainwashed. It immediately became "brown" versus "white," "oppressed" versus "oppressor."

These are the Brownshirts of our time. That they are women of color and womanists/feminists is all the more chilling and tragic. And unbelievable. And to me, practically unbearable.

Afterwards, my son who was present and who is ever-wise, said, "Well mom, you have your answer. The Jew-haters will never allow you into their wider, wonderful world. You can't go back."

(11/19/03)

3 JEWS ON THE PRECIPICE

Today, the danger to Jews is far graver and more complex than it ever was before, including the 1930s.

Czarist-, Nazi-, and Stalinist-era anti-Semitic stereotypes (the Jews control the media and the banks and seek world domination) have been added to the pre-existing Islamic views of Jews as subhuman infidels.

Jew-haters are creating a situation in which another mass murder—perhaps even a Holocaust-like mass murder of Jews—might be possible. In my view, it has already begun, certainly not in America, not yet in Europe—but in Israel.

I was among the first to characterize the new anti-Semitism as an alliance between Islamofascist terrorists and "politically correct" Western intellectuals. Both groups have remained morally blind to the slaughter of innocent civilians in Israel and America. Worse, they have blamed that slaughter on Israeli and American policy. In their frenzy to scapegoat Israel for all human suffering, these new anti-Semites have joined the United Nations, international human rights groups, and the media in failing to condemn the most horrendous human rights abuses in the world, including genocide.

"Politically correct" Americans, including some Jews, have joined Islamists in embracing Palestinians as the most oppressed and most noble of savages whose misery, in their view, has been caused solely by a cabal of Zionists, Orthodox Jews, and Christian Republicans.

Israelis are being slaughtered not only because they live in a nation engaged in a local war with neighboring nations, but also because Israel is a *Jewish* nation that has been under almost perpetual siege since its birth in 1948. Twenty-one thousand Israelis have lost their lives in wars of self-defense and in acts of terrorism against the Jewish state since 1948.

I cannot imagine how Israelis must be suffering—those who have lived through so many wars of self-defense and whose parents and grandparents endured Hitler's Final Solution, the Gulag, Cossack pogroms, and persecution and exile from Arab and Muslim lands.

The slow bleed of Israelis from 1948 to 2000 has been barely noted among Western intellectuals. "Everybody dies! Other people also suffer! Enough with the Jews!" Jewish blood does not register with them—or, rather, Jews are supposed to die; they are not shocked when it happens. In an attempt to awaken such hard-hearted intellectuals, some of whom are, sadly, Jews, I decided to convert the Israeli reality into American terms.

From 9/29/2000 to 5/12/04, terrorists murdered 961 Israelis. This represents 0.00015% of the Israeli Jewish, Christian, and Muslim population of 6.4 million. Based on an American population of approximately 293 million, the Israeli civilian death count is the equivalent of 43,950 Americans killed by terrorists on our own soil, in pizza parlors, on buses, at Passover Sedarim, in our beds.

In addition, between 9/29/2000 and 5/12/04, a total of 6,344 Israelis were wounded by terrorists, often seriously, and permanently. This represents 0.00099% of the Israeli population. This is the equivalent of approximately 290,500 Americans wounded by terrorists.

Every Israeli personally knows someone—a parent, a child, a spouse, a co-worker, a neighbor, a friend—who has been killed. Every Israeli knows someone who has been wounded for life. Ads for hospital beds and orthopedic devices regularly appear in mainstream newspapers, not in medical journals.

Yet, our "best and brightest" suggest that the Jews are "paranoid," "alarmist," "neurotic" about anti-Semitism. Hitler killed millions of people who were not Jews ("Why do the Jews go on and on only about themselves as if they are the only victims?"); Israelis are now perpetuating a "Holocaust" upon the Palestinians (another way of saying that "Hitler should have finished the Jews off"); Israel is a "colonial" state that should be abolished—exterminated—and this suggestion, which is being made by progressives and intellectuals, is not supposed to have anything to do with anti-Semitism.

Meanwhile, as some Jewish American organizations launch major fundraising drives pegged to these latest alarming atrocities, their leaders hasten to reassure us that Jews in America are relatively safe, and that Israel has a strong military, including a nuclear strike capacity. All true.

What if Israel ceases to exist, and if America is fatefully weakened by the terrorist threat against it—what then? What if the Jews of Israel, Europe, and South America remain at peril—what then? Is it "okay" that we're "okay" in America?

Hillel asked three questions, not just one: "If I'm not for

myself, who will be for me? When I am only for myself, what am I? And, if not now, when?"

Many Jewish progressives gloss over Hillel's first question. Some Jews are often the first to demonize the Jewish state and the Jewish religion in their zeal to institute social justice as if doing so is their version of Judaism.

So, what must we do?

My most radical suggestion is a gathering of the twelve tribes, which must be undertaken in the same spirit that Theodor Herzl convened the first World Zionist Congress. So many Jews who hold passionate and opposing views have simply stopped listening and talking to each other. The silence is more awful than arguments. Many Jews no longer act as if they believe the "Other" has been created in God's image. We must come together in order to strategize about our very survival.

What does the Torah teach us about anti-Semitism?

Early on, we see that God accepts Abel's offering but rejects Cain's. Despite God's intervention, the heartbroken and enraged Cain kills his brother, Abel, whose offering was "chosen" by God.

Yaakov favored Yosef—and Yosef's older half-brothers envied, resented, and hated him. Some wanted to kill Yosef, but they settled for selling him into slavery. Divine destiny will have Yosef rescue his people from famine and forgive his brothers.

What happens when one is chosen, not only by one's biological father but also by God, one's heavenly parent?

One breaks the hearts of all those who have not been chosen, and such heartbreak often leads to envy and resentment. Oddly enough, despite the considerable hardship and danger, many people still want to be "the chosen one."

While Jews do not cause Jew-hatred—nor does Israeli policy—we must also quietly consider that our chosenness (or at least our perceived chosenness) does seem to have certain consequences. We are the first People of the Book, and we are, psychologically and theologically, the mothers and fathers of all those who have followed in our monotheistic footsteps. In addition, our Jewish ideas about God, mitzvot, justice, ethics, mercy, have gotten us into trouble with all those who wish to worship idols, engage in child sacrifice, and to murder, rape, slander, and steal. The glory of being "chosen" also constitutes a dangerous and difficult burden.

The sages say that Jerusalem is the source of the world's peace and light. When the source of peace is not at peace, the world is sorely troubled too.

(5/19/04)

4 Listener-Sponsored Hate Radio on the Left Coast

On May 26, 2004, I was interviewed on "Feminist Magazine" on KPFK in Los Angeles, which is run by Pacifica Radio. They wanted me to talk about Jew-hatred and anti-Zionism within the feminist Left. A small group of KPFK feminists finally wanted to combat the unchallenged, unbalanced, and omnipresent hate speech against Jews and Israel at the station.

There have been problems at KPFK for at least 13 years. Had you been listening in 1991, you would have heard Steve Cokely say the AIDS virus had been invented by Jewish doctors to kill black babies. Cokely, who is black, also urged the residents of Los Angeles to turn their city into another Crown Heights. Cokely was forced to resign.

In 1992, in a two-day 30-hour "African Mental Health" marathon on KPFK, you would have heard Louis Farrakhan describe whites and Jews as "the pale horse with death as its rider and hell close behind that had wreaked destruction on red, yellow, and black people, as well as Palestinians in the

Middle East." Farrakhan promised that a "reckoning for this slaughter was soon to come."

Professor Leonard Jeffries and others claimed the Jews had "stolen Bible stories from Black Egyptian Muslims," "taken leadership roles in the NAACP in order to limit the progress of blacks," and "slavery had been invented by Talmudic scholars." No one challenged such views on-air.

In 1992, the KPFK program "Middle East in Focus" devoted an entire edition to "Palestine Solidarity Day." One guest was introduced as a "victim of Manifest Destiny...and of Zionism, as a Palestinian." Another speaker specifically accused the Israelis of persecuting Palestinian women. Pacifica did not offer its listeners any counter-views to these outlandish allegations.

Ralph Schoenman of WBAI, who also frequently appeared on Pacifica, condemned the Israeli government by asking, "Security for the Israeli state? Do you call security for the Apartheid state of South Africa a condition for the self-determination of the people of South Africa?" Schoenman called for the abolition of the Jewish state as a usurper, colonialist, and aggressor.

In June of 1994, a coalition of Jewish leaders and disenchanted listeners formed a legislative campaign that tried, but failed to reduce federal funding to the Corporation for Public Broadcasting for such Pacifica "hate speech."

The homophobia and Jew-hatred of Black nationalists and leftists were seen as too hot to handle. Those at the station who disagreed with this state of affairs were either dismissed as reactionaries or patronized as misguided.

Years later, on October 21, 2002, Don Bustany, the producer and host of Pacifica's "Middle East in Focus," issued a memo to all programmers who shared Schoenman's view, saying that Israel did not have the right to defend herself, that "every time any of us uses 'Israel Defense Forces' on the air, we are subtly saying to listeners that Israel is on the defensive and that its adversaries are on the offensive—which of course, is patently ridiculous."

Tricia Roth, the programmer of "Feminist Magazine" and member of the feminist collective, said the L.A. chapter of Women in Black once invaded a meeting of the feminist collective after a Holocaust survivor had appeared on "Feminist Magazine." An elderly woman dared to express disapproval of Palestinians who teach their children to hate, and stated that she believed the Bible gave the Jews rights in the Holy Land. "Women in Black were outraged. They denounced us and demanded that we be taken off the air," Roth said. What's troubling is the refusal and inability to tolerate the slightest difference of opinion among presumed radicals.

After nearly four months of calling and writing KPFK's new general manager, Eva Georgia, about this problem, Roth received a response. Georgia announced she would be forming a committee to "look at anti-Semitism at KPFK." However, Roth discovered that such a committee had not been formed, and Roth's request to join the non-existent committee was never answered. On January 22, 2003, Roth resigned on the air.

A program aired on March 12, 2003. Three of the five guests were Jewish anti-Zionists, including Sherna Gluck from Radio Intifada, and Ralph Shoenman from WBAI, whose book, *The Hidden History of Zionism*, claims that Jews purposely collaborated with the Nazis in the extermination of European Jewry in the interests of achieving a Jewish state.

After her on-air resignation, Roth attended a workshop

in non-violence, and decided to return to KPFK. She did not wish to concede control of the airwaves to Jew-haters. With the support of the feminist collective, she would focus exclusively on pro-Jewish and pro-Israel programming as a "corrective," and as a way of injecting on-air sanity and diversity.

Roth chose me as her first guest. She had read my latest book, *The New Anti-Semitism: The Current Crisis and What We Must Do About It*, and wanted to feature my views on the program. The "Feminist Magazine" collective was still reeling from the continuing barrage of on-air and off-air hate and disinformation often leveled against them by Jewish left feminists.

On-air, a representative from the L.A. chapter of Women in Black, when asked about Muslim-on-Muslim oppression, responded that "Israel's transgressions in this area" were her main bailiwick; she was not "concerned" by anyone who oppressed the Palestinians other than Jewish Israelis.

Roth told me that the switchboard lit up while we were still on the air last month. She said many called to protest my views as neither progressive nor feminist. Calls mounted for the censure and removal of "Feminist Magazine."

Two days ago, a protest petition to KPFK listeners appeared on the Internet in which my entire interview had been carefully, painfully transcribed (thanks to whoever did that), as proof that the views expressed are "not in keeping with the Pacifica Mission." The petition claimed that my views and the views of "Feminist Magazine" are "irrelevant to today's feminism, racist, and not worthy of Pacifica."

Other charges include that I write for *Frontpage Magazine*, support the war against terrorism/the war in Iraq, and have said that I may vote for President Bush in the next election.

This all "proves" that I am no longer a feminist and do not belong on any feminist program. Any feminist program that interviews me has no right to Pacifica air time.

The Soviet and Communist Chinese Cultural Revolutions are alive and well in left feminist America.

The petition sends readers to a *Nation* magazine article, written by the anti-Zionist Jew Brian Klug, who reviewed my book. The petition writers seem to believe that The *Nation* is the Bible, and claim that Klug's article "totally refutes and rejects Chesler's claims."

Younger feminists, and those obsessed with issues of sexuality and transgender issues seem to be involved. A letter written by former feminist collective member Jessica Hoffmann, which is part of the online petition, refers to "uneven" distributions of power in the feminist collective, to "felt elites" and "unofficially powerful members." Hoffman is in her early 20s, Roth in her mid-40s, and I'm almost in my mid-60s. When I asked Tricia Roth what she believed was behind this she said, "For progressive Jews, this is the ultimate rebellion, both against the status quo, against their parents, against all authority. Their identities are deeply tied to being left-wing radicals. This is how they are proving their identities."

Roth also observed that some of the more vocal protestors, including members of Women in Black, were themselves the children of Holocaust survivors; Roth suggested a possibly traumatic origin to this struggle, one in which the victim remains forever guilty, and the aggressor remains too frightening to oppose, and thus, potential victims identify with the aggressor for safety's sake.

The petition writers sound like so many other leftists and left-feminists who blame 9/11 on American military and economic policy, and who view the beheading of Daniel Pearl and Nicholas Berg as somehow caused by Prime Minister Sharon's and President Bush's military and political policies.

While America's foreign and domestic policies are open to serious criticism, the "blame America and Israel all the time" crowd is delusional. As a psychologist and psychotherapist I understand it. When people feel threatened and powerless they tend to resort to "magical thinking." A battered woman and an abused child will often blame themselves for being beaten—this gives them the only control over the situation they might have. If they think they did something wrong that "provoked" the beating, next time they will not do whatever it was and will, hopefully, avoid being beaten again.

Progressives find it easier to blame the Israeli or American governments for their mistakes than to stare long and hard into the face of radical totalitarian evil. People often blame the victim. It's more dangerous to blame the perpetrator. He might come after you too. Because people are also good, they prefer to look away from the matter entirely rather than endure the guilt they would otherwise feel for doing nothing.

Long live the brave feminist collective of KPFK'S "Feminist Magazine." Tricia Roth and Melissa Chiprin, who also interviewed me, are the whistle-blowing Karen Silkwoods and Erin Brokoviches of their generation.

(6/18/04)

5 THE RACE AGAINST LIES

In the 1940s, when the media and the American leadership refused to inform US citizens about the extermination of the Jews, a band of activists took it upon themselves to get the word out to the American people.

In 1942, Palestinian Jew Peter Bergson (a.k.a. Hillel Kook, the nephew of the first Chief Rabbi of Israel) and a small group of activists began an extraordinary and heartbreaking "race against death" as they tirelessly campaigned for American assistance to rescue the doomed Jews of Europe. When Kook began, two million Jews had already been exterminated. Tirelessly, Kook lobbied Congress, staged public and theatrical rallies, and placed paid ads in the nation's leading newspapers. His ads asked, "They Are Driven to Death Daily, But Can They Be Saved?" and "How Well Are You Sleeping?"

America's failure to respond was due to the lingering effects of the Great Depression, nativism, anti-Semitism, and, perhaps, a pro-Soviet foreign policy. In addition, Kook's efforts were actively obstructed by the American State

Department, the media (especially the *New York Times*), and the leaders of organized American Jewry (especially Rabbi Stephen Wise, Congressman Sol Bloom, New York State Judge Samuel Rosenman, communal leader Nahum Goldmann, and Ira Hirschmann of the War Refugee Board).

However, Kook was backed by Ben Hecht, Max Lerner, media tycoon William Randolph Hearst, Orthodox rabbis, and many Christian legislators such as Congressman Will Rogers, Jr., and Senators Guy Gillette, Edwin Johnson, and Elbert Thomas. When the *New York Times* refused to print the truth about what was happening to the Jews, or when they buried it on back pages, Kook had Hecht compose eye-catching paid ads in the *New York Times* and other papers.

In their riveting book, *A Race Against Death: Peter Bergson, America, and the Holocaust*, Professors David S. Wyman and Rafael Medoff carefully and dramatically document all of this. The heart of the book is a never-before-released twelve-hour interview with Kook (Bergson), which Wyman conducted in 1973. The parallels to today's world are chilling. Actually, in some ways, the situation today is worse.

There are about 14 million Jews left in the world. Everyone—the Jews of Israel most of all—are being systematically and perilously endangered by a non-stop onslaught of propaganda.

The Western media has still not caught on to the way Arabs and Palestinians systematically use media technology to brainwash people with simplistic and highly biased versions of reality. The propagandists never show the numerous acts of kindness and ethical behaviors of the Israeli Defense Forces nor do they show the systematic slaughter of innocent Israeli civilians, nearly half of whom are women and children.

On August 12, 2004, HBO will air James Miller's BBC Channel 4 film, *Death in Gaza*, (in Arabic and English) in which he interviewed only Palestinian children. Presumably, Miller was going to interview Israeli children too but he never did. Miller's widow, Sophy, has gone on record accusing the Israelis of purposely killing him on his last day of shooting in Gaza; if this was indeed his last day then perhaps Miller did not plan to interview any Israeli children after all.

After his death, Miller's wife and colleagues finished the film, and began a campaign seeking "Justice for James Miller." The film has been aired at many film festivals to rave reviews. The fact that the script was written by acclaimed journalist, Saira Shah, with whom Miller worked on *Beneath the Veil*, which was broadcast by CNN, ensures a devoted and vocal following. Shah, who is the British-born daughter of an Afghan father, is the author of *The Storyteller's Daughter*, which is a beautifully written book about her search for her Afghan roots.

In the Miller/Shah film, we mainly see Israeli tanks and bulldozers moving ominously toward children and weeping women; the soundtrack which accompanies the Israeli military equipment is that of a horror movie. The only "human" faces shown are Palestinians: crying, suffering, burying their dead, visiting cemeteries. In the Miller/Shah film, there are no Israeli civilians or child counterpart interviewees. Although the Palestinians are shown as world-class haters and brainwashers, I still fear that the film will encourage further demonization of Israel and sympathy for the murderous Palestinians.

There is only one filmmaker who has presented the truth of the Palestinian-Israeli conflict and his nom de guerre is Pierre Rehov. His film, *The Road to Jenin*, shows us a very different Israeli army than Miller's *Death in Gaza* depicts. A far truer view of the Israeli Army may be gleaned not only from Rehov's film but also from Gil Mezuman's film *Jenin Diary: The Inside Story*, and from an important and moving book by Brett Goldberg, *A Psalm in Jenin*.

Rehov has not yet found a network to showcase his six films nor does he have a distributor in the United States. On the anniversary of the Park Hotel Passover massacre in Netanya (which led to the Israeli incursion into Jenin), Rehov showed his film about Jenin and dedicated it to the 23 Israeli soldiers who died going into Jenin on foot from booby-trapped house to booby-trapped house, vulnerable to sniper-fire every inch of the way. Rehov invited the families of the dead soldiers and the survivors of the Park Hotel massacre. He personally fed 400 people. A former Chief Rabbi of Israel presided at a Passover Seder table that stood in the exact spot where the human homicide bomb had blown himself and 30 Israelis to pieces.

In Peter Bergson's/Hillel Kook's honor I have resolved that I must, in a small way, act as Kook would have done at this moment in history. Thus, starting today, on August 11, 2004, my website (www.phyllis-chesler.com) will host Pierre Rehov's recent films. I want those people who will watch *Death in Gaza* to have the option to see "the other side," which Rehov captures in his films. *The Silent Exodus* is about the approximately 800,000 – 850,000 Jews who had to flee Arab countries and what their lives were like under Islam before Israel became a sovereign entity. *The Hostages of Hatred* is a film in which Rehov interviews Palestinians—including children—about their views. The hero of *Hostages* is, perhaps, Bassam Eid, the Director of Human Rights Monitoring for Palestine who bravely "tells it like it is."

As we all now know, the "Jenin Massacre" was a falsehood. Twenty-three armed Israeli soldiers and 52 armed Palestinian soldiers died. The Israelis were up against homemade napalm, rockets, human homicide bombs, snipers, booby-trapped roads, stores, fields, and buildings. Palestinian fighters were transported via ambulances, and snipers were shooting from mosque minarets. "Helping" civilians was a high-risk Israeli activity. Many Israeli soldiers were wounded and killed when they tried to do so.

Contrary to myth, Israeli soldiers not only gave out food and water, they also gave up their own rations to civilians. They stocked up on candies for children and diapers for infants. Israeli soldiers did not confiscate or destroy civilian property. They slept on floors so as not to soil beds; systematically rolled up oriental carpets to shield them from their muddy military boots; left notes apologizing for any damage and thanking absentee home-owners for their "hospitality." Sleepless, embattled, freezing, the Israelis refused to "borrow" blankets or coffee (only one caffeine-starved soldier did so and his commanding officer wrestled with whether or not to punish him). Israelis did not shell any hospitals. In fact, they treated every Palestinian civilian who was wounded. In one instance, when an Israeli soldier accidentally wounded an old Arab man who was deaf and who could not hear his orders, the soldier literally fainted; the Arab man was medically evacuated.

Unlike the Palestinians and Arabs who danced and cheered when they lynched, be-headed, or blew up infidels, Israelis mourned and wept when they had to destroy ancient orchards and homes because they sheltered terrorists. When one developmentally challenged Palestinian boy whom the Israelis had been feeding was wired up with explosives,

Israelis found a way to feed him from afar.

Mezuman's documentary, filmed while the invasion of Jenin was still in progress, shows us exhausted, traumatized, frightened, heartsick Israeli reservists engaged in soul-searching and criticism of Israeli Army policy. Rehov's film confirms all this and more. Brett Goldberg's book explores the characters, biographies, and conduct-in-battle of the 23 Israelis who died in Jenin as well as those of some Israeli survivors of the battle of Jenin.

If HBO and other American and European networks do not begin airing "both sides" of the Israeli-Palestinian issue so that people can really "make up their own minds," we are all the poorer for it. I hereby formally join the august ranks of Christopher Hitchens and Paul Berman in their view that what was once a "liberal" media has so quickly become a "totalitarian" and "Islamofascist-" friendly media—and all in the name of free speech, anti-censorship, and (Muslim-only) civil rights.

(8/11/04)

6 Duke's Terror Conference

Duke University in North Carolina hosted the fourth annual Palestine Solidarity Movement conference, draping anti-Jewish and anti-Zionist hate speech in the glorious colors of free speech.

Jews are assisting the Palestine Solidarity Movement (PSM) at Duke. To the best of my knowledge, no Palestinians are assisting Jewish groups in this way.

For example, an Israeli-South African Jewish graduate student at Duke, Rann Bar-On, belongs to Hiwar, the student group that invited the PSM to Duke. "Hiwar" means "dialogue" in Arabic. In response to questions about why he is supporting a group that endorses terrorism, Bar-On has been quoted as saying, "We don't see it as very useful for us as a solidarity movement to condemn violence." At least three Jews are speaking for PSM. (Why Left Jews are the first to condemn Israel merits a conference all its own.)

Emily Antoon, the president of Hiwar and a Duke junior, has refused to co-sponsor the "Jewish" rally for peace and against terrorism. Antoon has been quoted as saying, "I think it implicitly endorses state terrorism."

I wrote an open letter to the Duke administration. I appealed to the President "as a member of Duke's extended family of scholars" since my archives reside at Duke University:

I understand that Duke University will be hosting a Palestinian Solidarity Movement (PSM) conference and certain faculty members believe that doing so constitutes a commitment to free speech and academic freedom. Ironically, Duke will be supporting a group (also known as the International Solidarity Movement), which does not believe in free speech or democracy and which endorses violence, mass murder, Jew-hatred, and homicidal-suicide terrorism.

True, America prides itself on extending its civil rights, including that of free speech, to racist groups and to their hate speech. Let me respectfully suggest that, post-9/11, America may no longer do so without risking grievous consequences in terms of lives lost and truth abandoned.

Would you proudly host a Nazi Party or Ku Klux Klan conference in the name of academic freedom? Given your commitment to the First Amendment, would you still allow the meeting to take place behind closed doors with no press allowed? I understand that this is what the Palestine Solidarity Movement conference planners have demanded. As you know, a free and vigorous press is one of our protections against tyranny. What issue cannot bear the cleansing light of scrutiny?

Why is Duke giving any intellectual credibility to what is bound to be a hate-fest? Some say that PSM's/ISM's hate speech and lies are only words and cannot hurt anyone. At some other time in history, and perhaps in terms of other subjects, I might agree with you. However, the level of hate-propaganda against Israel and Jews is deadly. During this latest Palestinian-led Intifada (2000-2004), such propaganda has led to and yet rendered invisible the highest civilian body count in Israel's history. Only Israel's unilateral creation of a security barrier has begun to stanch the flood of Israeli blood.

Many good Jewish organizations and activists protested and infiltrated the Palestinian Solidarity Conference.

Rabbi Zalman Bluming, the Chabad Rabbi at Duke, brought the terrorist-destroyed bus #19 to campus for two days. He estimates that at least 4,000 students and community members saw it. Rabbi Bluming said, "When Jews stand up for Israel with clarity, without apology, the world respects this."

Rabbi Avi Weiss sent about 30 activists from AMCHA, who, under the soft-spoken leadership of Rabbi Etan Mintz, stood moral vigil outside the PSM conference. They sang peace movement melodies. In Rabbi Mintz's words, "We had come to honor the souls of the thousands who were murdered by terrorist attacks... (Not only were they slain), it was as if now they were being re-murdered... [Here] their murderers were being exonerated, even extolled."

Four Jewish organizations (StandWithUS, American Jewish Congress, Hasbara Fellowships and the Zionist

Organization of America) paid for two full-page ads that appeared in the Duke student newspaper several days before the PSM conference began. The ads showed graphic, color photographs of terrorism against Israeli civilians on buses, at universities, nightclubs, bus stops, shopping centers, and synagogues. They also depicted the Ku Klux Klan-like indoctrination of Palestinian children.

The activists-infiltrators, including Lee Kaplan, published the following information.

The PSM/ISM speakers proclaimed that Zionism is a "disease" and that Israel is an "apartheid" state. They viewed "Palestine" as the "epitome of freedom" and terrorists as freedom-fighters. They called for the abolition of the Jewish state through the use of suicide-homicide terrorism and through the adoption of a "one-state" solution in which Jews would be demographically overwhelmed, marginalized, persecuted, and ultimately driven out.

The conference proposed some startling new strategies.

They suggested that PSM's Jewish supporters "hijack" Project Birthright, and use it to get free trips to Israel. Upon arrival, they could slip into "Palestine" to assist Israel's enemies. They taught a session on how to lie to Israeli authorities and to the Birthright people.

The PSM/ISM announced a plan to use left-wing Jews, Christians, and Muslims to infiltrate and "take over" campus Hillels—as a way of indoctrinating American students with their ideology of hate.

The PSM/ISM also announced the need for a boycott of Jewish companies such as Estee Lauder, Clinique, and Bobbi Brown because they donate money to Israel and do business there.

In addition, the PSM conference called for the co-opting

of mainstream Christian groups like the Presbyterians and the Episcopalians to further the various divest-in-Israel movements.

This conference was not academic in any way, but it was hosted at an academic institution that paid for conference security.

Welcome to a Brave New Academic America.

(OCTOBER 2004)

7 Murder, Lies, and Videotape

Paradise Now is a brilliant and powerful piece of propaganda, which has already won a major award and has been sold to 45 countries, including Israel. The film was financed by Dutch, French, and German backers. The director, Hany Abu-Assad, who has lived in Holland for the last 20 years, describes himself as a Palestinian with an Israeli passport. Reviewers have described the film as an attempt to "humanize" human homicide bombs, to "dramatize" what goes through their minds.

Some reviewers have suggested that Abu-Assad actually endangered himself by portraying the terrorist-recruiters as cold and manipulative and by allowing two of his characters to question—rather passionately—whether suicide bombing missions are effective responses to oppression and occupation. Reviewers have also congratulated Abu-Assad on his careful research and solid documentation.

Nothing could be further from the truth—although he is certainly a very good artist. The film excels in irony, humor, character, and drama. Said (one of the human homicide bombers played by Kais Nashef) is as heartbreakingly soulful as Giancarlo Giannini was in *Seven Beauties* and *Swept Away*. Nashef actually resembles him. The tale is gripping and tragic—as long as you accept his exceedingly close-cropped informational frame. Israelis are depersonalized and demonized. We see Israelis only as soldiers: ominous, hard-eyed, helmeted, armed, in tanks. The film is anti-historical and based on a series of lies, omissions, and one outright fantasy.

First, what the film does right:

The film takes place in a 48-hour period in which two friends, Said (not Edward, but the choice of name is significant) and Khaled (Ali Suliman), who work at dead-end jobs in an auto repair shop, are told that their "suicide mission" will take place in Tel Aviv the next day. We see them at work, at home, relating to a woman, Suha, with their recruiter (the local schoolteacher), and with the handlers who film their prepared speeches, feed, shave, dress, embrace them—and then strap on their explosive belts that they can never remove.

For them, there is no exit. Quietly, but clearly, Abu-Assad shows us the enormously erotic element involved in Palestinian male bonding. He also shows us the casual cruelty with which older Palestinian men treat younger Palestinian men and boys. Most important, the film does suggest one very powerful motivation for becoming a suicide killer.

Said fulfills his mission, Khaled turns back. Why this difference? Arab and Muslim society is a shame and honor-based culture. Psychologically, Said feels that he must cleanse his shame: His father was executed as a collaborator by Palestinians when Said was ten. He blames the Occupation for his father's "weakness" and for his own decision to become a murderer. Said takes no personal responsibility for what he does. Khaled does not have such personal shame to expiate, nor does Suha, who is the daughter of a Palestinian hero. Both Khaled and Suha say the right things about non-violent resistance, but our hearts are with Said who is the film's tragic hero.

As to the lies:

Said decides not to board a bus that is filled with settlers because he suddenly experiences sympathy for the toddler on board. In reality, Palestinian human homicide bombs have deliberately targeted Israeli civilians, not soldiers. In the last five years, nearly 800 Israeli *civilians* have been murdered by Palestinian terrorists; thousands have been maimed permanently. Israeli soldiers have also killed Palestinian civilians, but only inadvertently in their attempt to kill Palestinian terrorists who use their own people as human shields.

Said, in his filmed "shahid" speech, claims that Israelis have rejected a two-state solution. This has been well-documented as a falsehood.

One of Said's handlers claims that this operation is the first they have tried in two years. Since Arafat unilaterally decided to break off negotiations and to launch the Intifada of 2000, the Palestinians have not stopped trying to kill Israeli civilians. Vigilant counter-terrorist and police work, and the security fence have increasingly stopped them. Still, they keep coming. Hamas says they will never stop until Jews and Christian infidels have been driven from Muslim holy lands.

Said also accuses Israel of having carried out "ethnic cleansing." This is untrue. "Ethnic cleansing" is what the ethnic Arab Muslims are currently doing in Darfur, Sudan to black African Muslims, animists, and Christians; what every Arab Muslim country did to Jews and other infidels for millennia.

Said is only a fictional character; he is entitled to his limited or distorted view of reality. This is exactly what a good film is supposed to do: get us inside the heads of its characters without judging them, right?

Well, yes—but here's the problem. The world has already been indoctrinated in favor of "the Palestinian narrative." Doctored film footage of fake Israeli massacres and fake Jewish and Israeli killings of Palestinian innocents have inflamed most of the world. *Paradise Now* is the first feature film on the subject by a Palestinian. Because this is a good film, it may have enormous influence over how an already heavily indoctrinated world audience views the phenomenon of Palestinian human homicide bombs.

Perhaps the biggest lie in this film is an omission: we do not understand how continuous the hatred of Jews and Israel is among Palestinians, how brainwashed the Palestinian population really is. Palestinian Media Watch has been translating what the Palestinians say in Arabic in textbooks, on television, in mosques, on videos, and in the electronic media.

A few examples will suffice: Jews and Israelis control the world media and the world's money; they behead Muslim children in order to obtain their blood for Jewish rituals; the Mossad was behind 9/11; they also control the U.S. government. Daily, Palestinians—who have been denied citizenship in every Arab Muslim country and whose corrupt leaders have lined their own pockets with money meant to ease the suffering of their people—are indoctrinated to hate Jews and Israelis, and are trained to kill them.

One cannot deny that Palestinian daily life has been interrupted by long lines at checkpoints, nor can one deny the discomfort involved in having to wait, often for hours, to use the bathroom. However, some of those in line, including women, are packing explosives. The number of human homicide bombing missions that Israel vigilantly intercepts is very high. Some days, *10-20* attempts are made. But Palestinian killers also get through. While Israeli soldiers can be irritable and jumpy (who wouldn't be?), it is preposterous to suggest that they behave as German Nazis did.

Also omitted are the bloody Israeli body parts, the screams, the terror, the pain, the life-long disabilities, the collective Israeli agony. In fact, we do not get to see Said blow up his bus of Israeli soldiers. We see him in a series of close-ups—and then the screen goes white. Slowly, we understand that he has detonated his bomb. Slowly, the screen credits come up in Arabic.

Finally, the fantasy in the film is calibrated to appeal to a Western audience. Suha, the pacifist hero, dresses like a fashionable European. She is a young and attractive woman who lives alone, drives her own car, and allows Said to visit her in the middle of the night. She makes him tea. Really? Women are killed for far less on the West Bank or in Gaza in honor killings. The presence of Suha (who shares a first name with Mrs. Arafat) suggests that the West Bank is not all that different from Paris or London, that Islamic gender apartheid does not exist.

Abu-Assad is a good film maker—possibly a great one—but will he ever do a film based on the autobiography of "Souad" who grew up on the West Bank and whose family tried to burn her alive in an honor killing? Will he ever challenge himself to "humanize" some Israelis, dare to render them sympathetic to both an Arab and Western audience? Now that would require real and considerable courage and artistry.

(11/1/05)

8 THE LAMENTABLE CASE OF JOAN SCOTT

Joan Wallach Scott has recently taken a high-profile position on academic freedom and the Middle East conflict. Given her prominence in the American Association of University Professors (AAUP) and her reputation as a serious historian, her writings on the academic dimension of the Arab-Israeli conflict betray a troubling partisanship.

Scott is currently the Harold F. Linder Professor at the School of Social Science in the Institute for Advanced Study at Princeton. She has also played a major role in the AAUP as the chair of its prestigious Committee on Academic Freedom and Tenure.

Scott's pronouncements are manifestoes in the culture war now paralyzing serious intellectual work on the problems that face democratic societies in the 21st century. A lengthy article by Scott, titled "Middle East Studies under Siege," appears in the current issue of *The Link*, a publication of Americans for Middle East Understanding.

Scott's article purports to be a plea for the protection of

academic freedom. The besieger, according to Scott, is "the well-organized lobby...systematically attacking Middle East studies programs." She detects "a pattern of coordinated actions, organized through networks that tie to, if not directly emanate from, the pro-Sharon, pro-occupation lobby." This lobby, Scott claims, has bullied courageous academics who speak out against Israeli abuses of human rights, has tried to cancel fair and balanced conferences that might include criticism of Israel, and has had a "chilling" effect on academic freedom reminiscent, she says, of the McCarthy era. To illustrate aggression against Muslim students, she reports that:

A week after the [9/11] attacks, at Orange Coast College, in Costa Mesa, California, Professor Ken Hearlson, a conservative, born-again Christian, was accused of calling his Muslim students Nazis, terrorists and murderers. And there were other incidents of this kind.

Note her strange circumlocution—"was accused of." The college, in response to accusations from the Muslim students in question, suspended Hearlson. Later, a hearing, reviewing transcripts of tapes of the class in question, found him innocent, and reinstated him. By "other incidents of this kind," Scott presumably means other incidents of conservative professors harassing Muslim students. Her anecdote actually illustrates the case of Muslim students harassing a professor who criticized Muslim extremism, and, indeed, that event is hardly unique.

Take for example the case of Professor Thomas Klocek. In September 2004, DePaul University suspended him without a hearing after he engaged in an argument with pro-Palestinian students at a student activities fair, and the students complained to an administrator. Other professors, including one at the University of Pennsylvania and one at Columbia University, have lost their jobs after receiving warnings from colleagues not to be too outspoken on behalf of Israel. These events are not on Scott's list, even though they clearly represent threats to academic freedom.

However, she devotes seven paragraphs to the case of a professor accused of harassing pro-Israeli students at Columbia University. Her saga begins with the David Project, an "off-campus, pro-occupation activist group" that funded a student film, *Columbia Unbecoming*. In the film, students accuse faculty in Columbia's Department of Middle Eastern and Asian Languages and Cultures of demonizing Israel and of attacking students who questioned that demonization. Joseph Massad, a Palestinian-American professor, was the faculty member most prominently mentioned.

Scott implies that because the film has never been publicly screened, the charges are trumped up. The film has not been publicly screened because some of the students who appear in the film are still afraid of reprisals, even though they have graduated.

Scott notes that a faculty Ad Hoc Grievance Committee exonerated the other professors named in the film and largely exonerated Massad; the committee's report describes Massad as "categorical in his classes concerning the unacceptability of anti-Semitic views." Neither Scott nor the grievance committee report explains that Massad is on record defining anti-Semitic to mean anti-Arab; nor does Scott inform us that the grievance committee itself was heavily weighted in favor of Massad and his colleagues.

Another Scott anecdote: In May 2002, competing rallies by pro-Israeli and pro-Palestinian student groups at San Francisco State University degenerated into an ugly clash of words. The administration sent a warning letter to the Jewish student group and cut off funds for one year to the pro-Palestinian organization.

"Competing rallies...degenerated into an ugly clash of words." Such a statement appears to blame neither side and allows her to imply unfairness in the administration's asymmetrical treatment of the two student groups.

Professor Laurie Zoloth, who was director of SFSU's Jewish Studies Department in 2002, but is neither "pro-occupation" nor a "lobbyist," has described the background, how she and others had to walk a daily gauntlet of posters proclaiming that Zionism=Racism and Jews=Nazis. When Hillel and Jewish students sponsored a pro-peace and pro-Israel demonstration, an angry mob carrying posters depicting food cans with babies on them labeled "canned Palestinian children meat, slaughtered according to Jewish rites," surrounded the Jewish students yelling "Go back to Russia;" "We will kill you;" and "Hitler did not finish the job." Zoloth was unable to persuade the campus police to maintain the promised separation of 100 feet between the demonstrators and the mob, or to make any arrests. Ultimately, the campus police had to escort the cornered Jewish students to safety. A colleague of Zoloth's described the Jewish students as having "provoked" the riot; the provocation, the colleague explained, was displaying the Israeli flag and pro-Israel posters.

Let us place these events in a larger context studiously avoided in Scott's article. In October of 2000, the Palestinian Authority initiated a global campaign of vilification of Israel and intimidation of anyone who objected. A wide range of media outlets and NGOs in the West, including many campus groups, served as amplifiers, broadcasting and affirming these demonizing messages. Most authorities in the United States and Europe failed to respond to this abuse of free speech. The vilification intensified steadily, from the hate-fest of NGOs at Durban in September 2001 to calls for boycotts of and divestment in Israel following the false accusations of a massacre at Jenin in April 2002. Lawns and plazas at many campuses like SFSU were filled daily with tables full of people and posters comparing Israel to the Nazis and spreading blood libels. Riots prevented pro-Israel figures from speaking on campuses such as Berkeley and Concordia.

What Scott, in rhetoric reminiscent of *The Protocols of the Elders of Zion* calls a "well-organized" Jewish lobby consists primarily of individuals horrified by the resurgence of a virulent anti-Semitism not seen in the West since the rise of the Nazis.

Although Scott claims that the "pro-occupation" lobbying groups were active in the 1990s, the only evidence she cites is criticism of Edward Said, who had been a highly lionized academic enemy of Israel since the 1970s. In reality, the SFSU incident and other similar incidents in the spring of 2002 marked a turning point; only after observing such naked aggression on campus did many individuals recognize the need to come to the defense of Israel. Scott scarcely mentions organizations like the Palestinian/International Solidarity Movement, which wages divestment and boycott campaigns against Israel, and she makes no mention at all of Arab/Muslim funding for such campaigns and other campus-based initiatives.

Scott implies that what professors of Middle Eastern studies teach about Islam and the Arab-Israeli conflict is largely accurate and reliable, and that any objections to it represent the intolerance of a privileged group (Jews) toward any criticism. In *Ivory Towers on Sand*, Martin Kramer describes a field paralyzed by Saïdian political correctness, in which any negative characterization of Arab culture is dismissed as racism, and professors intimidate dissenters and disseminate indoctrination. Our Middle Eastern studies "experts" have failed us precisely when we need them most. They do not help us to understand Islamic terrorism, the history of Jihad and its apocalyptic worldview, the dynamics of radicalization in Western mosques, or the oppression of minorities and gender apartheid in the Islamic world. They primarily obsess about post-9/11 "Islamophobia" and the "racist Israeli state."

Last spring, the AAUP joined other major academic, scientific, and professional organizations in a resolution of the British Association of University Teachers (AUT), a trade union of academics, to boycott all faculty of the University of Haifa and Bar-Ilan University in Israel. The boycott resolution was subsequently reversed. However, the AAUP recently obtained funding for a conference on academic boycotts, to be held February 13-17 in Bellagio, Italy. Of about 20 individuals invited to the conference, eight were outspoken and aggressive proponents of the AUT boycott. Three, who were faculty or administrators at the targeted Israeli universities, were invited—or perhaps, summoned—with less than three weeks' notice.

The AAUP claims to be unalterably opposed to academic boycotts. Therefore questions were raised about the rationale for the conference and its intended outcome. In response to those questions, on February 7, 2006, the Ford, Rockefeller, and Cummings Foundations, which were funding the conference, asked that it be postponed. The materials distributed for the conference inexplicably included "a deeply offensive article by a holocaust denier," as the AAUP described it in an apology posted on its website. On February 9, when the article came to light, the AAUP executive committee voted for postponement. But Scott has angrily protested that decision, arguing that critics of the conference are "lobbyists on behalf of the current Israeli regime."

It is unfortunate that this kind of conspiracy theorizing is common in American universities, but shocking that Scott, who for the past few years has been responsible for guarding academic freedom at the AAUP, should show such commitment to it.

That Scott also resides at one of the most distinguished private academic institutes in the United States, where 28 Nobel laureates and Albert Einstein have worked, illustrates the triumph of anti-democratic ideology over scholarship. We are only beginning to become aware of the extent and costs of this intellectual catastrophe.

(2/21/06)

9 ACADEMIC GOON SQUAD

In late May, after months of debate and rancor, the largest academic union in Britain advised its members to boycott any Israeli academic who would not publicly disavow the so-called "apartheid policies" of the Israeli state. This meant that any Israeli academic who did not subscribe to the political views of the National Association of Teachers in Higher and Further Education (NATHFE) could be blacklisted: prevented from speaking or participating in conferences at British universities, and from being published in British academic journals.

This was the third time in four years that British academics tried to censure and isolate Israeli academics. The vote came despite an international petition launched by three academic groups: the U.S.-based Scholars for Peace in the Middle East, the Israel-based International Advisory Board for Academic Freedom, and the British-based Engage, which together collected nearly 6,000 signatures.

The vote to boycott was close, 106 to 71, and a good number of the union's 70,000 members condemned it.

Moreover, since NATHFE recently dissolved and merged with another British academic union (the Association of University Teachers, which ultimately failed in its attempt to boycott Israeli academics last year), the NATHFE vote is not binding on the newly formed body.

Still, NATHFE's vote represents a disquieting turning point, one that attempts to chill academic freedom and place a political litmus test on scholarship. The treatment of these Israeli scholars is particularly troubling. They alone are held accountable for their state's policies while scholars from Iran, Syria, Saudi Arabia, Korea and China—all recognized human rights abusers—are not boycotted.

The vote is another example of anti-Zionism morphing into anti-Semitism. Just as Jewish individuals were once persecuted and demonized, now the Jewish state has become the punching bag of the world. Contrary to what British academics would have the world believe, Zionism is not "racism" or "apartheid." It is the liberation movement of the Jewish people, founded by people of all colors gathered together from all continents. The attempt to target Israel and its people is not new.

Seventy-three years after Adolf Hitler fired Jewish professors from German universities, and burned and banned Jewish books, a group of British academics led the pack against Israeli scholars. These academics claim that Israel's "illegal" occupation of Palestinian territory requires the same sort of campaign that once was waged against apartheid South Africa. They envision that such boycotts, divestment, and sanctions will ultimately end the "Zionist occupation." They, and their many European and North American counterparts, see themselves as freedom-fighters for the oppressed, waging a battle against Israeli and American imperialism.

The potential danger to Jews, truth, democracy, and Western values is as great today as it was in 1933. The culture war's propaganda is not confined to one country or even one continent. Today, it is global, constant, sophisticated, and highly contagious. Education, talent, even genius do not immunize an academic from the mental illness that Jew-hatred represents.

Such politically correct academics are in denial about Jihadic, Islamist danger, and they seek to appease Islamist violence by siding with it against various scapegoats, beginning with the Jews and Israel. Academics who should have more accurate views of geopolitical conflicts instead view the Jihadi aggressor as the "victim" and his true victims, including civilians, as the guilty perpetrators.

For the crime of defending themselves, some British academics characterized Israelis under siege as "worse than Nazis" whose "genocidal policies" justified the rash of Palestinian human homicide bombs. Such academics, however, did not condemn the anti-Jewish, genocidal Islamic propaganda that turned countless adolescents into brainwashed, brutal killers.

Leading anti-Zionist British academics responded to the war against the Jews by launching divestment and boycott campaigns against Israel and against Israeli academics. In 2002, 123 British academics published an "open letter" in the *Guardian* calling for a "moratorium" on all cultural and research links with Israel. From 2004 to 2005, the British Association of University Teachers voted to boycott two Israeli universities for their alleged complicity in their government's military policies. That vote was overturned only after a tremendous struggle and international condemnation.

Similar divestment and boycott campaigns against Israel

were launched throughout the Western world.

Thankfully, British and European academics do not speak for all academics and reasonable people of good will.

For example, the American Association for the Advancement of Science condemned the boycott, as did British and Scottish church groups and the British government. While some of these petition signers do not agree with all of Israel's policies, they also oppose boycotts that smack of collective punishment, and racial, national, and political profiling.

Many petition signers are professors of physics, medicine, math and computer science who, unlike professors of social science and the humanities, are not as politicized. They do not use their disciplines as launch pads for their political views. They respect the work of their Israeli scientific counterparts, who are world leaders in technology, science and research. One professor comments, "Science builds bridges. It is an example of collaboration without borders."

Academics who signed the Scholars for Peace in the Middle East petition characterized the boycott a number of ways: "shameful," "repugnant," "discriminatory," "indefensible," "antisemitic," "selective," "appeasement-oriented," "anti-academic" and an example of dangerous "group thinking."

Many petition signers view this boycott as reminiscent of the Nazi era. Petition signers note that no boycotts have been undertaken against academics whose governments engage in real "ethnic cleansing" and human rights violations; they also note that Palestinians, Arabs, and Muslims are not being held accountable for their savage persecution of academics and dissenters.

One academic notes that "the British are responsible for

the mess they see in Palestine. Let's not scapegoat the Jews again."

Another wonders, "Are they planning to boycott Iranian academics?"

One professor implores, "Don't become the Savonarola of modern academia."

Still another notes that "the first task of a fascist regime is to boycott academics."

The truth is that a "silent" boycott has already begun. Some British academics have refused to write for Israeli journals, and refused to publish or review the work of Israeli academics and creative artists in British journals. For example, Exeter's Professor Richard Seaford recently refused to contribute an article to an Israeli journal of classical studies because of the "brutal and illegal expansionism and slow-motion ethnic cleansing being practiced by the [Israeli] government." A U.K. publication, *Dance Europe*, rejected an article by an Israeli choreographer unless she "publicly condemns Israeli occupation."

Those who are pro-boycott or in favor of blacklisting have effectively cut themselves off from the international community of scholars. Nevertheless, it counts as a propaganda victory for intolerance. It is also a step in the wrong direction, one that targets, demonizes and punishes a group of people based solely on their national, ethnic, and religious identity.

(6/16/06)

10 Manifesto for Survival

In late November, mobs in Paris once again shouted "Death to the Jew"—the very chant that came to characterize the Dreyfus case. The Hapoel Tel Aviv soccer team had won its match with the Paris Saint-Germain team. An angry mob surrounded a French Jew named Yanniv Hazout and yelled "kill the Jew," "dirty Jew," "dirty Negro," with many raising their arms in Nazi salutes. A black French policeman rushed to Hazout's defense. The crowd threatened to kill them both. The officer fired his gun, and killed one demonstrator and wounded another.

I see the noose tightening around Israel's neck and the necks of the world's Jews. The fix is in—Arab oil money can do that over a 50- or 60-year period. Today, Jews and Israel can do no right—even or especially when that is precisely what we do—and the nations who persecute us and others can do no wrong, no matter how many genocides or human rights atrocities they commit.

The propaganda has no limits, and it does not stop coming. No matter how many Big Lies you defeat, ten more immediately spring up to take their places.

Today, the truth goes begging for a scrap of respectful attention. If one tries to tell the truth about radical Islam, especially about Islamic gender and religious apartheid, one quickly finds oneself a pariah, scorned as a racist and "white supremacist."

The cultural wars are as hot as the military wars. Those with views such as mine have been subjected to a silent boycott. We do not get invited to speak on campuses. Even some Jewish-American student groups are careful not to invite speakers who might "offend" Muslim students.

Simultaneously, those who are invited to speak on campus are mainly people who agree with the works of America- and Israel-bashers Norman Finkelstein, Noam Chomsky, and the late "post-colonialist" Edward Said. When views such as theirs are exposed as anti-scholarly and bogus, guess what happens? Those in charge cry "persecution," blame the "Zionist lobby," and attempt to silence all views but their own.

Careful exposure of such naked Emperors does not stop them. They move on from publishing a paper to having their shoddy pseudo-scholarship defended at great cost in full-page ads in the *New York Times*, and then they garner book contracts with prestigious publishing houses. I refer here to Stephen Walt and John J. Mearsheimer of "Israel Lobby" fame whose publisher is now Farrar, Straus, and Giroux.

Recently, Cambridge University in Britain invited me to deliver a keynote address at a major international feminist conference—then they disinvited me. Every other speaker is on record as being in favor of abolishing the Jewish state or has been signing petitions to boycott Israel. One keynoter, hailed as a champion of human rights, routinely conducts anti-American protests outside the American Embassy in

London. (They subsequently did invite me to deliver a stand-alone lecture but not when an international group would be present to hear it). As of 2015, they have not "made good" on this offer.

Often, pro-America and pro-Israel truth-tellers who are invited to address a college audience are subjected to a hostile work environment, peppered with hostile questions, booed, jeered, picketed.

The situation is quite Orwellian. And yes, we are facing a potential Islamification of America.

With that in mind, here is what I propose.

Iran's Ahmadinejad and those he serves are the Hitlers of our time. They mean what they say. They wish to annihilate Israel with nuclear weapons, and they wish to convert all infidels to Islam. They want a caliphate.

We are up against a new kind of enemy—people who love death more than they love life. According to German scholar and activist Matthias Küntzel, the Ayatollah Khomeini dispatched 450,000 children between the ages of 12 and 18 to fight in the war between Iran and Iraq. Few survived. They swept the fields for mines, they comprised human waves that did not stop advancing even as other *"basiji"* sent before them were shot down or blown up. They carried little plastic keys around their necks that would open the gates of Paradise—or so their handlers told them.

As Jews, we must continue to love life, but we must plan for war—a very long war. We cannot afford to hope for the best or wait for someone else to handle it for us. We cannot deny that we are at war, nor can we trust the UN (especially now that John Bolton will not be there), NATO, or our European allies. But, as Israeli Major General Yaakov Amidror has pointed out, Israel and America might find some unexpected, temporary allies among the Saudis, Egyptians, and Jordanians who do not want a Shiite, Iranian take-over of their region.

We must live life in the moment—but we must also remember that we are an Eternal People obligated to eternal tasks. We cannot expect the battle between Good and Evil to cease—at least not until the Messiah comes. Evil triumphs when good people do not oppose it.

I have a distinguished friend who prefers not to use his own name here. Let us call him Wolf Papiermeister. Let me share with you some of his suggestions.

- Name the enemy as radical totalitarian Islam and all those who appease it. Even though our enemy is not a single nation state, it has a name—Islam—and an address—Mecca.
- Propagandize against totalitarian Islam and against all those who appease it. Use the full force of modern media to expose the imperialistic and barbaric aspects of Islam.
- Make it a national priority to develop non-oil alternatives. Why are we providing Islamists with the resources to destroy us?
- Put the West on a war footing. Reinstitute the draft. Use the military to enforce oil conservation.
- Restrict massive Muslim immigration into the West. Insist that immigrants pledge to uphold religious tolerance and democratic values, including women's rights. Grant asylum to Muslims fleeing Islamic persecution.
- Leave the UN. Kick it out of the U.S. The UN is a disgraceful failure and a colossal waste of money.

- Secure our prisons from Islamic recruitment. Why do we allow the spread of Islamic hate groups among already violent criminals? We are creating yet another extremely dangerous fifth column.
- Declare that the law of our land is American civil and criminal law. Wherever Sharia, the Islamic legal code, conflicts with our law, our law should prevail.

(12/13/06)

11 CELLULOID FANTASIES

I have been hooked on movies from the moment I saw *Fantasia* and *The Red Shoes* at the Windsor Movie Theatre in Boro Park when I was six years old.

Things have now taken a turn for the worse. The celluloid presentation of the Intifada of 2000 is characterized by sophisticated doctoring of film footage and lethally anti-Semitic storylines.

Many Hollywood movies no longer function merely as escape entertainment. We can detect a coded propaganda subtext and a failure to connect the dots.

The Nativity Story, which premiered in Vatican City and opened worldwide last December, depicts Mary (played by the "ethnic" Keisha Castle-Hughes of *Whale Rider* fame) and Joseph as Palestinian Arabs—not as the Jews they really were, but as anti-historical pre-Islamic Muslims with faintly Arabic accents. The family of Jesus is depicted as persecuted Palestinians on the run from the evil Jewish King Herod.

Since Christians on the West Bank today are persecuted by Muslims and protected by Jewish Israel, is this film meant to hide these facts, or merely to inflame audiences against Jews?

Alfonso Cuarón's adaptation of P.D. James's *The Children of Men* is set in London in the year 2027—a bleak time. Nuclear wars and ceaseless terrorism have devastated the planet. The British government is ruthlessly brutalizing "refugees." Human extinction looms. No woman has gotten pregnant in 18 years. One might think this film was written by Swift, Orwell, or Atwood, but the film has no real politics. It is, however, rife with symbols that substitute for a real story line. Immigrants are horrifically herded into prison camps that bear the heavy-handed logo "Homeland Security," the Leftist, present-day equivalent to Auschwitz's *"Arbeit Macht Frei."*

In a final apocalyptic showdown, the "resistance" has degenerated into a mob of angry, armed, and keffiyeh-bedecked shooters who are carrying signs and shouting slogans in Arabic. The scene bears absolutely no relationship to the rather poignant story of the miraculous birth of a girl-child who is shepherded through hell to the safety of the mythical "Human Project." But because we have all been subjected to similar scenes of Muslim demonstrations on our television screens, the very sight triggers and symbolizes "relevance" or "important politics" precisely when none exist.

Even escape movies are increasingly functioning as pro-Islamist propaganda.

The presumably serious political film, Emilio Estevez's *Bobby*, is a fictional account of the lives of 24 people who were present in the Ambassador hotel when Robert F. Kennedy was assassinated. The film boasts many stars including Anthony Hopkins, Helen Hunt, Demi Moore, and

Laurence Fishburne. It also has archival footage of Robert Kennedy's speeches.

But the film pointedly erased all facts about Kennedy's killer and his motives. In the theater lobby, after watching the film, three women asked aloud, "But who actually killed Kennedy?"

I told them, "Sirhan Sirhan, a Palestinian, killed Bobby Kennedy."

"But why?" one woman asked.

"Because Sirhan was angry that the American government had sold military equipment to Israel."

This omission is ominous. In 1973, Yasser Arafat's Fatah and Black September terrorist groups kidnapped American diplomats George Curtis Moore and Cleo Noel Jr., and Belgian diplomat Guy Eid in Khartoum, Sudan. They demanded that Jordan release a Black September leader, that Germany release some members of the Baader-Meinhof gang—and that America release Sirhan Sirhan.

The demands were not met and the three diplomats were executed on direct orders from Arafat—the same Arafat who received the Nobel Peace Prize, was received as a king at the United Nations, and with whom American presidents subsequently dined.

The film got a seven-minute standing ovation at the Venice Film Festival and has been nominated for many awards.

Bobby pretends to a political significance it does not have. People come away feeling they have just relived an important moment in American history when in fact they've been fed a series of well-acted fairy tales.

(2/14/07)

12 STANDING UP FOR THE TRUTH SHOULD NOT MAKE YOU A HERO

*T*he state-owned TV channel France 2 sued Philippe Karsenty for defamation when he insisted its airing of a very brief portion of the 27 minutes of raw footage of Mohammed al-Dura, the 12-year-old Palestinian boy allegedly killed by Israeli army gunfire, constituted a blood libel. The event occurred on September 30, 2000 at the Netzarim Junction and al-Dura became the face that launched more than a thousand Islamist riots, anti-Israeli petitions, and Palestinian human homicide bombings.

This past September, almost seven years later, a Paris judge ordered that France 2 turn over the film to the court by November 14. The trial is set for February 27, 2008.

Karsenty is willing to name Israel's Ambassador to France, Danny Shek, who would not give him a fair hearing and who refused to shake his hand at a party. He also names Charles Enderlin (a Jew and an Israeli), France 2's bureau chief in Jerusalem, who recorded the voice-over for the al-Dura program. According to the *Jerusalem Post*, "Danny Shek enjoys warms relations with Enderlin."

Karsenty's comment: "Such treason by an ambassador should have him fired forever from the Israeli foreign ministry."

Most Israeli intellectuals have remained silent about this case. On October 2, Natan Sharansky finally wrote an important piece about it in the *Wall Street Journal*. Karsenty said he "is happy—even thrilled—to have the support of such an important public figure."

I quietly note two things: First, that Sharansky came forward only after the Parisian judge ordered the raw footage to be turned over to the court; after the IDF finally demanded the raw footage; after the Israeli government proclaimed that it now believes the event was staged; and after the Israeli Shurat HaDin Law Center announced it would sue Charles Enderlin and request that the Israeli Government Press Office cancel his Israeli press credentials.

Second, Sharansky is the only major internationally recognized voice of conscience to have come forward. Elie Wiesel has said nothing. Former president Bill Clinton, who publicly mourned the presumed death of al-Dura, has remained silent, as have former presidents Carter and Bush.

Where are all the voices against racism and for justice in "Palestine"? If they really cared about Palestinians more than they cared about defaming Jews, wouldn't they be pleased to learn that a Palestinian child had not met such a violent end after all? Wouldn't they be enraged about the Palestinian "fake-a-death-and-fool-the-infidel" propaganda industry?

Karsenty is sharply critical of the "treacherous" former French president, Jacques Chirac. He says, "Chirac was more dangerous than any Arab dictator because during his entire career he provided the enemies of the Jews and Israel with the most dangerous weapons."

Of the French media Karsenty says, "They have failed to cover this case, except very minimally. As far as they are concerned, I am already on the intellectual equivalent of Devil's Island."

Karsenty says the staging of news events by Palestinians is both well-known and accepted by the French media. He also notes that, with the exception of the president of CRIF (Conseil Représentatif des Institutions Juives de France), Richard Prasquier, the organized French Jewish community has been, at best, unnaturally quiet about the al-Dura affair. He mentions, in passing, that he has lost most of his friends.

Karsenty also names some heroes, such as Israeli physicist Nahum Shahaf, whose work proved the IDF could not have fired the shots and that it was a staged event. He also names the head of the Israel Government Press Office, Daniel Seaman; the French psychoanalyst, Gérard Huber, who first published a book on the case in January 2003; and the American professor Richard Landes, who has worked tirelessly to publicize the truth.

Karsenty names *Pajamas Media* and its Paris bureau chief, Nidra Poller, as the only media outlet that "covered my struggle consistently, accurately, and as befit an important, historical case."

Karsenty is not Captain Dreyfus. He says Israel, not he, embodies the Dreyfus Case today. I agree, but the fact remains that it is Karsenty who has been sued and treated as a criminal by the French state and who is being forced to defend himself. The French, who defamed and punished Dreyfus, are now defaming and punishing the very Jewish state that arose partly because of Herzl's response to the Dreyfus case.

Karsenty is zealous about the truth of this matter. No one is exempted from his high standards, not even his supporters. He pointed out that even I had not "gotten it" right five years ago.

He is absolutely correct. In *The New Anti-Semitism*, I carefully noted that many experts and a German documentary filmmaker had begun to question the veracity of the 59-second al-Dura report, that people had begun to suggest that the entire episode might have been staged.

Like everyone else, I assumed the boy had indeed been killed.

I did the best I could at the time with the information we had. Nevertheless, if I could be taken in, it goes a long way in explaining how the entire world was fooled—a world not nearly as vigilant as I try to be concerning the truth about Jews and Israel.

We simply cannot trust Arab, Muslim, and Palestinian media. We know too much about the staging of events, the doctoring of footage, the documentation of fake massacres. But we also cannot afford to trust the international media, which kept replaying this staged footage without asking any questions.

Karsenty assures me that three independent journalists who viewed the raw footage "saw a series of staged events, casual passersby, a man riding a bicycle, and no death agony, as was claimed." He said that two of these journalists were "pressured not to go public."

Karsenty is unafraid. "Unlike Dreyfus," he says, "I am not in prison. Only my social life is ruined. If they find me guilty, it will show that France is even more corrupt than we thought."

Karsenty seeks vindication outside of the courts as well. He wants the kind of political intervention that will make such a court decision official.

"President Sarkozy, as the effective boss of the state-owned TV France 2, will have to intervene," he says. "He could demand that the film be submitted to expert analysis. As France's president, he could ask his TV to apologize to the entire world."

When people wonder why he is doing this, since anti-Semites and anti-Zionists will only continue to defame Israel, he responds, "Sir, did you shave yesterday? And you will shave again tomorrow? Why bother?"

And then he says, "It is important to stand up for the truth, no matter the cost. That should not make you a hero."

(10/24/07)

13 Ms. Magazine Fails the Cause of Freedom

PHYLLIS CHESLER'S PREPARED REMARKS

Recently, in the pages of the *New York Times*, Gloria Steinem wrote that we should not hold the only female Presidential candidate to higher or different standards than we hold male politicians; when we do, Gloria explained, that's sexism. Since 1972, I have been explaining to Gloria and other *Ms.* feminists that we should not hold the only Jewish state to a higher or different standard than we hold all other nations states; when we do, it is called racism, Jew-hatred, or anti-Semitism.

Western feminists have praised and worked with Shirin Ebadi, an Iranian lawyer and human rights activist. She won the Nobel Prize, but she also lives in a country ruled by Islamofascists who have kidnapped and murdered American and Israeli civilians and who hold their own people hostage.

Yet, three Israeli women leaders who identify with the West cannot even buy their way into the pages of the Feminist

Majority's *Ms.* magazine in a full page ad that says, "This is Israel." One of these women is Dorit Beinisch, the President of the Israeli Supreme Court, who, in the matter of the Women of the Wall (I was a name-plaintiff in this legendary lawsuit), to her eternal credit, judged that Jewish women had the right to pray in a group in the women's section at the Western Wall.

Ms. magazine should give her a parade, not banish her from their pages.

Ms. magazine has the right not to run an ad in which three major Israeli women leaders are featured. In doing so, they reveal their political conformity.

For a long time, too many Western feminists have been more concerned with the alleged "occupation" of a country that does not exist (Palestine) than they have been concerned with the occupation of women's bodies worldwide, especially in Islamic countries.

Before I came here today I looked through some issues of *Ms.* online from 2000 to 2007. The editorial bias is blatantly and consistently anti-Israel and pro-Palestinian. This is not the *Ms.* I once knew and loved so long ago. This is a Stalinized, post-colonial, anti-imperialist, multi-culturally relativist version of *Ms.* This is a feminism that has been utterly Palestinianized.

This does not serve the cause of Palestinian women well, nor does it serve the cause of women anywhere. It is unwise to desert the one democracy in the region and give a free pass to barbaric, totalitarian, fascist regimes. This kind of feminism betrays the women and men in the Third World who need feminist support the most. I am not a cultural relativist. I believe in a feminism that is universal.

Israel is not perfect—what country is? —yet only

Israel has been universally demonized. The United Nations specializes in this; it is the only thing they do well. *Ms.* has learned its lessons well from the United Nations and from all the propaganda that has swirled through the Western democracies for the last 40 years.

From the start, feminism has been unfairly, even viciously attacked. I do not want to do that here today. World events have made feminism more important, but most Western feminists prefer to blame America and Israel for the indigenous barbarism of Third World countries. They are also very proud of their cultural relativism. They say they don't want to "judge" anyone else's culture or country, unless, of course, that country is Jewish Israel.

Feminists slander Israel when they describe her as an apartheid state.

When I say this on campuses, I need police officers to protect my right to speak.

Many Western feminists have not supported the ex-Muslim dissident and feminist, Ayaan Hirsi Ali. Some feminists have attacked her as too anti-Muslim and as too soft on American imperialism and Western colonialism. Feminists have not praised the ex-Muslim feminists, Nonie Darwish or Wafa Sultan, who are both speaking truth to power, but who are not blaming America and Israel for anything.

Ms. magazine has praised individual feminist activists who live in countries where women are genitally mutilated, secluded, routinely beaten, veiled, not allowed to drive, forced into polygamous marriages, publicly gang-raped, stoned to death, and honor-murdered if they protest any of the above.

The American Jewish Congress had the courage to stand up to the *Ms.* Empire "for the love of Zion," and for the love of truth. It is my honor to stand with them, and with Blu Greenberg and Francine Klagsbrun today at this moment.

(1/15/08)

14 Obama Is Our First Muslim Presidential Contender

Obama is our first Muslim presidential contender.
I am not saying that he secretly is or ever was a Muslim. However, since his father was a Muslim, the "ummah," the Muslim people, consider him a Muslim whether he agrees with them or not. He is a United Nations-style anti-American and postmodern multi-cultural relativist, and that means Obama may refuse to call barbarism by its rightful name if that barbarism is practiced by Muslims.

On at least one public occasion, there is a photograph of Obama failing (or refusing) to pledge allegiance to the American flag. When challenged on this and other questions of patriotism, Obama explained that the true American patriot is one who criticizes his country's faults, not one who merely salutes its flag.

When I characterize Obama as our first Muslim Presidential contender, I am not talking about the photo of

Obama wearing a turban or the headgear of a Somali elder. I am talking about his ties to Trinity United Church of Christ Pastor Jeremiah Wright (Obama has been a member for twenty years), and Pastor Wright's ties to Farrakhan—who just last night bent over backward in his praise of Obama as our new Savior. Farrakhan addressed only the "black, brown, red, and yellow" people of America and of the world, not the "white" people, and compared Obama to the founder of the Nation of Islam, Fard Muhammad, whose mother was white and whose father was black—like Obama's parents. Farrakhan claimed that both men were "Saviors" and that Obama might be the only man who can save America.

A reminder: Farrakhan is a black separatist and black-nationalist Muslim, and the man who described Judaism as a "gutter religion."

Where does Obama stand on Islamic gender and religious apartheid? Is he aware that it has been penetrating the West, including America, the country he wishes to govern? Does he have a plan as to how he will deal with it? Does he stand with the Islamists or with their victims, beginning with Muslim women and Muslim intellectuals? Where does he stand on the proliferation of arranged marriages, polygamy, face-veiling, wife- and daughter-beating, and honor murders in America? And on the Islamist use of American civil rights law to safeguard Islamic gender and religious apartheid and Islamic separatism in America?

Does Obama care about the persecution of "infidels," including Christians, in Muslim lands? Does he have a foreign policy vision that would demand reciprocity for all religions in Saudi Arabia, Afghanistan, and Iran *before* we allow American law to be used to construct mini-Saudi Arabias or Irans in America?

Has he called for an end to the Kassam rockets that rain down on Israeli civilians in Sderot? And for an end to Saudi, Iranian, and Syrian support for Hamas and Hezbollah as they all seek to annihilate the only Jewish state?

Why has no one been asking all the candidates these questions?

Obama's various alliances are worrisome. In addition, Obama has chosen a foreign policy team that has been consistently pro-Palestinian and anti-Israel; many of Obama's advisors have engaged in boycotts and urged divestment in Israel as if Israel really is "apartheid" South Africa.

Obama also wants to talk to Amadinejad who has referred to Israelis as "filthy bacteria," has funded countless acts of murderous terrorism against Israel, and has pledged to genocidally exterminate the Jewish state. "Talk," he said—and without pre-conditions. Of course, Obama's handlers are backpedaling on this one as fast as they can.

Obama is a thrilling orator. But he is vague and repeats himself just as an actor might. Yes, it is exciting that a bi-racial American who looks African is running for the American presidency, but it is equally important, or it should be, that a woman is a presidential contender as well. And we, the people should not be voting for—or against—anyone because of their race or gender. Their agenda alone is what should matter.

(2/26/08)

15 STOP THE ISRAEL BASHING IN THE MEDIA AND THE JEWS WILL NO LONGER BE HATED

Our era's Dreyfus has just been vindicated.

A few hours ago, a French Appeals Court decided that Phillipe Karsenty did not libel Charles Enderlin of France's Channel 2 in the matter of Mohammed Al-Dura. One wonders whether the world, which was so eager to lap up the base, visual propaganda against Israel, will now lap up the truth just as eagerly. I doubt it. Even if the world's mainstream media covers this legal victory widely, and accurately, it may still not be able to reverse the revulsion toward Israel that this staged photo of the twelve-year-old Mohammed al-Dura has provoked.

While most of the world is already primed to believe the worst about Israelis, this staged event at the Netzarim Junction has already done its vast and dirty work. Can a legal decision compete with a soul-stirring staged photo in the Arab speaking world? How about in the Israel-bashing global media?

Fausta Wertz tells us that France's Channel 2, which perpetrated the hoax, has not reported the verdict. Only Charles Enderlin, who sued Karsenty for libel, mentions the verdict on his own blog. His spin: The child died, the Israelis did it. No alternate comments are allowed on his blog.

Fausta tells us to "expect nothing more from the media." She might just be right.

The *New York Times* covered the decision as did *Reuters*, Britain's *Spectator*, the *Jerusalem Post*, and other Israeli media. The *International Herald Tribune* ran yesterday's AP dispatch. This story takes the same line as the *Times*, namely, that the court ruled that Karsenty was entitled to voice his opinion without that opinion being deemed "libelous."

There are no stories (at least, not yet) in which the mainstream Western media admit that, in the past, they have allowed themselves to be fooled, over and over again, by the narrative of Palestinian victimhood and Israeli evil because it suited them—the facts be damned.

Can the families of Israelis who were murdered and maimed during the Al-Aqsa Intifada sue France's Channel 2 and Charles Enderlin for money damages? Enderlin and his Palestinian cameraman knowingly perpetrated a hoax. Having just lost, Enderlin is now vowing to appeal the decision. (Enderlin-the-slanderer is the one who sued Karsenty for "libel.") As the excellent Professor Richard Landes notes in his ongoing coverage of this case on his blog *Augean Stables*, "Those whom the gods would destroy, first they drive mad."

(5/21/08–5/22/08)

16 STAGED PALESTINIAN HOAXES IN THE FIRST LEBANON WAR

The prominent Israeli academic, Dr. Marilyn Safir, of Haifa, just wrote to me about her personal eye-witness experience of Palestinian faux-tography in the *first* Lebanon war (1981-1982). I have known her for 36 years, and share her letter with permission. She writes:

> *In the first Lebanon War, just before I left for that feminist conference in Montreal, we saw two news reports on Israel TV. In one, the Israel news team followed a French film crew. The French media put several young children in a burnt out car and lit a fire on the far side of the car and then filmed the children in the "burning car" screaming and crying with the smoke and flames billowing in the background. Two days later I saw this clip broadcast in Montreal. If I hadn't seen them staging it, I would have believed these were*

kids who were directly attacked (by Israelis) and left to burn to death.

The other clip was of the Israeli air force attacking a "hospital" with a big red cross on the roof. We could see that the "hospital" was actually a base of the PLO who were (engaged in) shooting from it. That, too, appeared on the news. Interestingly, the Lebanese government took out a big paid ad stating that the (so-called) hospital was PLO Headquarters and was headed by Arafat's brother.

(The Montreal feminist) conference was the one that the PLO tried to take over to pass anti-Israeli Resolutions and that I more or less single-handedly fought to prevent—successfully—I might add.

Thank you, Marilyn. I wonder how many more such incidents people know about and when they will come forward. Will the mainstream Western and Arab language media ever cover this? And, if not, what do we propose to do?

(5/23/08)

17 A Day in the Life of the New York Islamic Times

This past weekend, the paper of record had a ball. One columnist attacked Israeli settlers. The lead story attacked American military interrogation methods as practiced on known, al-Qaeda terrorists. The magazine had a piece by journalist and Harvard law professor, Noah Feldman, who once more defended the rights of Muslims and Muslim immigrants in Europe. (Yes, he's the one who finds Orthodox Judaism barbaric but defends Islam's right to veil its women.)

I have written about Feldman before. This time, Feldman argues that Muslims are, regrettably, becoming "pariahs" in Europe and he cautions Europeans to remember that they once perpetrated a Holocaust on another "pariah" people: Jews. Feldman fails to note that Jews were never violent and, for the most part, wished to assimilate and did so with pride. The problem today with many first-, second-, and third-generation Muslims (of course, there are many exceptions) is that they do not want to become assimilated, modern

Europeans but wish to recreate the Punjab in Britain, Algiers in France, Istanbul in Germany, etc.

Feldman is sacralizing regrettably hostile, radically fundamentalist and anti-assimilationist Muslims by falsely, or at least glibly, confusing them with six million dead Jews. He is trying to transfer the sacred power of Ultimate Victimhood to all Muslim immigrants, including the Islamists and the terrorists. Feldman writes:

> This leaves another, more controversial explanation for anti-Muslim attitudes in Europe: Even after 60 years of introspection about the anti-Semitism that led to the Holocaust, Europeans are not convinced that culturally and religiously different immigrants should be treated as full members of their societies...Hitler's horrifying success at killing so many Jews meant that the burgeoning postwar societies of the continent never had to come to terms with difference.

Europe has reaped the karmic whirlwind. Because Europeans refused to integrate the non-violent, Semitic group that respected their ways and that were at their mercies (the Jews), Europe has inherited the Semitic group that is violent and wishes to Islamify Europe. Also, guilty but tired-of-being-blamed-for-the-Holocaust Europeans, including Europe's intelligentsia, are now ready to embrace a far more traditional Semitic group in the service of Thanatos, Death.

Ethan Bronner penned a piece in the *New York Times* that was somewhat sympathetic to Israelis who are being rocketed and shelled, which is like throwing a bare bone to a starving dog. This kind of piece is the exception, not the rule, and it will disappear beneath the radar of the steady propaganda.

Finally, there is Nicholas Kristof's column at the back of the Week in Review. This was unexpectedly shocking. Kristof's work on sexual slavery and Islamic gender apartheid is so inspiring. How did he come to write such a biased piece about Israel?

Kristof damns Israeli settlers, especially in Hebron, and praises both Palestinians and left-wing Israelis who critique Israeli policy. He fails to note that the Israeli left has few Palestinian counterparts.

I am not saying that what he saw with his own eyes is not true. He saw Palestinians waiting at checkpoints and he saw Israelis whizzing by on highways, but he does not present the history or context for either reality. Kristof repeats what he has been told about pregnant Palestinian women who lose their unborn babies because they are forced to wait at checkpoints. He has been totally taken in by both Palestinian/Islamist/Western propaganda and by the valorously obsessional propaganda of Left Israeli groups.

Kristof apparently has no idea that there has been a continuous Jewish presence in Hebron for thousands of years, that Abraham purchased a burial cave there thousands of years ago. Psychoanalyst Perry R. Branson, citing Professor Barry Rubin, has an excellent blog about how Kristof's piece demonstrates routine unconscious biases against Israel. Branson also quotes our mutual colleague, Ed Bialek, who musters the requisite indignation and information:

> How is it that the NY Times editorial page just outdoes itself Sunday after Sunday? How is that Nicholas Kristof talks about an impractical Jewish settlement (in Hebron) that has no right being there? How is it that he talks about Jews "stealing" the land? How is it that he paints a

picture of the Jews as a completely alien presence in a land where he implies the Palestinians are the sole indigenous population?

How is it he fails to mention that Hebron is the site of the oldest Jewish community in the world? How is it that he never mentions that the downtown area "expropriated from the Palestinian" by the Israelis is the site of the "expropriated" historic Jewish community? How is it that there is no mention of how and when that Jewish presence came to an end, how the Jews were "transferred" from that city? How is it that he states that the only decent Jews are the ones documenting and condemning these colonial, imperial Jewish settlers, these Jewish interlopers?

I have taken the time to visit only one issue of the *New York Islamic Times*. Imagine the effect of such a newspaper day after day, week after week, year after year.

Here is our problem. Many more people will have read Kristof's words than will have read Ed Bialek's words. Day after day, the mainstream media continue to publish disinformation, which brainwashes its readers. Yes, Ed and I have a First Amendment right to criticize propaganda, but how many people will read our words?

(6/23/08)

18 A Young Jew Is Savagely Beaten In Paris

In 2006, Ilan Halimi was brutally tortured for three full weeks in Paris by gangs of African Muslim immigrant torturers. The media did not describe them as "Muslims," but rather as "youth," "militants," "gang-members," "immigrants," and "immigrants from Africa." Neighbors took turns and joined in torturing Halimi. Other neighbors heard his screams and did nothing. Some came to watch. Halimi died on February 13, 2006. The ringleader of the gang, Youssouf Fofana, fled to the Ivory Coast but was extradited back to France. He and 18 others are facing a trial in his torture and murder.

Now, a visibly Jewish, kipah-wearing 17 year-old, Rudy Haddad, walking in a Jewish quarter, was set upon by 15-30 "African immigrants." No one is saying whether they are Muslims or not. According to a Jewish Telegraphic Agency report:

> While French officials were quick to condemn the attack, most fell short of identifying the crime

as anti-Semitic, saying the police first needed to complete their ongoing investigation. French President Nicolas Sarkozy told reporters while visiting Israel this week that he was "particularly shocked by what happened to a young French boy, on the pretext that he was wearing a kippah."

Sarkozy denounced the attack but did not conclude that the attack was anti-Semitic. Various representatives of the French Jewish community did.

Where are all the anti-racists now? The silence is chilling and all too predictable. Where are the mainstream media?

What is to be done? Do Jews world-wide, beginning in Europe, and particularly in the 19th arrondissement in Paris, need Israeli Defense Forces to guard them as they walk to Parisian synagogues?

Do French police officers need to guard individual Jews just as they have been forced to guard each and every synagogue and Jewish Center ever since Palestinian terrorist leader Yasser Arafat began his murderous campaign in the late 1960s of airplane hijackings, hostage taking, and synagogue and airport bombings?

Shall the remnant of Jewish life in Europe wearily pick itself up and leave, either to Israel, Australia, or America?

Will Europe finally consider not allowing any further immigration of African or Arab Muslims? Will Europe finally dare to consider outlawing radical and unevolved Islam as a criminal enterprise?

Clearly, Europe is willing to sacrifice its Jews to African immigrant and/or to Muslim barbarism.

(6/24/08)

19 A MUST-SEE PRO-ISRAEL FILM

A desperate handful of filmmakers have arisen these past few years to counter the mainstream media's Big Lies against Israel and Jews and to document the truth. Pierre Rehov has made many important films, including *Silent Exodus, Holy Land: Christians in Peril, The Road to Jenin*, and *Suicide Killers*.

Now comes *The Case for Israel: Democracy's Outpost*. Michael Yohay is the documentary film's award-winning director and producer (he was in charge of the news footage for IDF activities from 1993 to 2005), and Gloria Greenfield is its producer and marketing director.

The film is very important.

Alan Dershowitz, the Harvard law professor and prolific author, begins the film by explaining that he is pro-Israel "not only because I am a Jew...but because I am a civil libertarian" who fights for "human rights" and "women's rights," and "because I am a lover of peace."

Dershowitz discusses Jimmy Carter's cowardly refusal

to debate him face-to-face when Carter's book, *Palestine: Peace Not Apartheid*, came out. Dershowitz characterizes Carter's book as "essentially congratulating the Palestinian leadership for rejecting Camp David and Taba."

Former Prime Minister Benjamin Netanyahu reminds us that "there has been a reversal of the facts of history," and suggests that "the only way to make the case for Israel is to go back to the historical facts."

Eilat Mazor, the prominent archeologist, talks about Jerusalem's biblical-era Jewish roots. Archeologist Gabriel Barkay notes that "Jerusalem is mentioned by name 667 times in the Bible but is not even mentioned once in the Koran."

Ambassador Dore Gold points to Israel's excellent record in terms of allowing religious diversity to flourish and fears that "turning over the old city to the Palestinian Authority would be disastrous for the holy sites because we have seen across the Middle East...that radical Islam shows no tolerance for the holy sites of other faiths."

Authors Michael Oren and Benny Morris, along with Netanyahu, Professor Gerald Steinberg, and Alex Safian, are our history teachers as to what actually happened in 1947/1948. Netanyahu points out "that the Arabs have very cleverly turned the result of their aggression (in 1947 and again in 1967) into [their] cause." Arabs claim they attack Israel "because of the Arab refugees which are the result of the Arab aggression against the tiny Jewish state."

Eloquent experts (police and army officers) explain the Security Fence, the nature of a Kassam Rocket, the history of Palestinians who literally hide behind children to launch rockets at Israeli children, and the agonizing military and moral decisions Israel must carefully make and at great expense to itself.

Secretary-General Ban Ki-moon should summon the General Assembly, lock the doors, and screen this film at the United Nations.

(11/5/08)

20 THE PALESTINIAN CON: PAYING OFF THE THUGS

*L*ast night, in response to my article about the Holy Land victory in Dallas, jihadists and "useful idiots" began flooding my site with semi-literate factoids and insults that border on anti-Semitism. Their rage is palpable. They blame all evil and human suffering on the (small case) "zionists." Defenders have also emerged. Their spelling and sentence structure is a lot better, which suggests that ignorance still remains a great enemy.

The Palestinian leaders (not the people) are heavily funded by the entire world. They siphon off money for their own bank accounts, villas, and lifestyles while the people continue to suffer. Palestinian "handlers" manipulate the misery of the people and turn sad young men and women from impoverished and often fatherless families into human homicide bombs.

The apt phrase, "sad young men," is Dr. Anat Berko's. Dr. Berko is the author of *The Path to Paradise: The Inner World of Suicide Bombers and Their Dispatchers*. She is a

Lt. Colonel in the Israeli Defense Force. We met recently in New York and she showed me photographs of a father, a grandfather, and a great-grandfather all wearing full Arab dress. The Iraqi government threw them out "like dogs, like Jews," and confiscated their properties and businesses. Like so many Palestinian refugees, Dr. Berko's parents still have keys to their homes and factories in Baghdad, but they have not run an elaborate con game on the entire world, demanded perpetual aid and support, hatched wildly unrealistic plans to return.

If any Palestinian dares challenge *Palestinian* tyranny, they are killed or forced into exile.

There are only a handful of exceptions. Last year, Bassam Eid came to visit. He is the brave Palestinian who founded the first organization to monitor Palestinian-on-Palestinian violence, including corruption, intimidation, censorship, lynching, etc. When I asked him about the oft-repeated accusation that Israelis are "humiliating Palestinians at the checkpoints," he laughed. He said, "Real humiliation, even danger, is what Palestinians face if they visit Cairo or other Arab capitals." I asked him why he was still alive, was his family a powerful one? Again, he laughed. That, indeed, was the reason. Bassam Eid was in New York because *Rabbis* for Human Rights were honoring him. I wonder how often he's been honored by mullahs?

(11/25/08)

21 MADOFF THE JEW: THE MEDIA'S HYPOCRITICAL OBSESSION WITH THE FRAUDSTER'S FAITH

*F*or days now, I have been following the media coverage of the Madoff scandal. The *New York Times* kept emphasizing that he is Jewish and moved in moneyed, Jewish circles—not once, but time and again, in the same article, and in article after article. How exactly is Madoff's religion more relevant than Rod Blagojevich's religion? The *Times* has not described Blagojevich (or Kenneth Lay of Enron) as "Christian," nor do they describe the Arab or south Asian Muslim terrorists as "Muslims."

As I've previously noted, the *Times* goes out of its way to describe terrorists who are ethnic Arab Muslims and south Asian Muslims as "gunmen," "attackers," "fighters,"— never as terrorists—and they rarely use the word "Arab" or "Muslim" to characterize the perpetrators of a deadly rogue action. However, the paper of record will use the word "Muslim" to describe an aggrieved victim who has alleged "Islamophobia" or "racism."

People often wonder: What did they know and when did they know it—referring to political corruption scandals or to the cover-ups of monumental disasters like genocide? We now know that the *Times* knows precisely what they are doing.

Just as Bernie Madoff did.

Yes, of course, Madoff's betrayal is unforgivable. He has gutted an entire generation of Jewish philanthropic wealth, destroyed trust within the Jewish philanthropic world, but, far more important, impoverished widows, orphans, and the elderly, and, in so doing, endangered and shamed the Jewish people at a time when we have many real, not merely neurotically imagined, enemies.

That Arab and African oil sheikhs and countless tyrants on every continent impoverish and destroy their own people, their neighbors, and their enemies every single day is irrelevant. The world does not hold non-Jews accountable for the harm that they do. Only Jews are expected to meet their own high Jewish standards (for which they are hated and envied).

In the Middle East, graft and nepotism make the wheels turn. Everyone is on the take. Beggars aren't beggars; entire civil services are staffed by one or two clans. In Central Asia, everyone, from the Afghan president on is on the take and opium is a most abundant and attractive cash crop. The Afghan drug lords are addicting, infecting, and murdering entire global populations with their poppies as are those who buy and sell the heroin. No one holds the Afghans accountable. But woe to the Jewish people that have harbored, abetted, profited from, or has even been fleeced by Madoff, the greed master.

(12/23/08)

22 ISRAEL'S QUIET NIGHTMARE

*T*ry to imagine sitting in a bomb shelter, shaking with terror, day after day, year after year. Try to imagine having to run to get to that shelter; once the siren screams, you'll have only one minute before the rocket will strike. Imagine that you're elderly or disabled; imagine that you're diabetic but have forgotten your insulin; imagine that your children are freaking out or that you can't find them.

Do you seek shelter yourself or do you keep looking for your children? Do you give up your job, and keep your children at home and out of school? Do you scatter them among your relatives elsewhere in the country? How does a person resign herself to not being in control of ordinary life "for the duration?"

This has been the reality for Israeli civilians who live in Sderot, and it is now the reality for those living in Ashkelon and Be'er Sheva. The media has not covered this: Not enough blood, too little death, the photo opportunities are not...sexy. Thus, the world did not open its heart to this nerve-wracking, soul-deadening suffering, only a handful of protests were ever held, international pressure never built, the UN did not preside over urgent meetings.

Now, this utterly demoralizing reality, together with the grim fact that kidnapped Israeli soldier, Gilad Shalit, is still missing—well, it all does not seem to "count" as much as a photograph of one dead *Palestinian* child—one of Hamas's smaller human shields. You can see her on the front page of yesterday's *New York Times*. Hamas is not blamed for putting her in harm's way for purely propaganda purposes. Israel is blamed for daring to finally try to put an end to the endless barrage of artillery aimed at its civilian citizens by exterminationists.

Still, it is a terrible image. Strange, there are no front page photos of the three-month-old Israeli infant who has just been "lightly wounded" by Hamas rocketry in Gadera.

How can we capture Israeli suffering in a single photograph—assuming the world wanted to see it? In this instance, a few words might be worth a thousand pictures. I have begun to write to Israelis I know. Yesterday, I asked one woman to help me "humanize" Israel's plight. Here's the first response, from Jennifer Roskies. Her words are ironic, bitter, thoughtful, eloquent, and manage to convey both the "larger" and the more personal picture (so to speak). She writes:

> Unfortunately, I don't think that I have much to offer that would "humanize" what Israel is experiencing, because there is nothing that compares to the morbid orgasmic effect of dead children and babies' corpses. In terms of what the 900,000 hostage-citizens of Israel's south, "the south" is a half-hour drive from my door), there is not much to say, either.

There is nothing that spectacular about a government doing pretty much what it is supposed to do—namely, equip shelters, build protective structures, put an entire branch of the army, the Home Front Command, in charge of a comprehensive infrastructure of resources and personnel that provides information, hot lines, supplies, essential services, and most of all, makes sure that all public spaces and vulnerable areas are evacuated when the alarms sound.

I mean, what's the emotional thrill of seeing a kindergarten with a hole blown through its ceiling, or a crater in a soccer field after it's been evacuated and is now empty, when you could look at panic stricken civilians running through, (or buried under), dilapidated, unenforced structures without a shred of a notion of where to go. No place to run to—because the game plan was to leave them exposed and vulnerable, wedged deliberately between the rocket launchers and terror masterminds and the Israeli attacks.

Not only that: the seething hatred from Palestinian masses and fanatic fervor, (along with the self-righteousness in demonstrations around the world), bring such a high voltage rush that everything else is bland in comparison. That includes the unassuming nobility of young warriors who march into harm's way to try to stop the rockets, knowing that nothing can quell the hatred.

Jennifer Roskies has brilliantly captured the public relations nightmare that Israel is facing. Israel is being punished because she is taking care of her citizens, or at least, trying to do so. Israel is not supported to defend herself. Leftist Jews believe that Israel can only be deemed a "good Jewish" nation if it agrees to endure endless wars of attrition and to participate in the evisceration of its already small territory. Islamists agree with the leftist Jews that the only "good" Jewish nation is one that is not so... "Jewish," one that is, perhaps, dead and gone.

Hamas is being rewarded with sympathy and international support precisely because it uses civilians as human shields and has spent the last three years, after Israel unilaterally withdrew from Gaza, not in creating a Palestinian state, but in trying to destroy the Jewish state.

(1/6/09)

23 BRITISH LIES

I grew up believing that the "truth" of a matter really existed and that it mattered. Today, the intellectual elite believe that truth does not exist; that there are many truths and -isms; that everything is relative, that all points of view are "equal."

People have been taught to worship lies, paranoid projections, linguistic reversals, and manipulated images. False accusations are mass produced and continue to pass for sweet truth in every language under the sun.

If anyone thinks these are just words (no harm done, everyone is entitled to their opinion), please note that the entire world "cares" about Gaza and Palestine like no other places on earth. In the last month, the *New York Times* published two articles a day, accompanied by large photos, about Gaza. They also simultaneously featured op-ed pieces, editorials, and letters on Gaza in the very same issue.

The mainstream media that once wrote about the alleged "massacre" in Jenin has now spread the lie that more than 1,000 Gazans, including many women and children, were killed by Israelis in battle. Now, too late for the world's brief attention span, we learn that no more than 600 Gazans died, and that they were mainly Hamas warriors dressed as civilians—not civilians, not women and children. Compare that to the daily death tolls in Darfur and Congo and you will understand how very yellow this journalism truly is.

Once, barbarians ate their enemies' hearts in order to incorporate their power. Today's barbarians assert that *they* are the victims, thus hoping to incorporate the moral stature of those whom they envy, defame, and victimize.

Over the weekend, I published a piece about Douglas Murray's disinvitation as a moderator by the London School of Economics. Now, several commentators suggest that the matter was really more complicated, that LSE was not exactly, precisely, in the wrong. But is this true?

Based on my own experience with how Cambridge University disinvited me but then denied having done so, and based on what Douglas has told me, I think not. Once world media attention took note of the disinvitation, the London School of Terrorism and Appeasement tried to cover their sorry-ass exposure. According to Murray:

> The LSE has been desperately trying to firefight since the press here started on them. They even tried to "re-invite" me an hour and a half before the event started. All their earliest media responses are different from the later ones when they tried to pretend there was no problem. They were caught off guard by the amount of media interest and decided to try to come up with a new "narrative." Pretty pusillanimous from a university, or to be expected!
>
> Their press officer has been in a terrible spin and has been writing to blogs and papers

everywhere. But the *Telegraph* and *Evening Standard* here saw the original emails (which I'm very happy to send to you too) disinviting for all the reasons shown in the original press reports.

Of course the LSE actually IS a hot-bed of radicalism and has repeatedly produced terrorists—not least the murderer of Daniel Pearl. Each time they are revealed to be a hot-bed of extremism they express embarrassment at the information becoming public knowledge—but never do a thing to change the situation.

A few years ago, I was invited by the Women's Studies/ Gender Studies program to deliver one of four keynote speeches at an international conference marking their tenth anniversary. They said that I had made quite a good case in my book *The Death of Feminism: What's Next in the Struggle for Women's Freedom*. I was amazed and immediately agreed to come. Then I reviewed who the other speakers would be and realized that I would be the "token" critic of Islamic gender and religious apartheid and the token pro-American, pro-Israel, and pro-Western democracy voice.

I stressed that I would come, one way or the other, but asked them to review the possible need for campus security. They promptly disinvited me, but only to the international conference. They were canny enough to write that in the future, I would be welcome to address a small, non-international group. I never heard from them again.

According to Douglas Murray:

> The current line the LSE is trying to pursue is that the particular international circumstances made it impossible this time, but that on other

occasions (during peacetime?) I would be allowed on campus again. It's worth noting what "normal" circumstances at the LSE are.

I spoke to the Jewish Society at LSE last term. The Islamic society there heard of my visit and threatened the J-Soc with various things they said would happen if I came. The J-Soc held firm. They invited the I-Soc to attend. The talk passed peacefully and no member of the I-Soc even tried to challenge me. A few of them merely sat in silence and recorded the event without asking permission (presumably hoping I was going to say something they could then object to: of course they were disappointed).

However, the next issue of the LSE student newspaper contained a front-page article dictated by the I-Soc with all of their propaganda, libeling me in most grotesque way: accusing me of "Islamophobia" and "racism" among other allegations. I wrote to the editors, journalists and head of LSE warning them that unless they printed a full front-page retraction immediately I would sue them for libel. The next issue duly contained a full and complete retraction.

This is not just happening in England. I want Americans to realize that our campuses are also under siege. Islamists and Marxist-Leninists, with lots of Wahabi-Saudi funding, have taken them over. Their Palestinianized point of view prevails. The disinvitations are happening here too—as are the non-invitations. And, the rage of the Muslim and pro-Palestinian pro-"peace" marchers is very frightening. In London over the weekend (very much like the marches for Gaza across America), a march on the Israeli Embassy turned ugly. As I watched it, I could hear one of the marchers clearly screaming "police brutality," over and over again. The marchers were attacking the unarmed police and one of their leaders made sure to claim victim status.

How long will the world continue to fall for such tricks, persist in believing that Lies are true?

(1/26/09)

24 JEWS: TO THE MUSLIM GAS CHAMBER

We have grown used to seeing Palestinian and Hamas supporters goose-step, Nazi-style, and shoot out their arms as they deliver the Hitlerian "Sieg Heil" salute. They chant and scream, "Jews to the ovens," "Hitler did not kill enough of you," "Jews to the gas chambers."

This is raw, rank, Jew-hatred; that much is clear. We are also faced with a major paradox. These same Palestinian and Hamas supporters routinely hold signs that accuse Israel of being a "Nazi" state. To them, Gaza is "Auschwitz," and the Israelis have "occupied" it with "genocidal" intentions. Of course this is not true. According to my colleague, Dr. Barry Rubin:

> In 1939, there were seven million Jews in continental Europe. At the end of the Holocaust, only one million Jews survived. There are currently 1.2 million Palestinians in Gaza. At the end of the 2009 war, 1,199,000 Palestinians

are still there. The percentage of Jewish civilians killed by Germans and their allies was 86 percent. The percentage of Gazan Palestinians killed by Israelis is 0.1 percent. The number of Jewish civilians *deliberately* killed by Nazis and their allies is 6,000,000. The number of Palestinian civilians *deliberately* killed by Israelis=0.

But the truth no longer matters. Everyone has piled onto such metaphoric overkill. Thoughtful and moderate voices are no longer heard, only shouting, shocking, attacks seem to register.

Europeans and North Americans who support such a false Nazification of Jews are merely continuing the Holocaust-era determination to genocidally exterminate Jews. This time, they hope that by doing so, the Islamist hordes will spare them, allow them to survive as dhimmis, as inferior and subordinate citizens, in an Islamified Europe.

I asked Dr. Nancy H. Kobrin, the psychoanalyst and Arabist, what she thinks is going on. She said, "If we (the Jews) exist, the Muslims might have to acknowledge their own Jewish roots. They can't do that. Therefore, they must destroy us."

"So, they're trying to destroy the living witnesses?" I asked.

"Well, they are pandering to people who like Nazi insignia and the Nazi ideology. But they are also trying to drive the Jews crazy. They must know how seeing Nazi insignia makes us feel. This is very primitive, non-verbal behavior."

Dr. Kobrin calls this "psychological splitting. They want to have it both ways." What she means is that the Palestinian propagandists and Muslim jihadists want to both identify with the Nazis as triumphant, death-cult destroyers, and also with the (past) preferred sacred status accorded to dead Jewish victims. The Palestinians and other Islamists offer up their own babies, women, elderly, and civilian populations as human shields, human sacrifices, in order to obtain this grisly goal. They also engage in faked staged photos to approximate such Jewish-style deaths as well.

Dr. Kobrin reminds us that "paranoids" are obsessed with "purity" and therefore with "cleansing." This is accomplished by having a "scapegoat" upon whom one projects all the "dirty" components of oneself or of one's group-self.

The use of Nazi images are meant to terrify and intimidate all who view them—especially those who have, in the past, been jailed, tortured, exiled, and wounded by those who display such symbols. These images are forms of visual hate speech. They are meant to re-traumatize real victims and their second- and third-generation descendants and to intimidate bystanders.

But those Muslims who display Nazi imagery also feel that *they* are the wounded ones. They seek public redress for their real and imagined wounds. What wounds? For starters: painful, shameful, anal penetration by trusted relatives in childhood; beatings in childhood; painful, public male circumcision between the ages of five and thirteen; cruel parents, cruel teachers, cruel religious leaders, and equally cruel peers. Add to that a culture that takes cruelty as a given: poor nutrition, illiteracy, and/or no productive future—mainly due to Arab leaders who demand reverence and obedience even as they hoard the wealth meant to alleviate their people's suffering. Street theatre/political protest/mob merging is the only approved form of social life or group "orgasmic" activity.

According to Lloyd DeMause, there is a "paranoid" underside to anti-Semitism. It is caused by "child abuse, paedophilia and incest." He writes:

> I would like to refer to a careful survey in the journal, *Child Abuse & Neglect* that showed that when questioned 652 Palestinian undergraduates concluded that 19% were sexually assaulted by a family member, 36% by a relative and 46% by a stranger. Since this adds up to more than 100%, obviously many were abused by more than one person, but the overall conclusion I detailed in my *Journal of Psychohistory* article entitled "If I Blow Myself Up and Become a Martyr, I'll Finally Be Loved" (Spring 2006) was that most Palestinians are sexually abused, that men routinely have young boys they rape and that this is not because of poverty because the college students reporting such horrible memories have upper-class families.

This partially explains the Arab street. The Westerners who support them are a more curious matter. Are Westerners trying to both hide and atone for their racism by masquerading as anti-colonialists and by "slumming," dressing as impoverished Arabs? Or, is this a symbol of a Western wish to (psychologically) die, to be done with the demands of freedom, to be cleansed of all our filth—our greed and lust, our burdensome choices?

There is something else. The jihadic use of European Nazi images is essentially a "fakeout." The jihadists are projecting all the sins of Islam towards Jews onto Christian Europe. In their use of Holocaust-era imagery, the jihadists are trying to pretend that there is no long and genocidal history of Muslims towards Jews, Christians, and other infidels; they deny a 1,400 year history of Islamic Jew (and infidel) hatred and genocide—one that is very much alive today, one that is supported by Muslim religious sources.

Historically, despite individual exceptions and moments of respite, Jews were routinely and relentlessly subjected to pogroms in the Muslim world and were ultimately driven out of the Muslim Middle East. The Jewish refugee story is the larger and more hidden story of 1948 - 1956. The Christian Crusades took place because imperialist, colonialist, and genocidal Arab Muslims were slaughtering Christians throughout the Middle East and Central Asia in what was once known as Byzantium; Zoroastrians in Persia and Buddhists and Hindus in Afghanistan, too. Christians are still persecuted by Muslims today; many have been forced to flee Muslim lands.

The use of Nazi images in pro-Palestinian, anti-Israeli demonstrations cannot be countered with reason, fact, or truth. The hoarse demonstrators who scream hate speech slogans, who seem hypnotically in thrall to genocide, are not capable of rational conversations in which any truth other than their own prevails. If one presents a True Believer with objective facts that challenge their version of reality, they will either physically and verbally threaten to attack, actually attack, or they will walk away.

Bullies, including terrorists, must be defeated militarily. They will comprehend absolutely no other language.

(1/30/09)

25 JEWISH STUDENTS CORNERED, HUMILIATED, CURSED AT YORK UNIVERSITY

On February 11, 2009, aggression against Jewish students at York University in Toronto reached new heights. A press conference was underway in which student activists reported that they had obtained the necessary 5,000 signatures required to peacefully and lawfully impeach the existing student government, which had supported the student union that shut down York University for three months.

In other words, the students wanted to learn. The teachers wanted to teach. York University did not want to lose more students. They had experienced a 15% decline in applications for the next school year due to the closure and bad press.

A pro-Palestinian student government turned into a frightening Gaza-like mob, which screamed out anti-Jewish as well as anti-Israeli curses, banged on the floor and on the walls, and refused to disperse. The campus police could not handle the situation. They locked 20 Jewish students into a room to keep them safe and then called in the Toronto police; they determined that they could not provide security for the

Jewish students, whom they led out to safety amidst a hate-filled mob, chanting "Die, bitch, go back to Israel," and "Die, Jew, get the hell off campus."

On February 12, 2009, Jonathan Kay published Jonathan Blake Karoly's eye-witness account in the *National Post*. Karoly describes the verbal tactics used by the mobsters to try and rush the already overcrowded room; "Let the colored people in," "Maybe if my friends bleach their skin they'll be let inside," "Zionism is Racism." Karoly notes that as he took pictures of the melee, the Middle Eastern student who had yelled many of the racial slurs saw that Karoly was also wearing a kipah and threatened to "take his camera and smash it." They threatened no other student, only the Jew.

According to Karoly, after the press conference was over, the mob outside the student press conference came and stood outside the Hillel office on another floor. They chanted, banged, yelled, menaced, and would not leave. When the Toronto police finally came, "one pro-Palestinian student [pulled his] Kaffiyah scarf all the way up to his eyes." As the police led the 20 Jewish students out, single file "through this unruly mob, they were pointing, laughing and chanting that we were 'racists on campus.'"

In addition to an alarming number of anti-Semitic incidents that took place in Canada during the first intifada, the suffocated intellectual atmosphere on many campuses was also noted. On December 17, 2002, 100 well-known Canadians signed an ad in the *Globe and Mail* that read "[a]n increasing number of students in universities and colleges say that they fear reprisals if they challenge prevailing pro-Palestinian, anti-Israeli views. If they argue that Israel has the right to exist, they are often greeted with threats, even physical assault."

On September 9, 2002, Benjamin Netanyahu was scheduled to speak at Concordia University in Montreal. One thousand Palestinians and their supporters gathered to scream vitriolic hate. They also taunted, spat at, and physically and verbally harassed all those who had come to hear Netanyahu speak. The police cancelled the event, but they did not intervene as individuals were attacked. I personally knew some of the people who were attacked at Concordia, including Concordia professors who were badly beaten and highly traumatized.

In an ADL press release, Abe Foxman links a "pandemic" of anti-Semitism to Israel's military action in Gaza to defend its citizens from non-stop, relentless rocket attacks. He writes that no one imagined that the war in Gaza would "so explode in an epidemic, a pandemic of anti-Semitism." The press release goes on to say that the global fallout from the Gaza crisis is the biggest threat to the safety and well-being of Diaspora Jewry in decades. He said, "This is the worst, the most intense, the most global that it's been in most of our memories." As usual, the ADL's Abe Foxman is dead wrong.

In Foxman's 2003 book on the subject, he viewed the danger of anti-Semitism as coming mainly from the Christian right-wing. He totally underplayed the danger Jews, Israel, the West, and America face, which is coming our way courtesy of Muslim jihadists and their left-wing and liberal supporters in the West.

Just as the student press conference at York, these days, on campus, whatever the subject is, it is always about "Palestine." And, those who support "Palestine" behave like Brownshirts—or worse.

(2/16/09)

26 ISRAELI TENNIS TEAM UNDER GUARD IN SWEDEN: ANTI-SEMITISM AND THE POLITICIZATION OF SPORTS

*A*thletes and anti-Semitism: Who can ever forget the Munich Olympics under Hitler? In the Nazi era, Jewish-Austrian and Jewish-German athletes had to have their own swimming and fencing clubs, since they were not allowed to compete with "Aryans."

The trauma of the 1972 Palestinian massacre of Israeli athletes at the Olympics in Munich, and the mishandling of the situation—especially by the German police—was enraging, unbelievable.

More recently, Israeli tennis player, Shahar Peer, was not allowed to play tennis in Abu Dhabi. Although Venus Williams denounced this decision, she still played there.

Today, another kind of situation faces the Israeli tennis team in Sweden. Andy Ram writes about it in *YNet News* today:

> In almost every respect, the events of the past week in Sweden are a sad moment for tennis, for sports in general, and certainly for Israel. Never in my career as an athlete have I encountered such hatred and such blend of sports and politics.
>
> Up until the last moment, the protestors attempted to prompt the cancellation of the Davis Cup match between Israel and Sweden. After we already landed here, their leader met with Swedish team captain Mats Wilander and asked him to call off the contest.

Ram goes on to describe how the Israeli team had to be sequestered in their hotel, guarded there, en route, and at the stadium by many police officers and anti-terrorist squads. Sadly, the stadium was empty since people feared riots or worse. He concludes:

> The feelings within the Israel team are very grim. All the innocence that prompted us to play tennis has disappeared, and this match, which was supposed to be a beautiful moment of sports, has become completely worthless. Nothing here is reminiscent of the Davis Cup; what we have is a war atmosphere, tension, and the feeling that something very bad may happen at any moment.

This is how it feels when one tries to present the truth about Israel on the American campus. It is a similarly politicized war-zone; there are empty chairs, an absent professoriate, and ugly threats. One also requires police protection.

(3/8/09)

27 Our Eternal Struggle

*W*ho would have believed that Jews would be in such danger again? That Israel and Zionism would become such dirty words in the world, despised by Western intellectuals and Islamic mobs alike?

Who would have predicted that the United Nations would remain ineffective in all things except one: the legitimization of Jew-hatred? And that so many members of international human rights organizations and the mainstream Western media would join Muslim leaders to accuse Israel of running an apartheid Nazi state bent on genocide?

Who would have thought that the Islamic jihad against Jews, which long preceded the establishment of the state of Israel, would still be going strong—a jihad that began during Muhammad's reign when he slaughtered the Jewish tribes of Arabia?

Who would ever have suggested that the largest refugee story in the Middle East—800,000-850,000 Jews expelled from Arab countries—would be forgotten and replaced with a Palestinian-only persecution narrative that would seize the imagination of the world? That Israel, which absorbed its refugees at its own expense, would be demonized and that Palestinian leaders, including terrorists who devote themselves to the destruction of Israel, would be glamorized as righteous and noble victims?

Who would have dreamed that Israel would be condemned for trying to defend its civilians? Or that Israel would reap hatred for exercising restraint in its treatment of Palestinian civilians? Or that Israel's terrorist enemies would be praised for hiding behind their own women and children or would themselves be counted as civilians (even as they fire rockets at Israel) because they craftily choose to dress as such?

Who could have imagined that such Big Lies would be championed by Western intellectuals and students—including Jews and Israelis?

Orwell would laugh. Or cry.

What is new about this anti-Semitism? The old, mad virus never entirely disappeared, but now anti-Zionism is the new anti-Semitism and the existence of the Jewish state is being used as justification to attack Jews everywhere.

The Arab world continues to accuse Jews and Israelis of spreading cancer and AIDS, of poisoning Palestinians, of perpetrating apartheid and genocide against the Palestinians. The reality, of course, is that Islam is the largest practitioner of apartheid in the world.

Demonizing Israelis as "worse than Nazis" allows Europeans to resume wallowing in the Jew-hatred that has defined their history while it provides them with the illusion that by doing so they render themselves safe from fundamentalist Muslim hostility. It is also a way of scapegoating Jews and Israel for the crimes of European racism and colonialism.

Neat trick.

Sixty years ago, would anyone have been pessimistic enough to fear that Jews would once again be physically menaced and verbally attacked, or that synagogues, community centers, cemeteries and schools would become targets in countries all over the world? That Jewish students would be attacked on campuses and at pro-Palestinian demonstrations in the West?

I never foresaw that pro-Israel sentiment and general truth-telling about the Middle East would be censored and mocked—and that those who held such views or who wished to share them on campus would require armed protection.

What's different about the new anti-Semitism is that Israel, Jews, and Judaism are being condemned by politically correct anti-racists, Westerners who condemn Israel for being nationalistic while they praise the so-called national liberation movements of tyrants. They condemn Judaism and Christianity as misogynistic but give a free pass to Islam. They refuse to criticize an imperialistic, intolerant, slave-holding religion in whose name Islamist terrorists are blowing up civilians globally, because the perpetrators live in areas formerly colonized by the West and are people of color.

Since early 2004 I have been saying that we are potentially looking at another Holocaust. This level of hatred and demonization never ends without the mass murder of Jews. The surreal can become real in an instant.

In many ways Jews today face a graver threat than they did in the 1930s because much of the world, rather than just one or two nations, is now involved in the demonization of Israel.

So what must be done?

We must understand that anti-Semitism is an illness—a

madness—something evil that is not caused by Jews. We may not be able to appease those who are afflicted with it any more than we can please Hamas or al-Qaeda, but we must successfully defend ourselves against it.

We must also shed our illusions—permanently. We cannot expect that conditions will always improve, or that one country or another will always be a safe haven for Jews.

Our ancestors suffered in exile for nearly 2,000 years, and while we are privileged to live in a time when our homeland has been restored to us, it was foolish to have thought that Jew-hatred would suddenly become extinct or that Israel would not remain under permanent siege.

As Jews, as Israelis, as members of a nation holy unto God, we must understand, and never forget, that ours is an eternal struggle.

(3/25/09)

28 Pierre Rehov: The Lion in Exile

Pierre Rehov is *the* documentarian of the Al-Aqsa Intifada, the filmmaker who showed us what Jenin was really about (*The Road to Jenin*), and who the human homicide bombers really are (*Suicide Killers*). In *Silent Exodus*, Rehov documents the story of Arab and North African Jews who were forced to flee their homelands. In *The Trojan Horse* and *Holy Land: Christians in Peril*, Rehov documents the persecution of Christians in the Islamist Middle East.

Rehov is an Algerian Jew: warm, serious, playful, seductive, expressive, sophisticated, secular—and an active participant in the new Great Game of Barbarism versus Civilization. Rehov went into war-zones in Gaza and the West Bank. His weapon is his camera.

I am proud to have championed Rehov's documentaries by posting them on my website in 2004. At the time, more than 30,000 people viewed two of his films in five weeks. Now, his films are available for sale at his own website, and have been shown in many film festivals. He has also begun to post short video clips on YouTube.

Last month, I unexpectedly ran into Pierre at the Hudson Institute luncheon for Geert Wilders. There he was—as warm as ever. I asked Rehov how long he would be visiting the States. His answer startled me. He said that he was here to stay, for good, that he was here with his daughter, his girlfriend, and his dog, and that he expects his son to soon join them. Pierre said that he could no longer live in Paris, that the very air there had become poisoned with anti-Israel sentiment that his pro-Israel activism had led to unending legal and financial problems for himself and for other pro-Israel activists. He said that, "daily life in Paris, France is simply unacceptable. The entire country has been invaded by six to ten million Muslims who do not want to adapt. The French non-Jews are scared, they are happy to sacrifice their Jews and all of Israel if it means they will be safe."

Rehov grew up in Algeria where he was seen not as a fellow Algerian (his ancestors had lived there for 500 years), but rather as a "hated" Frenchman and Jew. When he was seven or eight years old, Pierre saw eleven of his classmates blown up in a Muslim terrorist attack. He saw more people blown up in a café. Rehov endured a Muslim pogrom against Jews; he was spared, some of his relatives were not. He left Algeria in 1961, "together with 250,000 other Jews who were also expelled." Of course, the French were kicked out too—as were many of the Algerians who had helped the French.

Rehov's family hoped for a better life in France. Alas, they were met with "anti-Algerian (racialized) hatred"; they were also cursed as "dirty Jews." Like so many Jews, Rehov became a citizen of the world: someone whose view transcends the provincial, who does not belong to one nation, but to all nations, a bridge person, a boundary-leaper, a river-crosser: An Ivri, a Hebrew, a man who knows he might have to get out of town quickly.

Rehov flourished. He married and had children. His business ventures took him everywhere, including to Morocco. In the mid-1990s, Rehov was sharing a friendly, at-home dinner with a Moroccan Muslim business client and his wife when the man, albeit under the influence, suddenly began weeping uncontrollably. His host sobbed and said, "You're a really nice guy but you're a Jew and I know that one day I will have to kill you."

We are talking about secular, educated Muslims; politics was not being discussed, nor was Israel or Judaism. Yet, out of such alcoholic depths warriors sometimes spring.

This was a turning point for Rehov. He vowed not to remain a bystander, minimizer, or appeaser. Rehov said, "I believe that Israel is the miracle of the 20th century. It is also the result of the worse injustice that has ever been visited upon a people. No other people but the Jews have been exterminated, non-stop, for 20 centuries." He asked, "How many Jews are going to be killed before we wake up and decide to fight back? I don't want to be among the last to start fighting. I'm starting to fight right now."

Brave words—soon followed by even braver deeds.

Rehov told me that "Jews are not allowed to pre-emptively attack. Sometimes, they even get blamed when they dare to defend themselves."

When the Intifada of 2000 broke over Israel's head, Rehov was ready. He was the first person who challenged the Al-Dura Blood Libel. Rehov *sued* Channel Two; he even persuaded the French B'nai B'rith to back his lawsuit because only an organization, not an individual, could bring such a suit. Rehov spent eight months researching the matter—only to see his case dismissed in six weeks—with no explanation given. (Such cases usually take two years to be resolved).

Philippe Karsenty, another hero, was sued *by* Channel Two for defamation because he, too, continued to insist that the Al-Dura matter was a hoax, a fakery. Had Karsenty lost, he could have been jailed. Rehov told me that "The French hired the very best lawyers. They really wanted to win the case against him. They did not want Charles Enderlin, a veteran French journalist, and a Jew, to have to admit that he'd been 'had' by his Palestinian cameraman. Even now, Enderlin refuses to apologize or to admit any wrongdoing."

After seven hard years, Karsenty was vindicated in a French court—a victory which Channel Two is currently appealing.

Both Rehov and Karsenty swam uphill against the tide. The Islamic jihadists and their Western collaborators, including the French government and world media, fought against them. Neither man was supported (or believed) by most Jewish and Israeli organizations. There were a handful of exceptions, including the Zionist Organization of America in Karsenty's case. Both men insist they were sometimes sabotaged by Israeli and American-Jewish organizations. Karsenty has recently criticized David Harris and the American Jewish Committee for having sabotaged his efforts in France.

Rehov believes that the Arab-friendly French government, especially under Chirac, is partly responsible for the enormous harm caused by the Al-Dura Blood Libel. In his view, that valuable footage was immediately given away to the world media for free is a dead giveaway. "Suddenly, Channel Two tells us that it can't make money on the death of a kid," Rehov is incredulous. He said, "This is precisely what the media makes money on."

We may recall that Arafat and his family were treated like royalty in Paris. This is where Arafat came to die his mysterious death in November of 2004, long rumored to be of AIDS. (Arafat allegedly liked boys, not girls.) The French military Honor Guard held a funeral for Arafat at a military airport near Paris. President Jacques Chirac stood alone beside Arafat's body for about ten minutes. He described Arafat as "a man of courage." The French national anthem, the Palestinian anthem, and Chopin's Funeral March were played.

Even dead, Arafat still had Chirac in his back pocket.

Meanwhile, Rehov tried to rally French Jewish organizations to hold the French government legally responsible for having defamed the Jewish state. Then, he went to Israel (he holds an Israeli passport) to further research the Al-Dura case. A German filmmaker, Esther Schapira, made a film in which she challenged the veracity of this latest Blood Libel. Rehov persuaded a Jewish organization to buy the rights to her film so that they could distribute it widely.

Still, neither the Israeli government nor worldwide Jewish organizations wanted to make a fuss. Perhaps they wanted the world to forget the Blood Libel.

This did not stop Rehov. With his French passport in hand, Pierre assembled a crew and took his digital camera to the West Bank and Gaza. In each of his films he exposed the Palestinian propaganda-and-hate machine as non-stop and exterminationist in intentionality—*before* Israel evacuated Gaza and Hamas was voted into office.

Still, Rehov could not persuade a single channel to show any of his films in France. (I failed to interest HBO and PBS in airing his films here as well—even though they aired films with very opposite points of view.) Then, Rehov ingeniously used the French freedom of expression laws in order to distribute his films. He created a political magazine which he called *Contre-Champs* (Reverse Angle) and inserted a copy of his documentaries in each magazine. His magazines sold like hotcakes.

I asked Rehov why he had chosen exile, yet again. He is not as young as he once was, and he has expended a fortune to get his work done. This is what he said.

> My daughter was very friendly with Ilan Halimi, the poor Jewish boy who was lured to his death and endured three weeks of torture by Muslim barbarians. The whole neighborhood took part in the torture or came to watch it. My daughter knew that he'd been kidnapped before it made the newspapers. She could not live in France anymore. I came here to be with her.

I sighed. I told him that America was also undergoing an Islamification process and it remained to be seen as to whether or not we will stand up to it.

He said, "I am afraid that no one will understand this until there is another terrorist attack on American soil."

And so we sat with each other, sipping coffee and enjoying his enchanting little dog, Nougat, a Yorkie. We remained together in the den until it was time to joyfully welcome the Sabbath and my other guests.

(4/1/09)

29 FROM TREBLINKA TO GLEN COVE, LONG ISLAND

When I first arrived at Congregation Tifereth Israel, in Glen Cove, Long Island, a man who was seated at my table asked me if I wanted to buy *his* book. I was there to lead a discussion after a screening of the film *The Case for Israel*. His name is Eddie (Yehudah Yankov) Weinstein and his book, published by Yad Vashem Publications, *17 Days in Treblinka. Daring to Resist, and Refusing to Die,* is powerful and moving.

The book is a very specific, first-person account of Weinstein's deportation from Łosice, Poland, on August 22, 1942, to his liberation by the Soviet army on July 31, 1944. Weinstein managed to escape six times during the Holocaust.

Weinstein shows us how quickly and brutally the successive restrictions upon Jews and their deportations were; how the trapped Jews clung to illusions—things had been bad before; they will also survive slave labor camps or life in a ghetto; surely, the world will learn of their fate and rescue them; the Germans will be defeated. Weinstein describes how older people were unable to uproot themselves overnight. He shows us how surreal Treblinka's killing fields truly were where at least 870,000 Jews were rapidly and relentlessly murdered.

The gratuitous cruelty is heart-stopping. Deported Jews were subjected to torturous thirst, hunger, cold, filth, smothered, and dehydrated in box cars or broken by forced marches before they were killed. The Nazi killers kept screaming, beating, shoving, and striking their prey. Laughing killers shot infants down into huge burning pits. Random killings, mass killings never stopped.

In Treblinka, Weinstein was shot in the chest, "into the lungs," but he did not die; he managed to hide under a vast pile of Jewish clothing, which was being sorted; then, he became a sorter of the clothing for 17 days, "each of which was more like a century." Miraculously, Weinstein and some young friends managed to dodge death in Treblinka and escape. Their troubles continued because now they were at the mercy of roving German soldiers and of their fellow Poles who *sold* water to the dying Jews for valuables, like gold or jewelry; who had already occupied Jewish homes, appropriated Jewish money, food, or valuables, who were already wearing and selling Jewish clothes—and who were, themselves, at the mercy of a ravenous German army.

All of Weinstein's relatives perished—except his father, whom he found in a slave labor camp. Together with a few others, they escaped and for two years faced death every moment as they lived in hiding, first under a pigsty, a fishpond, then a forest bunker. Some Poles risked their lives to bring them food, which they only did for exorbitant sums of money. Even then, they were always threatening to turn them in and often tried to kill their Jews-in-hiding in very primitive ways.

Weinstein's personal anecdotes of deadly Polish anti-Semitism, envy, and avarice, after Poland was liberated by Soviet Russia are unbearable to read. Anyone who suggests that Jews return to Poland should read his book. (And yes, of course, there were Poles who heroically hid and saved Jews. Their stories must also be told, their deeds memorialized, as Israel routinely does.)

Since I am not a Holocaust scholar, each detail of this brief but remarkable book is as fresh, vivid, outrageous, memorable, as when Weinstein first wrote about it in the mid-1940s in a DP camp.

Where did Weinstein get the gold with which to survive? Again, miraculously, he found it in the clothing of the dead Jews and somehow managed to secrete enough gold coins to last for two years.

When he arrived in America, Weinstein worked for ten years as a Singer sewing machine operator in the garment district. Then, he went into business and began a sweater factory that lasted for 45 years. Now retired, Weinstein lectures on his Holocaust experiences. He told me that he "speaks every day in schools, synagogues, and museums." He spoke to me about his two sons and then, with characteristic spirit, asked me "if I wanted him to come and lecture, because if I did, he is ready."

Eddie Weinstein's survival is a miracle. His written account is another. Our meeting was coincidental, unplanned, but, going forward, it will immeasurably strengthen how I present the case for Israel in the future.

(4/6/09)

30 THE LEGACY OF ISLAMIC ANTI-SEMITISM. A BOOK REVIEW

*D*r. Andrew Bostom's *The Legacy of Islamic AntiSemitism: From Sacred Texts to Solemn History* is an overwhelming and powerful book, perhaps the first of its kind: a major "J'Accuse." Bostom challenges the prevailing view in the West and among Jews that Islam was kinder and gentler towards Jews than Christianity. Bostom also refutes the notion that Islamic Jew-hatred was only recently learned from the Nazis; in his view, Islamic anti-Semitism is as old as Islam itself.

The myth of the Golden Age in Spain as one in which Jews, Muslims, and Christians lived in peace and harmony has now been laid to rest by Bostom's (and Bat Ye'or's) work.

Bostom's work is chilling, comprehensive, heartbreaking, and persuasive. I want to share one very dramatic story, one of hundreds, which is contained in Bostom's book. It is a haunting and awful tale.

In 1834, Sol Hachuel was a devout 17-year-old Jew whose impoverished father was a Talmud scholar. She lived in Tangier, Morocco. Somehow, she became friendly with a Muslim woman named Tahra de Mesoodi who was eager to convert a Jew to Islam. Tahra falsely claimed that Sol *had* converted. Sol disagreed, but was still viewed as an apostate, which is a capital crime—even today. Dragged before the governor, Sol said, "A Jewess I was born, a Jewess I wish to die."

The Basha of Tangier, Arba Esudio, threatened, "I will load (you) with chains...I will have you torn piece-meal by wild beasts, you shall not see the light of day, you shall perish of hunger...in having provoked the anger of the Prophet." Amazingly, Sol responded, "I will patiently bear the weight of your chains, I will give my limbs to be torn piece-meal by wild beasts; I will renounce forever the light of day...I will smile at your indignation, and the anger of your Prophet: since neither he nor you have been able to convert a weak female!"

Sol was chained both hand and foot and confined to a "lightless dungeon" with an iron collar around her neck. The Muslim authorities threatened her distraught father with 500 lashes if he did not immediately come up with the cost of Sol's transport to Fez and the cost of her execution. In Fez, the Jewish community was threatened with extermination if their leaders failed to persuade Sol to convert to Islam. They tried but failed. The Sultan condemned Sol to death in the public square. She fasted and prayed. She was dragged along the ground like an animal with a rope around her neck.

The executioner asked her one last time if she would convert. According to an eye-witness, "Sol, then raising her streaming eyes to heaven, repeated with the utmost devotion, the Shema (the central prayer in Judaism), which having concluded, kneeling and casting her eyes to the ground, she said to the executioner: 'I have finished, dispose of my life.'"

Sol became known as a heroic martyr among Moroccan Jews. According to Jewish law, she was buried immediately—and in a place of honor, right next to a revered Jewish sage.

(4/10/09)

31 THE BLOOD LIBELS AT NATIONAL GEOGRAPHIC MAGAZINE

*M*ost people barely notice menacing anti-Israel demonstrations in the street, rabid anti-Israel resolutions at the United Nations, obsessive anti-Israel boycott resolutions among Western academics, and relentless anti-Israel headlines in the world media.

What worries me more are the movies and plays that subtly and inexorably shift the civilian point of view, movies that glamorize Arab tyrants and terrorists and demonize Israeli soldiers, "settlers," and politicians. Gradually, imperceptibly, ordinary people have come to believe that the Muslim world is peaceful, friendly, safe; that its "rough edges" are due to its having formerly been oppressed by Europe; that Islamist terrorism has been caused by the United States' invasion of Afghanistan and Iraq; that much of this is Israel's fault—or rather, that much of this may now be solved if only America sacrifices Israel for the sake of world peace.

The pre-eminent, planet-friendly magazine, *National Geographic,* which boasts a readership of nearly eight million people, arrives here faithfully, courtesy of a gift subscription. Sometimes I look at it, often I don't. But the cover story in this issue immediately caught my eye: "The Christian Exodus from the Holy Land." So, I thought, the animal-friendly magazine "gets" it. My hopes raised, I turned to the article, which is also titled "The Forgotten Faithful: Arab Christians."

Here's what the article does: It essentially blames the Christian Crusaders, American Christians, and Israel (!) for the persecution and disappearance of Arab Christians from the Middle East. The lies, omissions, and biases are mind-boggling. For example, the article, written by Don Belt, does not explain *why* the Crusades ever took place—namely, to protect the Christian Arabs from being slaughtered and forcibly converted by Muslims. Belt writes that "ironically, it was during the Crusades (1095-1291) that Arab Christians, slaughtered along with Muslims by the crusaders and caught in the cross fire between Islam and the Christian West, began a long, steady retreat into the minority."

How has Belt managed to minimize the Arab Muslim conquest of the Christian and Jewish Middle East? What Belt fails to note is that more than *four centuries* of such Arab Muslim persecution of Christians is precisely what led to the Christian Crusades.

It's true: some caliphs were temporarily kind to their dhimmi populations; an Egyptian ruler granted asylum to the great Jewish scholar and philosopher Maimonides—who was, however, in flight from *Muslims* in Spain. Maimonides became the ruler's personal physician. The Turkish Sultan granted asylum to the fabulously wealthy, and attractively taxable Donna Gracia HaNasi, who was, herself, in flight from Christian persecution in Spain and Portugal. But mainly, the Jews of Islam lived in enormous poverty and were routinely murdered, jailed for ransom, their goods confiscated, and exiled.

After blaming the Crusaders for accidentally slaughtering Christian Arabs, Belt goes on to blame contemporary Israel for persecuting Christians—without mentioning that Palestinian terrorists have routinely used the holiest churches as toilets and as places to stash weapons and hostages. Belt quotes an Arab Christian from Bethlehem who attributes his suffering mainly to the "giant (Israeli) Wall" and to an Israeli bureaucracy, which does not allow him to live with his wife, who is an Israeli citizen, in Jerusalem.

Omitted entirely is the horrendous reality of Islamic religious apartheid. No Arab or Palestinian government has ever handed over total control of Christian and Jewish holy places to Christians or Jews. They have pillaged and destroyed those places, sometimes built mosques over them, forbidden Christians and Jews from worshipping at the ruin or in the intact building, or have allowed them to worship there at considerable risk.

Belt also blames American Christians for the disappearance of Arab Christians from the Holy Land. Belt quotes Razek Siriani, who works for the Middle East Council of Churches in Aleppo, Syria. Here's what Siriani (dancing for his life, I might add) has to say:

> "We're completely outnumbered and surrounded by angry voices," he says. Western Christians have made matters worse, he argues, echoing a sentiment expressed by many Arab Christians.

"It's because of what Christians in the West, led by the U.S., have been doing in the East," he says, ticking off the wars in Iraq and Afghanistan, U.S. support for Israel, and the threats of "regime change" by the Bush administration. "To many Muslims, especially the fanatics, this looks like the Crusades all over again, a war against Islam waged by Christianity. Because we're Christians, they see us as the enemy too. It's guilt by association."

Belt manages to blame Christian Crusaders, Israelis, and American Christians who are pro-Israel and are therefore viewed as the new Christian Crusaders. Belt blames the Lebanese Christians who fought back against Palestinian terrorist gangsters for an increase in Islamic anti-Christian attitudes.

Who is barely "blamed" for the persecution of and the radically dwindling numbers of Christians in the Middle East? Muslims, of course, who, according to Belt, have always lived in peace with Christians and Jews in the Middle East. Belt shows us touching scenes of Muslims who worship at Christian shrines for miracles. In Syria, Belt quotes a mother, Miriam, whose family "used to be Christian" (I wonder why they converted?) and who now says "I believe in the prophets—Muslim, Jewish, and Christian—I believe in Mary, I've come here so my boy will be healed." Belt presents the forced conversions to Islam from Christianity as benign, free choices.

The Committee for Accuracy in Middle East Reporting in America (CAMERA) has been writing letters to *National Geographic* since 1996. CAMERA has also documented and protested their inaccurate and highly biased articles. Each time, the editors refused to make any change, issue any apology, or write any articles without a blatant anti-Israel bias.

(5/18/09)

32 HOMEGROWN ISLAMIC JIHAD IN THE BRONX

Riverdale, in the Bronx, is a gloriously leafy, hilly, and peaceful suburb. I have visited its extraordinary gardens and gracious homes, which overlook the Hudson River. I've visited a close friend and her family who live there, have studied and prayed with them, and have attended and lectured at Riverdale synagogues. Riverdale is as close to me, personally, psychologically, and geographically, as was the World Trade Center.

Four African-American converts to Islam, all of whom converted to Islam in prison, have been arrested by the FBI just as they attempted to bomb two Riverdale synagogues (the Riverdale Jewish Center and the Riverdale Temple) and Stewart Air National Guard Base in Newburgh, New York, where they lived and attended a mosque.

Why do I clearly state the race and religion of the terrorists? Because the liberal mainstream media refuses to do so, or buries such facts on its back pages. See the *New York Times* coverage. What starts as a bland, front page story continues on page 33 where the *Times* writes, "some of the men were of Arabic descent, and one is of Haitian descent."

I am not in favor of "profiling," i.e., discriminating against or persecuting people because of their skin-color or religious beliefs. However, what is one to do when these facts are crucial to the matter at hand?

According to counter-terrorism expert Frank Gaffney, the Saudis have been funding Wahabi-style political-religious conversions among racially marginalized men in prison in the West for a long time. The Islamic Society of North America has allegedly placed many imams and mullahs in the American prison system where they prey mainly upon men of color whose lives have already been shattered by poverty, absent fathers, drug addicted parents, racism, drugs, mental illness, gang life, and a long history of criminality. Islam may be presented to them as a religion that is especially friendly to men of African descent. Jihad may also be presented as a way to overcome "oppression."

A radical doctrine that preaches hatred of "white racist America" might be balm to their shamed spirits. Perhaps jailed men of color are also attracted by the possibility of polygamy, or by female co-religionists who are subservient to men on American soil; or by the possibility of permissible violence. Perhaps men also convert because they want the perks that Muslims receive in prison: protection, halal food, incense, prayer rugs.

Can prison officials restrict an inmate's access to religious teachings and services without violating the inmate's Constitutional right to freedom of religion? According to Frank Gaffney:

> The cumulative effects of Islamist recruitment in the U.S. penal system are as stunning as they are

ominous. Currently, there are said to be roughly 350,000 inmates in federal, state and local prisons who identify themselves as Muslims. Some 30,000-40,000 more are being added to that population each year. Official estimates suggest that roughly 80% of prisoners who "find faith" while in prison convert to Islam and that the percentage of the prison population that is "Muslim" today is somewhere between 15-20%. In fact, prison conversion alone is a major contributor to the rapid growth of Islam in the United States.

Onta Williams of the Bronx Four is quoted as saying, "They (the United States military) are killing Muslim brothers and sisters in Muslim countries, so if we kill them here (in the United States) with IEDs (improved explosive devices) and Stingers, it is equal." James Cromitie, a.k.a. Abdul Rahman, stated that he was part of a Pakistani-based terror group and wanted to kill Jews and Americans. According to the *New York Post*, "Cromitie pointed to people walking on the street in the vicinity of a Jewish community center and said that if he had a gun, he would shoot each one in the head."

It is crucial that we see the larger patterns and even more crucial that we act to stop Saudi funding of Islamic conversions in America, beginning with recruitment in our prison system. We must also reform our prison system so that it is does not provide such a fertile breeding ground for anti-American and anti-Jewish Islamic terrorism.

(5/21/09)

33 END THE ILLEGAL OCCUPATION OF JERUSALEM

*J*ournalist Aaron Klein's important new book, *The Late Great State of Israel: How Enemies Within and Without Threaten the Jewish Nation's Survival*, illuminates, infuriates, saddens, and cries out to both heaven and humanity.

Klein is neither a diplomatic insider, nor is he a scholar. He is a passionate and courageous journalist who talks to Palestinian terrorists all the time.

Klein indicts the world's governments and the global media, including the Israeli government and media, for having conspired in covering up the fact that the late Yasser Arafat was a bloodthirsty terrorist; for continuing to present Fatah, under Mahmud Abbas, Arafat's right-hand man, as a "moderate," when this is not the case; for being so "entrenched in their accepted narratives that they will completely invert the truth or blindly repeat proven falsehoods…(all in order to mask) the murderous ways of their Palestinian or Arab state partners."

According to Klein, the city of Jerusalem, like many

European cities, now has its own "no-go" areas. "Israeli police units stay off the streets" of certain "densely populated Arab neighborhoods," which, in effect, constitutes a "significant terrorist apparatus now based in eastern Jerusalem. The clear aim is to keep up a steady stream of attacks on western Jerusalem neighborhoods in order to pressure Israel into ceding eastern Jerusalem."

Over the years, Israelis have allowed more than "100,000 Palestinian Arabs to occupy tens of thousands of illegally constructed housing units in eastern and northern Jerusalem." Criminals, mercenaries, soldiers dressed as civilians, human homicide bombers and their terrorist handlers, may all live among them. This other illegal occupation or settlement activity began long *after* 1967, when Israel won a third war of self-defense launched against it by the major Arab powers. These Palestinian Arab immigrants were not living in these places before 1948 or before 1967. Klein argues that under Jordanian rule, one of these Jerusalem neighborhoods, Shuafat, was a forest.

These crowded Palestinian Arab housing complexes, schools, villas, palaces— even a Saudi-built polo club—are now filled with weapons and fighters. According to Klein, Palestinians have built their illegal settlements on land owned by the Jewish National Fund (JNF), which was entrusted to buy land for Jews in the Holy Land.

In an exchange with Klein, Russell Robinson, the CEO of the JNF, insisted that the land in question had been acquired by the JNF in the early 1900s but was subsequently either under Jordanian rule and/or is now under the Israel Land Authority and that the entire matter is "more complicated." Klein persuasively disputes both of Robinson's claims.

There has been no outcry about this because Jews and

Israelis do not want to be seen as—many do not even want to *be*—discriminatory or "racist" in terms of Palestinian Arabs.

Many Jews believe in the importance of treating the stranger at our gate with compassion. For years, Jews signed petitions and demonstrated against "the occupation" and for a "two-state solution"—well before it became fashionable. I was among them, but it turns out that I was a dreamer and a fool, tricked by master propagandists and by my own desire to do good.

To demand that Israel "make peace" with a people who are armed to the teeth is nonsense. For Jews and Israelis to call for a further Palestinian right of return and for a two-state solution is suicidal, given that there is only one tiny Jewish state while there are 57 Muslim (and Muslim-dominating) states in the world, 22 of which are in the Middle East. No Jews, including "politically correct" two-state solution Jews, can safely live in any one of the 22 Muslim Arab states in the Middle East.

Until recently, Jews, if they were very wealthy, could live well perhaps only in Tunisia and Turkey, but that happy little chapter may be drawing to a close. And, although the 35,000 Jews held hostage in Iran publicly insist that they are quite happy there, let's remember that Jewish-American diplomat Dennis Ross is not acceptable as an *American* envoy to Iran presumably because he is Jewish. The Obama White House has reassigned him.

Muslim countries are totally "apartheid" nation states.

Israel, on the other hand, counts 1.2 million Muslim and Christian Palestinian Arabs as Israeli citizens. Palestinian Arabs are Members of Knesset and sit on the Israeli Supreme Court. Israel has safeguarded the places of worship of all religions and has given the Baha'i, who fled Iran, a safe harbor in Haifa. In contrast, Palestinian Arabs have desecrated and destroyed Jewish and Christian places of worship. Klein has a horrific chapter on the barbaric Palestinian destruction of Joseph-the-Dream-Interpreter's Tomb.

I (and most Israelis) would have no problem with Israel's having Muslim or Christian Palestinian Arab residents in Jerusalem or anywhere else—just as long as Jews could also live safely in Nablus, Ramallah, Hebron, Amman, Cairo, Damascus, Mecca, Baghdad, Tehran, etc. That is, without armored troops to accompany them to and from peaceful prayer services or to the market to buy fruits and vegetables. This lack of reciprocity is infuriating, especially since our leaders fail to mention and refuse to criticize such a glaring and obvious disparity.

How can President Obama, a graduate of the Harvard Law School, not understand that the catch-phrase "two-state solution with the Palestinian right of return," by definition, means the death of the Jewish state?

(6/17/09)

34 VIENNA, MY CITY OF DREAMS/NIGHTMARES

This past Saturday evening, Chabad Rabbi Dov Gruzman conducted the annual ceremony to light the public Chanukah menorah in Stefenfaltz Square in Vienna. A local Muslim rushed over, began cursing Jews, then "hurled himself" at the rabbi, punching and kicking him. As the rabbi tried to hold off his attacker, the Muslim suddenly "bit his victim, severing part of his finger." The attacker was caught and arrested; the rabbi was hospitalized, and doctors tried to reattach his finger.

Rabbi Gruzman has just planned a much larger public lighting of the menorah and increased the usual order of 50 sufganiyot (jelly doughnuts) to 700.

I hope that this attack is not minimized as another example of one deranged individual. While Sudden Jihad Syndrome may indeed be practiced by deranged people (Ft. Hood's Major Nidal Hasan comes to mind), such attackers are also acting out the wishes of a specific culture of hatred. Terrorists are not necessarily "deranged." They may, indeed, be high-functioning "sociopaths." Hitler certainly was.

Hitler loved Vienna. The Viennese loved Hitler, too, once he came to power.

Just because we can psychiatrically diagnose people does not render them less dangerous. They can carefully plan attacks, use terror as a means of control in order to get their way—not as an expression of how distressed they are.

Like Rabbi Gruzman, Israel's response to increasing global anti-Semitism is a proactive one. The Israeli government has convened a global conference to combat anti-Semitism that will take place December 16th-17th in Jerusalem.

Austria ought to convene such a conference. Remember: Even when it became clear that former UN Secretary-General Kurt Waldheim had a Nazi past, the Austrians still voted him in as President. Recently, Vienna was the unembarrassed city that did not have the Israeli national anthem on hand to play in case the Israeli fencing athletes happened to win the competition. The Israeli female athletes did win top honors—and after a long and humiliating silence, they sang "Hatikvah" themselves, a cappella. In addition, the Austrians have an abysmal track record in terms of returning property and belongings that Austrian's stole from Jews during the Holocaust.

Herzl, a highly assimilated Viennese Austrian Jew, "got it" when he covered the Dreyfus case in Paris. In 1897, Herzl convened the first Zionist gathering in Basel, Switzerland. And, in 1949, Herzl was re-buried with honors in Israel. Freud, another Viennese son, "got it," when, as a Jew, he could not gain an appropriate appointment to a Viennese medical faculty. Still, Freud refused to leave his beloved Vienna behind until 1938, when Hitler was already on the march and Freud's life was at stake. Freud and his family fled to England, where he died and was cremated in 1939.

Vienna is a very inviting city. I was quite enchanted by it when I visited it for the first time in 1982 after delivering a lecture in Salzburg. When a journalist asked me what I thought of Vienna, I startled him by saying, "It reminds me of Tel Aviv." "What do you mean?" he sputtered. Said I, "The Austrian Jews whom you did not kill or who were forced to flee all have Viennese-style furnishings, polished wood tables, and lace curtains. Thus, when I'm next in Tel Aviv, I will always remember Vienna."

My maternal grandmother loved the Emperor "Franz-Yosief;" she thought he had been kind to the Jews. And, my mother of blessed memory used to play a certain saccharine tune on the piano and I'd sing along, "I hear you calling me… Vienna My City of Dreams."

Yes, Vienna is a dream alright—a perfect nightmare where Jews are concerned.

(12/14/09)

35 ARTISTS4ISRAEL 2 THE RESCUE

*L*ast night, I attended the Artists4Israel debut theatrical presentation on Bleecker Street. The theatre had a coffee bar; the lobby had the excited, "crazy" energy of an opening night.

Craig Dershowitz, the Executive Director of Artists4Israel told me, "You don't have to be Jewish to be pro-Israel. You don't have to be Jewish to work with us. We are not a *Jewish* talent show. You have to be an artist and a good one. We do Art, not Propaganda."

Craig wears his hair in a long and friendly ponytail and his arms are covered with tattoos. "Wanna see the angel Michael? Here he is. D'ya know who Ze'ev Jabotinsky was—here he is too," Craig said.

Artists4Israel is less than a year old. It has been something of a whirlwind year. The group came together when Operation Cast Lead and the propaganda fallout against Israel began.

According to Dershowitz, "Hamas started a culture war. We decided to be pro-active rather than defensive... Artists4Israel is the offense. Rather than countering the misconceptions, lies, and hate preached by the terrorist-funded Hamas culture war against Israel, A4I utilizes the arts to tell our own stories and create our own narratives highlighting the rights, beauty, and strength of Israel."

Lawyer Racquel Reinstein produced the evening *Love and Licenses*, which consisted of two plays: One, *At a Loss*, was a staged reading that starred Equity actors Charlotte Cohn, Jason Odell Williams, Andrew Rein, and Norma Fire. The second play, *Te Busco*, starred Amir Levi (who also conceived of the theatre program), but Jason Najjoum (the ghost lover) danced as well as toyed with Levi's character.

In both plays, the comedy was hilarious, and the acting and the choreography were superb. The plays are serious, funny, mystical, surreal, and could not take place anytime sooner than the 21st century. The characters are Israeli, American, Mexican, Christian, Jewish, gay, straight, transnational, and transgressive, even transgender. Both plays present characters who happen to be Jews and Israelis. But in an era of lethal Blood Libels against Jews and Israel, they humanize our people in the same way that other previously marginalized groups have "branded" and glorified their "differentness."

These are genuine actors, playwrights, and directors, not propagandists.

Artists4Israel also created pro-Israel posters and stood with them at the United Nations. They stood outside a showing of the Rachel Corrie play and tried to arm theatergoers with facts since they were about to be entertained by a gripping series of Big Lies. Very quickly, A4I integrated themselves into the graffiti community, the downtown art gallery world, the world of street performers and political performance artists—and then, all youthful exuberant energy, they began a series of projects that almost defy description.

They developed the Fashion Police project. This consists of at least two or more "provocatively dressed" artists patrolling the streets and "ticketing" any woman or man who is dressed "immodestly," especially any woman who is wearing a short skirt or a tight top. What they give her is a consciousness-raising postcard about the "brutal crackdown" on women's rights in Saudi Arabia, Gaza, and Egypt. Were she dressed this way there, she'd probably be beaten, hauled off to jail. The "ticket" is a postcard addressed to the Royal Embassy of Saudi Arabia.

Or take this project: "The Keffiyeh Exchange Program." They have modeled this on NYPD's Cash for Guns program. Artists4Israel offers "Free Stuff for Stupid Scarves." With full respect for the diversity of customs in the Middle East, Artists are trying to make people aware that identifying with keffiyeh-wearers (which so many young Americans do at anti-American and anti-Israel demonstrations) may mean glamorizing or identifying with human homicide bombers who are neither free spirits nor life-loving.

Artists4Israel teaches art on campuses. They have already participated in Art Basel. Their inaugural event was "Bombin' for Israel." Artists collaborated with top urban art and culture magazine BOMBIN'. Four hundred people turned out, braving snow and rain. BOMBIN's publisher, Taylor Levin, said, "A lot of these kids saw the World Trade Center fall and they see that Israel is being attacked by the same kind of terrorists. They hope that art can provide the moral clarity they don't see in the press."

Artists plans to visit Sderot to do "art therapy" with rocket-traumatized children. The proceeds from Wednesday evening's performance on Bleecker Street are meant to pay for this trip.

A4I comprise a dynamic, profound cultural resistance to the demonization of Israel. The Living Theatre's Judith Malina would love them—as would Peter Bergson, aka Hillel Kook, who tried to awaken American Jews to the unfolding tragedy of European Jewry via Broadway theater. To Bergson's sorrow, he failed. Let us hope and pray that Artists4Israel succeeds.

Artists4Israel was founded by Craig Dershowitz, Tara Gordon, Seth Wolfson, Sarah Brega, Alicia Post, Marianne Pane, Brian Dershowitz, Brandon Margolis, and Jenny Kagan.

(1/7/10)

36 LANCET STUDY BLAMES PALESTINIAN WIFE-BEATING ON ISRAEL

*B*ritain's premier medical journal *The Lancet* has been Palestinianized. It no longer bears any relationship to the first-rate scientific journal it once was. *The Lancet* has become part of the global movement in which standards have plunged, biases have soared, and Big Lies now pass for serious academic work.

The post-colonial academy is colonized by the false and dangerous ideas of Edward Said—please read Ibn Warraq's book *Defending the West: A Critique of Edward Said's Orientalism*. I once believed that Said's perspective had infected only the social sciences, humanities, and Middle East studies. We now see his malign influence at work in a new article by professors who work at the Harvard Medical School, University of Minnesota's School of Public Health, the Boston University School of Medicine, the School of Nursing at the University of Medicine and Dentistry of New Jersey, and the School of Social Work and Social Welfare at

The Hebrew University of Jerusalem.

Their study is titled: "Association between exposure to political violence and intimate-partner violence in the occupied Palestinian territory: a cross-sectional study." They have found that Palestinian husbands are more violent towards Palestinian wives as a function of the Israeli "occupation"—and that the violence increases significantly when the husbands are "directly" as opposed to "indirectly" exposed to political violence.

Arab Muslim men, including Palestinian men, are indeed violent towards Arab Muslim women. War-related stress, including poverty, usually increases "intimate partner violence," aka male domestic violence. But beyond that, how does one evaluate this study?

First, let's follow the money. This study was funded by the Palestinian National Authority, the Core Funding Group, and the Program in Health Disparities Research at the University of Minnesota. The Palestinian Authority is not a disinterested party. The data was collected by the Palestinian Central Bureau of Statistics. These are the people who told the world that Israeli soldiers shot young Mohammed al-Dura, committed a massacre in Jenin, and purposely attacked Palestinian civilians (who just happened to be jihadists dressed in civilian clothing or hostage-civilians behind whom the jihadists hid).

Second, let's note that the study has a political goal that trumps any objective academic or feminist goal. This study wishes to present Palestinian *men* as victims, even when those men are battering and murdering their wives. It wishes to present Palestinian cultural barbarism, which includes severe child abuse, as also due to the alleged Israeli occupation.

Third, the study has omitted the violence, including

femicide, which is routinely perpetrated against daughters and sisters in allegedly "occupied Palestine" and has, instead, focused only on husband-wife violence and only on couples who are currently married. The honor-murders of daughters and sisters by their parents and brothers are a well-known phenomenon in Gaza and on the West Bank.

"Souad," the author of *Burned Alive*, barely survived being set on fire by her family in the West Bank because she became pregnant out of wedlock by the man who promised to marry her; Israelis nursed her back to health. She fled the region for Europe, where she wrote a book about her near-death experience. Journalist Asma al-Ghoul, whom I interviewed in 2008, was fired for writing a series of articles about honor killings on the West Bank and in Gaza. These barbaric customs are not due to any alleged political or economic occupation by Israelis.

Hamas and other Palestinian terrorist groups have lured young Palestinian women into becoming human homicide bombs. In 2002, they manipulated Wafa Idris, a clinically depressed woman. In 2004, they lured Reem al-Riyashi, a wife and mother of two, into an affair and then threatened to shame her (which would have led to her being honor-murdered). Instead, they offered her a path to glory.

This study chose not to include such terrible violence against women because it could not be attributed to the alleged Israeli occupation—or to the matter of the disputed territories.

Fourth, had *The Lancet* wished to truly study the effects of war on women they would also have studied or referred to studies about the fate of Israeli women in terms of "intimate partner violence"; after all, they are also women and they are on the other side of enormous aggression. A comparison might have been academically sane and arguably more feminist.

In 2002, in an updated version of her book *Price of Honor*, British-American (and anti-Zionist) journalist Jan Goodwin claims that the Israeli military policies of self-defense have emasculated Palestinian men. Curfews keep grandiose, woman-hating, and honor- and shame-reared men at home for long hours. Based on anecdotal evidence, Goodwin believes that such men take their considerable frustrations out on women and children. Here, Goodwin quotes Suha Sabbagh, who says that the "Palestinian male, a father, the authority figure in the house, has lost all his authority." Goodwin dwells on the systematic "humiliation" of the Palestinian man by the Israelis. She writes, "Much of this belittling has taken place in front of their children and womenfolk," which in turn has "cut down" the image of the Palestinian man as the family's "hero" figure; "for Arab men, this is the same as losing their masculinity."

But Arab Muslim overly vigilant paternal authority is precisely what has brutalized Arab Muslim women. In 1992, Jean Sasson published *Princess: A True Story of Life Behind the Veil in Saudi Arabia*, and in it the unnamed al-Saud princess describes the typically cruel way that fathers, brothers, and husbands treat their "womenfolk." She writes, "The authority of a Saudi male is unlimited; his wife and children survive only if he desires. In our homes, he is the state...From an early age, the male child is taught that women are of little value...the child witnesses the disdain shown his mother and sisters by his father; this leads to his scorn of all females... [the] women in my land are ignored by their fathers, scorned by their brothers, and abused by their husbands."

Iranian-Swiss Carmen bin Laden, in her book *Inside the Kingdom*, portrays life for women under Saudi male rule similarly. Women cannot travel without a male escort and they cannot leave the house or the county without male permission and accompaniment. A daughter can be married against her will; a father can seize custody of his children and not allow their mother to ever see them again. Bin Laden writes, "I rarely met a Saudi woman who was not afraid of her husband... Women in Saudi Arabia must live in obedience, in isolation, and in the fear that they may be cast out and summarily divorced."

Saudi Arabia has not been "settled," "colonized," or "humiliated" by Israelis.

Jordan has not been "settled," "colonized," "occupied," or "humiliated" by Israel, and yet Jordan has a high rate of honor killing. According to Elaine Sheeley, in her 2007 book *Reclaiming Honor in Jordan*, between 19 and 100 honor killings take place in Jordan each year. Based on another author's use of United Nations statistics, Sheeley cites a much larger number of honor killings in Jordan, Gaza, and the West Bank. I am not sure how they came to this figure or if it is accurate, but the number given is "2,550 honor killings per annum."

Egypt is not colonized by Israel, and yet serious violence against women is common there. This includes female genital mutilation, wife-beating, daughter-beating, forced marriages—and, with the rise of the Muslim Brotherhood, forced veiling of previously modern women.

War is hell and women often bear the brunt of war-related male frustration at home. Israel alone is being blamed in this study for a war that was declared long ago against the Jewish state by the Arab League, the Palestinian Authority, and more recently by Hamas and Hezbollah. The "politics" of both this study and of *The Lancet* aim to scapegoat Israel for the barbarism and misogyny that is indigenous to Arab and Muslim culture.

(1/24/10)

37 Israel's Rebirth "A Boring Story" to U.S. Jews: An Interview with American Zionist Hero Dr. David Gutmann

*F*rom 1947 to 1948 I lived in Boro Park where, against parental and rabbinic advice, I joined a Zionist group. By 1950 I was packing machine gun parts for Israel in a home not far from the young Israel. But what I did as a child does not compare to what my friend and colleague David Gutmann did for love of Zion at that very time on the dangerous open seas.

Dr. Gutmann was a 21-year-old Jewish-American volunteer sailor for Aliyah Bet, the name given to "illegal" Jewish immigration into British-controlled Palestine (1939-1948). These boats tried to run the British blockade. One boat was stranded on the Danube and its passengers later sent back to Vienna and executed; another was bombed by the Soviets.

Once Hitler was defeated, British disdain for Jews quickly became visible. Most Holocaust survivors were captured and imprisoned on Cyprus; more than 1,600 drowned. The British sent some boats right back to Europe, to Germany, as was the case with the *SS Exodus*. This public relations fiasco backfired; my friend Ruth Gruber's on-board photo of the *SS Exodus* made the cover of *Life* magazine.

On behalf of the *Jewish Press,* I met with Dr. Gutmann. His generation of heroes is mainly gone but he is still here.

The Jewish Press/Phyllis Chesler: **How did you become a sailor?**
Dr. Gutmann: I served in the U.S. Merchant Marine during World War II.

The manifests list you as serving on two ships, the *Paducah-Geulah* and the *Ben Hecht*. Were they the same kind of boat? Who served with you?
I served first on the *Hecht*, after that on the *Geulah*. I was an engine room oiler on the *Hecht*, a second engineer on the *Geulah*. The *Hecht* was purchased and run by the Irgun. She was a German-built twin-diesel luxury yacht originally named *Abril* (April). She sailed for the U.S. Navy on anti-sub patrol during World War II. After the Brits left Palestine, the *Hecht/Abril* became part of the Israeli navy and was used to launch frogmen against Egyptian naval craft off Gaza. Last I heard, she was running tourists between Naples and Capri.

The *Hecht/Abril*'s crew was a mix of Jews and non-Jews, kids and veteran seamen, crazies and idealists. We ended up in Acco (Acre).

The *Geulah* was purchased and run by the Haganah. A twin-screw steamship built around 1905, she served during World War II as, I believe, a gunnery-training vessel on the

Great Lakes. She was scrapped in Naples in '49. The *Geulah*'s crew was more decorous than the *Hecht*'s complement. A mix of veteran sailors (Jews and non-Jews) and Zionistic college kids.

We also had a few exiled Spanish loyalist sailors and our second mate was Don Miguel Boeza, who had been high admiral of the loyalist navy. Our captain was Rudy Patzert, an old commie married to a Jew. He wrote a book about the voyage—*Running the Palestine Blockade*. Our Haganah commander was Moka Limon, a legendary hero of Aliyah Bet who later became admiral of Israel's navy. We all ended up in the Cyprus prison camps.

Are Jews still eager to hear your stories?
Despite the fact that I'm willing to speak without honoraria, even during 2008—Israel's 60th anniversary year—the response from heads of congregations was tepid. Since then, perhaps one in three rabbis show interest. Some who showed initial interest never followed up. Nowadays, they might suggest 10-minute gigs at men's club breakfast meetings.

Why the disinterest?
Rahm Emanuel reportedly said, "I've had it with Israel." I think a lot of Jews now feel that way. They're tired of worrying about Israel, unendingly, from crisis to crisis. The Palestinians are the heroes of our victim-adoring age; accordingly, many liberal Jews have come to believe the Palestinian "Nakba" revision, the lies that turned a miracle into another Jewish blood libel.

But whatever their politics, modern Jews have little sense of history. I speak about the '48 war, and the lies about it that are now believed by too many Jews. For most U.S. Jews, the '48 war is an old and perhaps boring story. They saw *Exodus*;

they don't want to see it again. They don't realize that history is the present, and that [post-Zionist] revisionist history is central to the attack on contemporary Israel. It is one of the manifold attempts to bring it down, first morally and then physically.

Did you stay in touch with others from Aliyah Bet?
Yes. I was one of the founders of the now defunct American Veterans of Israel organization. I held office and attended their reunions in Israel and the States. But that was then. Most of us are dead now, and I haven't had a drink with an old shipmate in years. Bob Levitan, our captain, participated indirectly in the breakout from Acco. With his Leica, he took ID-type photos of all the Irgun and Lehi prisoners, and these were later used in the phony ID cards issued to them prior to their escape.

Do you see any similarities between American Jewish attitudes in the 1930s and 1940s and today?
In the 1930s and 40s, American Jews sanctified FDR. Now they are equally loyal to Obama. Despite their growing awareness of the Holocaust, during World War II American Jews mostly stayed silent—few mass protests and little covert action.

My fear is that too many contemporary Jews are preparing to repeat this pattern. They will not embarrass the great and good Obama with their selfish concerns for what they view as a victimizing country—Israel—that no longer deserves their loyalty. Too many will follow Obama's lead and stay silent while Israel is weakened or destroyed.

(3/29/10)

38 Jews Confront the Abyss: "The Absence of Outrage Is Outrageous"

By now we know that Jew haters are never deterred by facts—only by force. We know that the Arab-Muslim world has brainwashed its citizens and the world with a steady stream of Blood Libels against Jews and Israel. The United Nations, international human rights organizations, the world media, and the world's so-called intelligentsia have all piled on, as have President Obama and his carefully chosen advisors. Obama, who bowed to the Saudi King and who publicly shamed the Israeli Prime Minister, has also, for the first time, decided not to sell bunker buster bombs to Israel; to deny Israeli scientists who work at Dimona visas to study in the United States; to manufacture a sham crisis over Israel building apartments in north Jerusalem—all in order to "impose" a Solution (hopefully not another Final Solution) on Israel.

The Man wants to show the world he's "tough" where the Jews are concerned so that it will not notice how "weak" he is in terms of confronting Iran's Ahmadinejad, Afghanistan's Hamid Karzai, North Korea's Kim Jong-il, Sudan's Omar Hassan al-Bashir, etc. But many see that Obama is "weak," beginning with the Arab and Muslim countries he most wishes to impress.

Jews cry, "Never again." Jews cry, "No more will we be silent." During the Holocaust, most American Jews were more concerned with their own survival than with that of their endangered brethren; they were misled by most of their Jewish leaders and by the Court Jews of the day. America is rapidly changing in terms of its relationship to Israel and to Islamism. Others are worried, just as I am: Daniel Greenfield at Sultan Knish, Marc Prowisor at Yesha Views, and Ed Koch at *The Huffington Post*.

In early 2004, I wrote that a new Holocaust had already begun in Israel.

The leaders of the major American Jewish organizations paid absolutely no attention to this. They did not invite me to speak or to lead workshops. Once, when we found ourselves on a panel at Columbia, Ken Jacobson of the ADL mocked me as "the Jewish Cassandra." I hope I am no Cassandra; no one listened to the Trojan princess and Troy went down in flames.

From the beginning of the Intifada of 2000, well-heeled professional American Jews in handsome three-piece suits, herd animals, self-important cowards, continued to deny and minimize the danger. They assured their funders that the alarmists were wrong, that they—the men in the suits—had it "all under control." How could it be otherwise? They were dining with Arab oil Sheiks and attending interfaith conferences at five star hotels. They were okay—it must have meant that the rest of us were okay too.

In the fall of 2003, Abe Foxman of the ADL finally published his book about anti-Semitism; the book saw little danger emanating from the Islamic world or from Western intellectuals. To Foxman, the Christian Right still remained the major threat. In 2003, when Congressman Tom Lantos wanted to create a U.S. government Office to Monitor and Combat Anti-Semitism, I was repeatedly told that Foxman was trying to block this effort. My sources will not go on record because Foxman wields far too much power. In 2004, when Lantos's Office was, nevertheless, created, Foxman immediately issued a press release "welcoming" the government's move and appearing to take some credit for it, too.

In 2004, Foxman raised holy hell about Mel Gibson's film *The Passion of the Christ*. First, he saw Gibson as "anti-Semitic," saw the film as "painful." Foxman feared it could "fuel latent anti-Semitism." However, Christians have not perpetrated pogroms against Jews or against anyone. Only *Muslims* have perpetrated countless pogroms against infidels in the Muslim world.

Every so often, Foxman will issue a press release about "Islamic extremism," but really taking it on would offend his largely liberal Jewish base and so he comments on specific incidents but has not launched a campaign of any kind against fundamentalist political Islam. Nor has he conducted a campaign to condemn "Islamophobia" as a false concept. Foxman sees "Islamophobia, anti-Semitism, and Christianophobia" as similar realities.

In 2010, nearly ten years after the Al-Aqsa Intifada began, after the Jewish liberals voted for Obama and continue to work or stand by their man, Foxman has, for the first time, called for a *Jewish* march on Washington to demonstrate support for the state of Israel.

The Office, envisioned by Lantos, is now headed by Obama's appointee, Hannah Rosenthal, who sits on the board of J Street.

This is not the time to appeal only to Jews to support Israel. There simply aren't enough Jews in the country or in the world. Foxman's call, and any similar calls, must go out to Christians, Hindus, Sikhs, Buddhist, atheists, Muslims, and ex-Muslims who oppose political Islam. There are at least two organizations that are already working in such coalitions. None are funded like the ADL. I am sure that if Foxman views it as profitable and fashionable to embrace such a vision, he will pretend that it was his idea all along, buy up some of the grassroots activists, and continue to make no difference.

This vision has already been embraced by the Human Rights Coalition Against Radical Islam, of which I am a member. The vision has also been undertaken by one man: Jeff Imm of Responsible for Equality And Liberty (R.E.A.L.); Imm will not work with racists even if they understand the need to combat jihad.

I know: Israel is a well-armed nuclear ghetto and is also strong culturally and economically. Still I sense our vulnerability. Jews are irrationally hated in a world that stood by and did nothing to stop the massacres of civilians in Bosnia, Rwanda, and Sudan—and the world had no blood lust for any of these victims.

Wisely, Israeli Prime Minister Netanyahu chose not to attend the Nuclear Security Summit in Washington, D.C. Why cross oceans to be insulted? Why waste time when the 46 countries in attendance are not yet prepared to stop Iran from going nuclear—and would rather stop Israel's launch of a pre-emptive attack than stop Iran from penetrating

Tel Aviv (or Mecca) with a nuclear bomb? Prime Minister Netanyahu just delivered a speech at Mount Herzl as part of Yom HaShoah Day. He said:

> Today, 65 years after the Holocaust, we must say in all honesty that what is most outrageous is the absence of outrage. The world gradually accepts Iran's statements of destruction against Israel and we still do not see the necessary international determination to stop Iran from arming itself with nuclear weapons. But if we have learned anything from the lessons of the Holocaust, it is that we must not remain silent and be deterred in the face of evil.

I call on all enlightened countries to rise up to forcefully and to firmly condemn Iran's destructive intentions and to act with genuine determination to stop it from acquiring nuclear weapons.

(4/13/10)

39 THE PALESTINIANS ALREADY HAVE TWO STATES: THE TRUTH ACCORDING TO KHALED ABU TOAMEH

*T*he world has gone mad—or at least, the American leadership has now formally joined the Islamist and international madness about "peace in the Middle East."

President Obama has just claimed that American "vital national security" is linked to finding—or even imposing—peace between Israelis and Palestinians.

I strongly recommend that President Obama consult with Khaled Abu Toameh, an Israeli/ Palestinian Arab Muslim journalist who lives in Jerusalem and really "gets it."

Abu Toameh used to work for the PLO newspaper as a translator and fledgling journalist. He confirmed that journalists and visitors to the "territories" cannot just go anywhere on their own; they risk being barred from future visits or even death if they report something that the Palestinian militias do not want the world to know. "All the news is controlled in Gaza and on the West Bank," he said.

In 1988, Abu Toameh began working for the *Jerusalem Post*. He has been attacked as a "traitor" on campuses in California. He understands how dangerous Hamas is and yet he reads that Hamas is becoming moderate—in Toronto's *Globe and Mail*.

I urge, I implore, I demand that all those who keep talking about a "peace process" listen to what Abu Toameh has to say. I feel so strongly about this that I am sharing his words almost verbatim. He spoke on the Upper West Side, at Aish HaTorah, an Orthodox Jewish religious center.

Abu Toameh confirms that the worst possible thing *for the Palestinian people* were the various peace processes that were highly misguided, insincere, and unworkable. He said that "before the Oslo Accords, Palestinians had high hopes that we would have a democratic Parliament just as the Israelis do and a free media. Since Oslo, things have gone in the wrong direction."

In his view, "Oslo was based on the assumption that Arafat and Fatah were reliable peace partners." But once Arafat was returned in triumph "the show began, a one man show. Thirteen to fifteen militias roamed the streets. Most of the money given to Arafat for Palestine went down the drain, into secret Swiss bank accounts, and to his wife, Suha, in France. He built a casino—right across from a refugee camp."

In his view, everyone was afraid to report the truth because Arafat and his goon squads would kill truth tellers. Thus, Arafat and the mythic peace process embittered and "radicalized" the Palestinian people and they turned to Hamas, an Islamist organization funded by Iran. "People lost faith in the peace process," he said. Abu Toameh also confirmed that in English Arafat kept speaking about peace, and in Arabic kept inciting people against Israel.

Israeli President Shimon Peres defended Arafat. Abu Toameh thought to himself, "How stupid can this man be? Doesn't he know that Arafat is describing the Jews as the descendants of pigs and monkeys? Why make peace with the Jews if they are this terrible?"

In 2006, Hamas won a democratic election—an election that was held under American supervision and that was supported by both President Bush and Secretary of State Condoleezza Rice. Abu Toameh knew Hamas would win. He said, "Israel also facilitated the election of Hamas by allowing Arabs in Jerusalem to vote in that election. Israel did not know what every Palestinian child knew: That Hamas would win."

Fatah has lost, Mahmoud Abbas cannot deliver peace nor can he make peace with Hamas. Hamas is not stepping down. "This civil war among the Palestinians has so far claimed 2,000 lives," Abu Toameh said.

Hamas kicked Fatah out of Gaza. Abu Toameh reports that he personally "saw Palestinians running away from Hamas towards Egypt, saw Egypt close the border to those in flight. Only Israel helped Muslims who were about to be slaughtered by Muslims." Ironically, Abu Toameh concludes:

> We got our two-state solution. The Palestinians got two states. Hamas is funded by the Muslim Brotherhood, Syria, and Iran and I would not want to live there. The West Bank is being run by Arafat's former cronies. But Mahmoud Abbas is afraid of his own people. I have not once seen him in a village. He has no credibility. He cannot deliver peace.

What does Abu Toameh suggest is the way forward?

> Dismantle all the Palestinian militias, start building Palestinian infrastructures, solve the Palestinian-Palestinian problems—and only then, sit down with the Jews. Obama thinks the ball is in the Israeli court. That is not true.
>
> If I were Netanyahu, I would offer Palestinians ten states. Bring Obama over, ask him: To whom do I give the Palestinian states? To Hamas? Abbas? Islamic Jihad?

He cautions Israel to be "careful about unilateral measures. Any land you give back, any land you give to Abbas, will end up in Iran's hand. See how Gaza ended up. The same thing will repeat itself. The majority of Jews support the Palestinian state not because they love Palestinians but because they want to get rid of them."

And then he issued a warning to Israel which had nothing to do with two-state solutions or with a peace process.

> Israeli Arabs have been loyal to Israel. They are still discriminated against. No, Israel is not an apartheid state, but discrimination exists against 1.4 million of its own citizens. If Israel does not implement an emergency plan to solve this then the radicalization of the Arab and Muslim world will explode. The next Intifada will be in Haifa, Umm al-Fahm, Nazareth, Rahat, Yaffo.

(4/15/10)

40 Jews Not Wanted on Campus If They Support Israel—Not Even at Brandeis

*M*ichael B. Oren is the distinguished historian and author of *Six Days of War* and *Power, Faith, and Fantasy*. He is Israel's Ambassador to the United States and has been invited to deliver the keynote address at Brandeis's 2010 commencement exercises.

Recently, Ambassador Oren got a taste of campus life at the University of California at Irvine where his speech was constantly interrupted; the choreographed disruptions led to eleven student arrests. In 2002, Prime Minister Netanyahu's speech in Montreal at Concordia University had to be canceled for security reasons.

The world is watching. Will Brandeis behave like the University of California or will it model individual achievement over mob rule? Will it defend free and academic speech?

Some Brandeis students and faculty have denounced this choice while others have applauded it. The denouncers claim that Ambassador Oren will be "political," and as such "divisive" and "polarizing." According to Professor Gordon Fellman, "His role obligates him to defend Israeli policies... that include defending the Israeli incursion into Gaza, housing policies of the occupation, and so on. I think for many people that's a third rail."

In 2006, Jordan's Prince Hassan bin Talal delivered the keynote address at graduation. Students did not protest Jordan's human rights record vis-à-vis the Palestinians in 1970 and in 2010 or its abysmal record on honor-related violence, including honor killings and the torture of its own citizens. No one held Jordan accountable for its systematic desecration of Jewish holy places and for its evacuation of Jews from the Jewish quarter in 1948. A prince who represents a country and a regime that behaves in this way is as "political" as Oren could ever be. The only difference is that one man is an Arab, Muslim prince; the other is an intellectual Jew and an American-Israeli. Students did not create online petitions to debate the merits of choosing Jordan's prince as a speaker.

I write this as the mother and mother-in-law of two former Brandeis students who both loved the school and as someone who once happily taught a course there. I have the fondest memories of Brandeis and appreciate its commitment to gender, religious, and racial equality, and its ability to make everyone feel warmly embraced.

The problem is bigger than this one instance. The question is whether or how well the Brandeis community will now be able to withstand the politically correct tides of anti-Semitism, censorship, and self-censorship, which threaten to engulf the world and the tiny Jewish state.

Do the anti-Oren students and faculty at Brandeis really understand what is going on? I fear not. Israel's critics are as merciless and unbalanced in their criticism of Israel-only. While holding an endangered Israel's feet to the fire, these critics practice compassion and understanding towards the non-Jewish barbarians of the Middle East and Islamic world.

In the name of anti-racism, Jews are the only group whom it is fashionable to "hate." If you stereotype Jews and believe that the Jewish state should be destroyed or abolished, you are exercising free, politically correct speech. However, if you support Jews and the Jewish state, you are a racist. You will lose your friends and funding. And you will be heckled and menaced on Western campuses, assuming that you are still invited to speak.

Even if a speaker might want to address a subject other than Israel (as Ambassador Oren conceivably might do), once it is known that a speaker supports rather than condemns the Jewish state, one loses credibility and their right to free, academic speech.

How did this all come about?

First, it took years of Soviet-, Arab League-, Saudi-, and Soros-funded hate propaganda, doctored footage, and Big Lies, all of which were meant to toughen people up for the simultaneous and subsequent legal, social, cultural, economic, and military attacks against Israel.

Just as President Obama and Secretary of State Clinton publicly shamed Israel's Prime Minister, Benjamin Netanyahu (but not Saudi Arabia's King Abdullah or Iran's President Ahmadinejad); just as academics Mearsheimer and Walt condemned what they described as the Israel Lobby (but did not mention the far more powerful Saudi Lobby); just as academics the world over continue to argue for boycotts against Israel, including against leftist Israeli academics (but do not suggest boycotts against Sudan, Iran, or Congo); just as intellectuals and First Amendment Freaks are busily romanticizing sophisticated misogynists and fascists such as the Muslim Brotherhood's Tariq Ramadan (but not the feminist hero Ayaan Hirsi Ali, who was offered no post in Women's Studies when she fled Holland for her life)—so, too, have the Islamified mobs set upon individual Jews and Israeli diplomats.

Just days ago, a pro-Palestinian mob tried to attack an Israeli diplomat outside the University of Manchester in the UK after she lectured at the university. Israel's Deputy Ambassador, Talya Lador-Fresher, believed that the mob of 300 "genuinely wanted to physically hurt me. If I had not had the police and security team, I would have been beaten up... no foreign diplomat should have to go through what I went through."

We must stand up for the truth and for the Jews—no matter the cost. We must name and reject radical evil. Heroism is now our only alternative if we want western civilization and the values of the Enlightenment to survive.

The world is watching. What will Brandeis do?

(5/3/10)

41 Turkey Attacks Israel: Does The Old Ottoman Empire Want to Lead the Caliphate?

One may describe the Turks on board the "freedom flotilla" as "humanitarian activists," but they are really Turkish jihadists on a mission to kill Jews. Their mission was to further demonize the already shamefully tarnished reputation of the Jewish state by forcing a violent confrontation in which Israeli soldiers would be forced to defend themselves. Muslims would probably be martyred—good public relations, useful for international lawfare against Israel.

Palestinian terrorists call themselves "freedom fighters;" Turkish terrorists call themselves "humanitarians." When propagandists appropriate and misuse language, reality is blurred, confusion reigns. When "good" people label Israeli "self-defense" as "aggression," one despairs—or at least hopes that serious people will see through the deception and set matters right.

The so-called "humanitarians," at least on one Turkish boat, came armed with metal bars and knives. A video shows Israeli soldiers being beaten with long, heavy metal rods. They were fighters, not pacifists, and they called out traditional Islamic battle cries, "[Remember] Khaibar, Khaibar, oh Jews! The army of Muhammad will return!" According to Palestinian Media Watch:

> Khaibar is the name of the last Jewish village defeated by Muhammad's army in 628. Many Jews were killed in that battle, which marked the end of Jewish presence in Arabia. There are Muslims who see that as a precursor for future wars against Jews. At gatherings and rallies of extremists, this chant is often heard as a threat to Jews to expect to be defeated and killed again by Muslims.

Israel's Deputy Foreign Minister Danny Ayalon said that the Turkish-led flotilla was:

> An armada of hate and violence in support of Hamas' terror organization and was a premeditated and outrageous provocation. On board the ship we found weapons prepared in advance and used against our forces. The organizers intent was violent, their method was violent, and the results were unfortunately violent. Israel regrets any loss of life and did everything to avoid this outcome.

The death count currently stands at 16 (mainly Turkish). Six IDF soldiers have been wounded. Predictably, the Arab, European, and liberal media are viewing Israel as the vicious aggressor. Al Jazeera's website calls what happened "a massacre." They refer to the dead as "martyrs."

This latest Turkish-Palestinian attack on Israel, disguised as a "peace" or "humanitarian" mission, was televised live— first, by the attackers, but also by the Israelis. One passenger on the *Mavi Marmara* was Bishop Hilarion Capucci who was convicted and imprisoned in Israel for smuggling weapons from Lebanon to the PLO. We also know that the Turkish jihadists came equipped with weapons: stun guns, knives, sharpened weapons, clubs, rocks, smoke bombs, slingshots, large metal poles—and the most important weapon of all: cellphone cameras. The terrorists streamed what was happening as it was happening. They actually got the jump on the Israelis who had planned—but failed—to jam the airwaves. At least, this is what Noah Shachtman, writing in *Wired*, claims.

This time, IDF cameras were also used, and rather successfully. We were able to click on YouTube to see how the "peaceful" passengers were beating up Israeli troops. The IDF showed how it was unloading "humanitarian cargo" from the ships and into Gaza. All along, the IDF provided a stream of Twitter updates and blog posts to "reinforce its position."

According to Shachtman, the other side live-streamed the battle.

The IDF footage may have neutralized some public opinion. This is a major "win" for Israel. Some of the mainstream media in the West did not *immediately* condemn Israel for committing a "massacre," a "war crime," or an "atrocity."

American Vice President Joe Biden called the Israeli operation "legitimate" and insisted that Israel "has an absolute right to deal with its security interest... It's legitimate for

Israel to say 'I don't know what's on that ship, these guys are dropping [thousands of] rockets on my people'…Israel is at war with Hamas and has the right to know whether arms are being smuggled in."

But Schachtman does make an interesting point. He tells us that the very popular IDF YouTube channel was not started by the IDF.

A young Israeli soldier—born in a small town in Hawaii, and converted to Judaism at Yale—got together with another American Israeli who thought it'd be cool to share some of their videos online. That became the IDF's official YouTube channel, unexpectedly generating millions of views.

Why did Turkey attack Israel? How much Iranian support did they have?

I am waiting for the United Nations and for the United States to condemn this unprovoked attack on a sovereign nation

(5/31/10)

42 ALICE WALKER: STOP TELLING LIES ABOUT ISRAEL

*T*he African-American feminist and writer Alice Walker (with whom I go way back) has written a naive and rather hate-filled piece about the Israeli blockade of Gaza and the IDF response to the Turkish terrorist boats:

> My heart is breaking; but I do not mind. For one thing, as soon as I wrote those words I was able to weep. Which I had not been able to do since learning of the attack by armed Israeli commandos on defenseless peace activists carrying aid to Gaza who tried to fend them off using chairs and sticks.

Walker brings in Jim Crow, Medgar Evers, Rosa Parks, Martin Luther King, Montgomery, Alabama, and the civil rights movement in order to present her view as hallowed by history, as holy. But her facts are all wrong.

How can Walker compare these known terrorists and racists to non-violent civil rights activists? Why does Walker condemn, even abhor the Jewish state and idolize the Islamist tyrants who hold Palestinians hostage in Gaza? Why identify the aggressors as innocent victims?

To what extent do Walker's views reflect those of the administration and of those close to the president?

We now understand that the passengers on board one ship, the *Mavi Marmara*, came to fight, to kill, and to die. Some were Turkish mercenaries, hired to do the Turkish Prime Minister's bidding—or perhaps Iran's bidding. Many had ties to known terrorist organizations. Alice: Here is part of an email which an Israeli Navy soldier sent to a relative. He requests that this information be shared widely.

> *Dear Aunt X:*
>
> *As you know, it was my unit and my friends who were on the ship. My commander was injured badly as a result of the "pacifist's" violence. I want to tell you how he was injured so you can tell the story. It shows just how horrible and inhuman were the activists. My commander was the first soldier that rappelled down from the helicopter to the ship. When he touched ground, he got hit in the head with a pole and stabbed in the stomach with a knife. When he drew out his secondary weapon—a handgun (his primary weapon was a regular paintball gun)—he was shot in the leg.*
>
> *He managed to fire a single shot before he was tossed from the balcony by 4 Arab activists, to the lower deck (a 12-foot fall). He was then dragged by other activists to a room in the lower deck where he was stripped down by 2 activists.*

They took off his vest, helmet, and shirt, leaving him with only his pants and shoes on. When they finished they took a knife and expanded the wound he already had in his stomach. They cut his ab muscles horizontally and by hand spilled his guts out.

When they finished, they raised him up and walked him on the deck outside. He was conscious the whole time. If you are asking yourself why they did all that here comes the reason. They wanted to show the soldiers their commander's body so they will be demoralized and scared. Luckily, when they walked him on the deck, a soldier saw him and managed to shoot the activist that was walking him down the outside corridor. He shot him with a special non-lethal bullet that didn't kill him. My commander managed to jump from the deck to the water and swim to an army rescue boat (his guts still out of his body and now in salty sea water). That was how he was saved. The activists that did this to him are alive and now in Turkey and treated as heroes.

I'm sorry if I described this with too many details, but I thought it was necessary for the credibility. Please tell this story to anyone who will listen.

Stop the Lies. Alice Walker: My heart is breaking, too.

(6/6/10)

43 AN AVALANCHE OF ANTI-ISRAEL PROPAGANDA

Today, on the very day that President Obama is scheduled to meet with Prime Minister Netanyahu, the *New York Times* published a lead story of nearly 5,000 words titled "Tax-Exempt Funds Aid Settlements in West Bank." Before Bibi could even have breakfast, the paper was probably on his desk. The article is accompanied by six photographs and a map of the so-called "illegal settlements."

This article presents the settlements as "illegal," "isolated" "outposts," run by "militants" and supported by funds from abroad supplied by wealthy American Jews and by Christian Evangelical supporters of Israel. This is presented as if it is a damning and dramatic expose of shady characters.

"Illegal" and "militant" are an interesting choice of words for a newspaper that refuses to call Turkish assassins and mercenaries "terrorists," and refers to them as "humanitarian activists;" a newspaper that refused to describe the dreaded Sudanese Janjaweed as "ethnic Arab Muslims" engaging in "genocidal aggression" against black African Muslims, Christians, and animists.

After outlining the tax-exempt support for allegedly "illegal" settlements in the West Bank, the article fails the most minimal standards for even-handed reporting. It fails to mention the nearly half-century-long funding of an Israel-hating, corrupt, and tyrannical Palestinian leadership—by the United States, the United Nations, the European Union, and by the Arab and Muslim world.

The *Times* article is propaganda and advocacy, not even-handed journalism. The Paper of Record is doing some heavy lifting for the White House. This piece—so prominent, so lengthy, so carefully timed——is yet another way to pressure Prime Minister Netanyahu even before he sits down with President Obama. Just as you've unilaterally given up Gaza, give up the West Bank, give up East Jerusalem, accept the return of five generations of Palestinian "refugees," give up control of Tel Aviv and Haifa—in short, do what King Abdullah of Saudi Arabia wants and then maybe we'll let a remnant of Jewry live. True, only as second- or third-class citizens but if this means peace in the Middle East and an Arab world united with America against Iran, little enough to ask.

What needs to be said in the Paper of Record requires at least the same 5,000 words that comprise this misleading piece. It needs to be written by the world's leading historians and Middle East analysts. I am only one Jew, crying out, dependent on what I read in the mass media and on the internet.

(7/6/10)

44 JUST OUT: *TIME* MAGAZINE'S LATEST BLOOD LIBEL ABOUT ISRAEL

Time's cover story (9/2/10) is titled "Why Israel Doesn't Care About Peace." It is illustrated by a large Jewish star composed of daisies. Yes, daisies—as in: Israelis have nothing better to do than "count daisies;" they are sitting pretty.

This is journalist Karl Vick's precise point. He writes: "Israelis are no longer preoccupied with the matter [of peace with the Palestinians]. They're otherwise engaged: They're making money; they're enjoying the rays of the late summer…they have moved on."

Vick quotes an Israeli real estate agent in Ashdod, who tells him, "People are indifferent. They don't care if there's going to be war. They don't care if there's going to be peace. They don't care. They live in the day."

According to Vick, Israelis don't care about peace or about Palestinians because they are having too good a time:

sunbathing, swimming, café-hopping, profiting from start-up companies, etc. Vick suggests that Israelis resemble Californians more than they resemble Egyptians. Israel does not fit in. They are not a true part of the Middle East.

These are Vick's thoughts, not mine.

Of course, Jews are the original Palestinians and the most indigenous of the region's inhabitants. Why doesn't Vick point out that there are some Israelis who remain permanently on high alert for the next terrorist attack, permanently scarred by the last ones? Does he not know that Palestinians are also leading the high life in villas on both the West Bank and in Gaza, that they, too, are sunbathing, swimming, shopping, dining out, and relaxing at the beach—at least as much as the Islamist thugs who run the lives of Palestinians will allow it?

Vick writes that real estate is booming, as is business in general; Israeli "brainiacs" have helped their nation avoid the economic disasters that have plunged Europe and America into a recession. He writes, "Israel avoided the debt traps that dragged the U.S. and Europe into recession. It is known as a start-up nation—second only to the U.S. companies listed on the NASDAQ exchange."

Vick presents Israel's "success" as unseemly because it makes other nations look bad. Does he harbor the suspicion that Jewish prosperity has been "stolen" from non-Jews or is he merely advertising that Jewish gold is there, ripe for the taking?

Buried—but really buried—in Vick's four-page cover piece are snippets of true facts: The Israelis are weary of peace negotiations that never succeed because the Palestinians do not want peace—they want to destroy Israel. Vick fails to convey that negotiations cannot succeed as long as the Arab propaganda against Jews continues to turn out children who hate Jews and who become human homicide bombs.

Vick fails to comprehend that the Israelis are not living in la-la land à la southern Californians (hence, the Jewish star made of daisies on the cover). The Israelis are actually showing the entire world how to embrace life, even as they live, trembling, in the shadow of death. They are teaching the world how to "love life more than they fear death." A new and wonderful book, *A New Shoah: The Untold Story of Israel's Victims of Terrorism*, by Italian journalist Giulio Meotti, makes precisely this point.

The Jewish insistence on life may be the key to our survival as a people despite ceaseless persecution. It might be the lesson, the model, for all humanity in an era of genocides, civil wars, and totalitarian regimes. Why is *Time* turning things on their head and refusing to recognize the courage and the heroism of Israelis who choose to live in the moment when the moment is all they have? Against all odds, the Jews simply refuse to give up. As Meotti writes of the numerous victims of terrorism during the ongoing Intifada of 2000, "Israel teaches the world love of life, not in the sense of a banal joie de vivre, but as a solemn celebration."

Meotti understands that, in the last decade, Israel is the "first country ever to experience suicide terrorism on a mass scale: that more than 150 suicide attacks have been carried out plus 500 have been prevented." According to Meotti, there have been "1,723 people (murdered) and 10,000 injured" in Israel. Meotti also converts these numbers into the demographic equivalent of attacks on Americans. He writes that in American population terms, this means that "74,000 Americans" would have been killed and "400,000 injured."

What Meotti remembers are the lives and the deaths of these Israeli victims of Palestinian terrorism. These are unknown stories, unnamed victims, whose mortal remains have evaporated as surely as those Jews who went up in smoke during the Nazi Holocaust. His stories are mainly of victims who were unarmed and helpless and who, it turns out, were actually exceptionally kind to others, often to the very Arab Palestinians who shot them down, bludgeoned them to death, or blew them up into unrecognizable bone fragments, drops of blood, perhaps a few teeth.

I hope that people understand that *Time* magazine, as well as countless other media in the Western world can no longer be trusted to tell the truth.

(9/4/10)

45 A NEW KIND OF THEATER: ACTORS AGAINST ISRAEL

Once, the world's reigning Hollywood and theater people were satisfied with their glamour, wealth, fame, and torrid affairs. That is no longer enough. Now, theater people adopt "causes." They sign petitions. They march. They make unexpectedly long speeches at the Academy Awards apologizing for America's extermination of native Indians and for slavery. They also adopt politically correct children. Therefore, it is no surprise that the current crop have elected to join the worldwide delegitimization of Israel project.

Some *Israeli* writers and actors are refusing to perform at a new cultural center in the city of Ariel, located in Samaria (Shomron) and over the Green Line. Israeli authors A.B. Yehoshua, Amos Oz, David Grossman, and 47 other Israeli playwrights, directors, actors, and theater people are among those who sent a letter to *Haaretz* about their boycott of Ariel.

American-Jewish theater people are backing them to the hilt. Ed Asner, Theodore Bikel, Tony Kushner, Mandy Patinkin, Stephen Sondheim, Eve Ensler, Judith Malina,

Roseanne Barr, as well as non-Jews such as Vanessa Redgrave, Kathleen Chalfant, Julianne Moore, and Mira Nair, have signed a petition supporting the Israeli theater people who refuse to perform at Ariel. In all, 150 Americans have signed this petition. Many, but not all of them, are Jews.

The theater is wondrous but passing strange. There are all kinds of dues to pay—on the casting couch, but also personally and politically. If you don't "perform" a certain kind of politics, and/or if your plays don't toe certain party lines, your plays will not be produced, you will not even make it to the casting couch.

Theater people must share the views held by the Obama administration and by the American, European, and Israeli Left, namely, that the Israeli settlements are holding up the peace process—not Hamas's hatred for a Jewish state; not Abbas's inability to tame the wildest passions ignited by political Islam.

Once, Tel Aviv was considered a "settlement." In 1929, Muslims rioted and massacred Jews in the holy *Jewish* city of Hebron—simply because they were Jews, infidels; in 1938, Arab rioters infiltrated Kiryat Shmuel in Tiberias, killing 19 Jews, eleven of whom were children. They also set fire to Jewish homes and synagogues. In 1948, Arabs massacred a convoy of Jews bringing doctors and medical supplies to Hadassah Hospital; 79 Jews, mostly doctors and nurses, were murdered. Suffice it to say: In the 1940s and 1950s, Arabs kept right on massacring Jews in the Holy Land—long before Israel won any additional territory in the 1967 war of self-defense.

What Israeli "settlement" compelled them to do so?

Tragically, our new theater stars wish to be seen as "anti-racists;" yet, by holding Arab and Muslim countries to much lower standards and by condemning their inhabitants to continued Islamist barbarism, they fail their own standard of anti-racism. Their anti-Zionism is a profound form of racism—a fact which they absolutely refuse to understand.

(9/15/10)

46 WILL THE WORLD LEARN THE LESSONS OF THE HOLOCAUST IN TIME?

*T*he first conference I ever attended about global anti-Semitism took place in New York City in early 2003 at the Center for Jewish History. My son accompanied me. The more I heard, the unhappier I grew. My son could not understand why. He asked, "Mom, why are you groaning? They are saying exactly what you've written in your manuscript." My book, *The New Anti-Semitism*, was about to be published that summer.

I explained, "But they are the world's experts on this subject. I am only the new kid on the block. If they haven't taken it further than I have, then we're all in terrible trouble."

I have lived long enough to have this eerie, humbling experience any number of times. I am not saying that others have not analyzed the matter as well as I have; on the contrary. Many are far more scholarly. They are genuine experts who have devoted their entire careers to this subject—and more and more books are being published about this every month.

It is not enough. Our documentation of the impending Holocaust of Jewish Israel and the ongoing Islamic Jihad against the world is not enough to stop these calamities or to change minds that are closed to reason. I do not think we have enough time to deprogram the brainwashed, one by one. Only a military victory will do it.

Six weeks ago, I had a heavenly time working with a group of feminists at the conference on global anti-Semitism, which was sponsored by the Yale Initiative for the Interdisciplinary Study of Antisemitism. I unexpectedly chaired one session but was there primarily to discuss feminists and anti-Semitism on a plenary panel. (Thank you Dr. Charles Small.)

I was also part of another conference about Muslim anti-Semitism which was sponsored by the *Journal for the Study of Antisemitism*. I spoke and chaired a panel with Daniel Jonah Goldhagen of Harvard and Mark Weitzman of the Simon Wiesenthal Center

There were many wonderful people at the Yale conference and at the conference in New York City yesterday. Daniel Pipes, of the Middle East Forum was his usual reasoned and brilliant self. He said that he feared that Westerners, Americans, will not take jihad seriously, and will not do what is necessary, until one of the many planned terrible attacks succeeds, until thousands, maybe hundreds of thousands are killed.

Richard Landes and I were at both conferences. At Yale, I chaired a session with Landes, Alvin Rosenfeld, and Doron Ben-Atar. The panel title was "Self Hatred and Contemporary Antisemitism." When I told Landes that he really had to sum up, he said, "People, they are coming to schecht (slaughter) us, we had better do something."

The room was very quiet. Faces were extremely grave,

especially the face of the next speaker, Alvin Rosenfeld. I, never one to be called "light," wanted to lighten this moment. So I resorted to humor. I said, "So, what do we do after someone says that we are about to die? We call upon the next speaker to enlighten us further."

It worked. People laughed a little bit. Jewish irony and humor to the rescue.

(10/4/10)

47 DARKEST ANTI-SEMITISM IN HOLLAND

*H*olland prides itself on its religious tolerance. It welcomed Portuguese Jews, and, although they forbade them to join guilds or own shops, the Jews nevertheless flourished in Holland as publishers, physicians, and diamond dealers.

Holland also prides itself on its presumably heroic role as resistance fighters against the Nazi occupation. But the truth is something darker, more complicated, and not so heroic.

To me, Holland represents tulips, legalized marijuana, women selling sex in windows, multi-cultural tolerance, a huge Muslim problem—and the murder of Anne Frank and nearly all of Dutch Jewry.

I spent time in the mid-1970s with the late Meyer Levin in his home in Israel; he tried to persuade me that Broadway Jewish communists (Lillian Hellman in particular) had colluded with Otto Frank, Anne's father, to ditch Levin's screenplay about Frank and to present a far more "universal" and less specifically Jewish Anne. Hellman and others succeeded. They also managed to persuade Hollywood and Broadway to focus on Anne's "optimism," and to bypass her growing sense of the unfolding tragedy.

Levin became obsessed with the "whitewashing" of the Holocaust through this use of Anne Frank. I agreed with him. Others did not. He died a bitter and heartbroken man. Not until 1997 did Cynthia Ozick finally set the record straight in *The New Yorker*. She, too, found that Levin had been telling the truth.

Author Abigail R. Esman would have believed Levin. An expatriate Jewish-American, Esman, has written a powerful new book, *Radical State: How Jihad Is Winning Over Democracy in the West*, which is set in Holland, where she has lived for the last 20 years.

Esman reminds me that although Jews were given shelter in 1536, "the Jews of Amsterdam were able to practice their religion so long as they did so privately—one of history's first examples of the trait some Dutch now proudly call their 'tolerance' and others angrily describe as coldhearted standoffishness." Esman states that 75% of Holland's Jews were exterminated during the Nazi occupation (1940-1945), which means that "more Jews died per capita in the Netherlands than anywhere else in Europe outside of Germany." However, "the 1944 rail strike [in Holland constituted] the only public protest held anywhere in Europe against the persecution of the Jews."

In her beautifully written book, she gives us one chilling example after another of old-fashioned Jew-hatred and of its latest lethal Dutch-Muslim version. When Muslims riot in Holland or disagree with anyone, they demonize them as "Zionists."

After a showing of Geert Wilders's film, *Fitna*, "the

media reported that a handful of lone protestors had stood near the Parliament building in The Hague, carrying a banner that stated simply, 'Wilders is a Zionist.' On May 4, 2003 (Holocaust Memorial Day), in the Baarsjes section of Amsterdam, Moroccan boys were caught kicking memorial wreaths along the streets and chanting the popular refrain, 'Joden, die moeten we doden,' ('Kill the Jews,' or—literally translated—'We must kill Jews')."

According to Esman, newspapers reported that "teachers had begun receiving threats when they attempted to teach about the Holocaust."

During the worst year of the 2000 Intifada against Israel, in April, 2002, "anti-Israel demonstrations on Dam Square in Amsterdam were accompanied by cries of 'Hamas, Hezbollah, Jihad!' British, American, and Israeli flags were set afire. Overall, the Dutch Center for Information and Documentation on Israel (CIDI) confirmed a 140 percent increase in anti-Semitic incidents in the Netherlands between the last quarter of 2002 and the first quarter of 2003 over the same period a year earlier, most of them committed by Muslim youth."

Esman reports that "Kankerjood" ("cancer Jew") became a "favorite insult among the Dutch Muslim community; in Sweden, a Jewish couple I met told me that Muslims had begun greeting one another with the simple phrase 'Kill Jews' (as in, 'Hey, kill Jews. How's it going?') Dutch and Belgian rap groups recorded 'kankerjood' songs with lyrics like 'F--- the Jews, cancer Jews, the allochtonen (immigrants) will come and kill you...'"

Perhaps the most chilling document presented in Esman's book—which is also about jihad, not only in Europe, but also worldwide—is her presentation of the letter that the assassin, Dutch Moroccan Mohammed Bouyeri, stabbed into the nearly decapitated body of artist Theo van Gogh. Diabolically, Bouyeri cites Talmudic sources, which are taken out of context. He cites Bava Metzia, 114a-114b, which according to Bouyeri, tells us that "only Jews are (considered) people." However, the point made on these pages is only true in relation to an abstract point of law and is not a Talmudic rejection of all of God's creation. Bouyeri accuses Jewish texts of committing Koranic "sins." His letter, which is also a death threat to Ayaan Hirsi Ali reads, in part:

> It is a fact that Dutch politics is dominated by many Jews and is a product of the Talmudic Schools... What do you think of the fact that the Mayor of Amsterdam is at the helm of an ideology whereby Jews are permitted to lie to non-Jews? Baba Kamma 113a: Jews may use lies ("listen") to mislead gentiles. What do you think of the fact that you are part of a government that supports a State that pleads for genocide?

I have interviewed Esman and read her book. It should be required reading for Israeli and European leaders.

(10/12/10)

48 ANTI-SEMITISM CANNOT BE EQUATED WITH ISLAMOPHOBIA

*E*ven as Chancellor Angela Merkel pronounces the failure of "multiculturalism" in Germany, the English-language German newspaper reporter, Marc Young, writing for the English-language German news at *The Local*, proclaims that "bigotry towards Muslims is the new anti-Semitism."

Allow me to remind Mr. Young that one of the things that is "new" about this most ancient of hatreds is that it is pandemic in the Islamic world and in Muslim communities in the West, and that the multicultural relativists in the world's universities, media, and political leadership are collaborating with it in the name of "political correctness." Thus, what both Young and those who run the state-subsidized Center for Research on Anti-Semitism at the Technical University of Berlin have learned from the Nazi Holocaust is that Europeans should not discriminate against Muslims as they once did against Jews. German scholar Clemens Heni strongly disagrees:

> There is no other prejudice or form of racism which you can compare to this centuries-long hatred (anti-Semitism) which has no real justification. If you look at Islam today, there is a point to Islamophobia because Jihadists say, "We want to kill the unbelievers." Jews never said that. As a German I have a responsibility to deal with my own history. If I see that other Germans want to downplay anti-Semitism and to minimize the threat of Islamic jihad and other forms of anti-Zionism—I think there is something deeply wrong, they didn't learn the lesson from the Holocaust. Most people in Germany and in academia focus on anti-Semitism as one prejudice among many like racism, colonialism, imperialism, sexism, whatever. That was the reason why Robert Wistrich, the leading historian of anti-Semitism, was never invited to the Berlin Center for Research on anti-Semitism for the last 20 years. Usually an institute, well-funded, with hundreds of thousands of Euros a year—they have to invite the leading scholars. They didn't invite him. One must ask why.

Heni has paid a price for his views, both in Berlin and at Israel's leading "post-Zionist" universities, which have, so far, refused to hire him as a professor of German history who specializes in German anti-Semitism when such positions have been available.

Heni has written about anti-Semitism in Germany:

Antisemitism and German history, and has co-written a paper, *German Middle Eastern Studies and Islamism After 9/11*. He remains an independent scholar without a tenured position. In a recent interview, Heni explained to me:

> The controversy goes back to the conference in 2008 that equated Islamophobia and anti-Semitism, literally saying that the Muslims of today are in the same situation that the Jews were in during the late 19th century. I'm a scholar of German history, so I know a little bit about what happened at that time. We had specific parties dedicated to spreading anti-Semitism, and right now we don't have a single party spreading Islamophobia, saying "we don't want any Muslims in our country," or that they should be killed. Mr. Benz, the head of the Center, claimed that after the killing of Theo van Gogh in the Netherlands in 2004, we had an increase in hostility toward Islam. He did not say that he was sorry about what happened to Mr. van Gogh, which was one of the most powerful political acts of murder in the last decade in Europe because it was a very Islamist, jihadist action.

Leaping right over what is specific to the extermination of Europe's Jews, Germans, as well as other Europeans today, are generalizing this tragic and unique history so as to justify the absorption of a far more dangerous and increasingly radicalized Muslim population.

(10/19/10)

49 ISRAEL'S PR WAR NEEDS STUXNET

The global propaganda war against Israel is an avalanche, a veritable tsunami. Unchecked, it continues to gain both acceleration and mass and is, if anything, as dangerous as any human homicide bomb or rocket attack.

In the midst of a perfectly pleasant conversation, a (now former) colleague unexpectedly started yelling at me about my defense of "that" country—"you know, the one that sends its military to purposely blind young activists who have come to free Gaza."

This colleague knew absolutely nothing about the incident or about the war against Israel. She reads about Israel in the *New York Times* and *The Nation*, and given how propaganda works, she felt entitled to attack me because Israel had dared to defend itself against paid Turkish assassins—and because a young Jewish-American activist, mesmerized by the International Solidarity Movement, found herself holding a Turkish and Austrian flag and standing at the Kalandiya crossing, where she was accidentally blinded by a tear gas canister.

My former colleague probably believes that Mohammed al-Dura was killed by the IDF on purpose too.

A decade later, more American Jewish organization leaders are beginning to sound as I and a handful of others once did. The unfunded and poorly funded pro-Israel grassroots anti-propaganda and campus activist groups are way ahead of the Fat Cats. Now, because major Jewish donors are finally demanding that "something be done" to deal with the hatred of Israel on American campuses, the large Jewish-American organizations suddenly claim that they will do it.

On their watch we not only lost this propaganda war—we also did not fight it at all.

The other night a very knowledgeable man assured me that AIPAC was on the job. I told him that AIPAC has done an excellent job, but mainly in lobbying Congress on Israel's behalf. The problem is so much bigger than Congress. There is the Internet, the Western campuses, all the international human rights organizations, the United Nations, the Islamic world and for that matter, the governments of at least 195 countries. And then there are all the coming generations... by now, the Saudi lobby has poisoned countless generations with myths about Israel's evil.

It is not enough to lobby Congress. It is not even enough to document the anti-Israel bias in magazine and journal articles *after* they have already been published. We are up against a juggernaut of brainwashing. Where will the funding come from that will meet and raise this diabolical game of propaganda poker against the Jewish state? We need the equivalent of a series of Stuxnet viruses in the war of ideas. Nothing less will do.

(12/13/10)

50 IS IT NOT TORTURE WHEN THE PRISONER IS A JEW?

Last year, *The New Yorker* ran a piece about solitary confinement. The article concludes that this punishment amounts to torture, that it can induce "acute psychosis with hallucinations." The article describes the cases of two political prisoners or prisoners-of-war. AP's Middle East correspondent, Terry Anderson, was put into solitary by Hezbollah in Lebanon for six years. Anderson "felt himself disintegrating;" his mind went blank; he had hallucinations; he started to become "neurotically possessive about his little space;" he felt his brain was "grinding down." He also describes Senator John McCain who said that "solitary confinement crushes your spirit and weakens your resistance more than any other form of mistreatment."

Clearly, *The New Yorker*'s man, Atul Gawande, opposes this practice.

Gawande does not mention Jonathan Pollard, a man whose living head is on a pike in the public square for all to see (a message, a warning to us all): a man who killed no one.

Noureddine Malki—his name is one of five aliases—was loyal to a Middle Eastern country, the American military hired him as an intelligence officer and translator anyway—partly because he knew an important Middle East language. He was a poor choice. This man passed classified documents to "insurgents" in Iraq who were battling American forces; he also had conversations with members of al-Qaeda and kept their documents on his computer.

He pretended to be from Lebanon, the persecuted son of a Muslim father and a Christian mother, and on this basis allegedly sought and received asylum in America, naturalized citizenship, and a job as an Arabic translator for the Army. He received top secret clearance and was working in Iraq where he took bribes from various Sunni sheikhs and passed classified information on to them.

He was caught, tried, and, in 2008, sentenced to—*ten* years. Currently, Noureddine Malki (if that is his real name) communicates with people from his jail cell. He claims that he was once held in solitary for six months and wants the ACLU to investigate.

Jonathan Pollard was held in solitary for *seven years* and has been held captive for 25 years. What crime did he commit? Did he spy against America for the Soviets or for the Chinese communists? Did he aid one of America's enemies?

American Navy Seaman Michael Walker operated a Soviet spy ring; he was arrested in 1980, pleaded guilty, was sentenced to 25 years and released after 15.

CIA Agent David Barnett sold the Soviets the names of 30 American undercover agents. He was arrested in the mid-1980s, sentenced to 18 years, and paroled after only ten years.

In 2010, Chinese-American engineer Dongfan "Greg" Chung operated as a spy for China against America for 30 years. He received a 15-year sentence.

What is "different" about Pollard? Pollard is the only Jew. The others are Christians, Muslims or atheists.

What else is different? Pollard is the only one who shared secrets with an American *ally*. Pollard shared information with Israel. Pollard was the scapegoat for another man, also a Jew, but a Jew who did not like being a Jew, whose mother was Christian: a former Jew who wanted to prove how tough he could be on Jews and on the Jewish state.

Pollard's nemesis was Secretary of Defense Caspar W. Weinberger whose paternal grandparents were Jews and whose father was a Jewish lawyer. When Caspar was a boy, he was supposedly taunted for being Jewish. His mother was a Christian and he was raised as a Christian. When he visited Yad Vashem, the Memorial to the Jews who were murdered in the Holocaust, he said loudly, "I am not a Jew." He said this in response to the guard who told him that "he, too, would have been murdered in the Holocaust."

Weinberger submitted a 40-page affidavit in which he insisted that Pollard should be harshly sentenced. In later years, he said that "the Pollard matter was comparatively minor." Weinberger is now dead and no doubt roasting in hell. One wonders: What did he have over CIA head George Tenet (who threatened to resign when President Clinton suggested pardoning Pollard)? What did Weinberger have over President Bush's Dick Cheney and Donald Rumsfeld, both of whom went along with Weinberger's revenge? Based on a recent article by Leo Rennert about the Pollard case:

> It is now clear that Pollard, in failing health, has been the victim of a CIA cover-up of a massive intelligence failure, with the agency blaming Pollard for the damage caused by a real "mole"

inside the CIA who passed to Moscow the names of more than a dozen U.S. informants in the Soviet Union—namely Aldrich Ames, the head of CIA's Soviet-Eastern Europe division, who fingered Pollard to keep the CIA from discovering his own treachery. The CIA did not discover Ames' role until well after Pollard was behind bars and it still isn't willing to acknowledge its mistake in blaming Pollard for Ames's crimes.

Where are all the anti-torture activists when it comes to Pollard? How can it be that our most prominent American political prisoner has never made it onto their honor roll of causes with which to browbeat America?

Over the years, first Orthodox Jewish rabbis and then slowly, cautiously, nervously, large Jewish organizations began to call for Pollard's release and pardon. Recently, the Conference of Presidents has done so as have other large Jewish-American organizations. Over the years, Israeli Prime Ministers Rabin, Netanyahu, and Olmert have requested that Pollard be pardoned. Reagan (two terms), Bush, Clinton (two terms), and Bush Jr. (two terms) have all refused to do so.

Does Pollard stand a better chance under President Obama? Yesterday, Prime Minister Benjamin Netanyahu formally asked President Obama to pardon Jonathan Pollard. I stand with the Prime Minister in this matter.

(12/22/10)

51 PERETZ-THE-LEFTIST DEFAMES POLLARD AS "REPELLENT VIPER"

*I*n the last days of 2010, Marty Peretz, the recently retired editor and publisher of *The New Republic*, published two rambling and gratuitously cruel pieces that advised President Obama *not* to pardon Jonathan Pollard.

No one asked Peretz to weigh in on the matter; he could simply have remained silent. After all, Peretz has lived the life of a wealthy, influential, and outspoken Jewish public figure—a life of honor and freedom. Pollard has been dishonored, despised, and imprisoned for 25 years, seven of which was spent in solitary confinement. He is a sick man whose supporters have finally, after many years, begun to gather serious support for his release.

Noblesse oblige should have required Peretz remain silent. Instead, at *The New Republic,* Peretz comes at Pollard with 800 pounds of shockingly anti-Semitic language in which he makes the case against the prisoner. Peretz describes Pollard as "the single repellent figure," a "sleaze bag transmogrified into not only a hero but a saint," a "viper," a "convicted espionage agent...who got paid for his work... His professional career reeks with infamy and is suffused with depravity."

Peretz also accuses the prisoner of spying for Pakistan; there is no evidence of this in the public record.

Peretz not only despises Pollard, he despises Pollard's supporters and characterizes them as "brazen...professional victims, mostly brutal themselves, who originate in the ultra-nationalist and religious right. They are insatiable. And they want America to be Israel's patsy."

Peretz damns Pollard because he does not like some of Pollard's supporters who, he claims, engage in "incessant special pleading." If released, Peretz fears, Pollard will be greeted by "triumphant hustlers in the streets of Jerusalem... dancing the hora, of course, ecstatic." Why? Because they will have "pulled one over on [President Obama]. Over America too."

This language and these ideas are reminiscent of Hitler's *Der Stürmer*, not of a Left liberal Jew who taught at Harvard for many years, bought *The New Republic*, and is now temporarily living and teaching in Tel Aviv. Peretz warns President Obama:

> If you release Pollard, you would be encouraging the kind of ideological blackmail that has paralyzed Israeli politics not just in the ongoing diplomatic torpor... Today they want Pollard free. Tomorrow they will be arguing the justice of racial discrimination against Arabs. The day after they will be pressing for limitations on civil liberties. Oh my, they already have.

In other words, Peretz is telling Obama that if he pardons or grants Pollard clemency that Obama will be contributing to Israeli "racial discrimination against Arabs." Peretz assures Obama (whose candidacy he supported) that "Israel's place in the American mind is quite secure... American solidarity with Israel is quite firm." Peretz does not view Pollard's unending imprisonment as a case of "anti-Semitism," and Obama will not lose Jewish support if he fails to pardon the prisoner; Pollard is "not Natan Sharansky held captive after a twisted Soviet judicial hearing."

What if the charges against Pollard are not true? What if only some of the charges are true, but pale in comparison besides far more major betrayals by other *non-Jewish* American spies whose hands, unlike Pollard's, are tainted with American blood? What if others, whose crimes have been far more grievous, have been freed far sooner?

Might Caspar Weinberger's own assistant Secretary of Defense Lawrence Korb, who is now part of the effort to have Pollard pardoned, know something that Peretz refuses to understand? Korb has been working together with law professor Kenneth Lasson, former senior staff member of the Senate Intelligence Committee Angelo Codevilla, and former U.S. prosecutor and Army intelligence officer John Loftus on the Pollard case. Korb is speaking to the world media on this issue. With Barney Frank assuming a leadership role, 39 members of Congress are also asking President Obama to release Pollard. Former head of the CIA James Woolsey, former Chairman of the Senate's Select Intelligence Committee Dennis De Concini, and former U.S. Attorney General Michael Mukasey have urged clemency for Pollard.

Peretz stands alone. What can explain this? In my view, here is one possible explanation.

Recently, Peretz was accused of being a "racist rat"—and at Harvard on the very day Peretz's former students had chosen to honor him. I defended Peretz from his campus harassers. Now, in retrospect, I must reconsider that defense. While campus public shaming tactics are totalitarian in style and intent, it is clear that Peretz's unexpected attack upon Pollard is his bid to gain favor with the politically correct anti-racist Left. How does a liberal Zionist Jew do this? He sacrifices and scapegoats the most vulnerable Jew, the Jew already accused of being a Jewish "traitor." *Pollard* is guilty of dual loyalty—not Peretz. Pollard-the-dastardly-Jew chose Israel above America. No one should mistake him for Peretz-the-good-Jew.

While Peretz has, in the past, defended Israel among his left colleagues, ultimately, Peretz will not choose a right-wing, nationalist religious Israel over and above his loyalty to the secular anti-Zionist "Left." His wild accusation against Pollard is meant to prove that once and for all. Peretz has struggled with his own dual loyalties, but he is now, publicly and emphatically, choosing the liberal Left which has rejected him, and he is doing so on the near-corpse of a Jew who has already been punished more than enough.

Peretz is casting the last stone or, rather, the only stone that counts, the stone aimed at Pollard at precisely the same moment when a host of wiser, kinder voices are being heard at the White House.

(1/3/11)

52 ISRAELI APARTHEID WEEK: POLITICAL THEATER AT ITS WORST

*T*he mob roars its hoarse, ear-splitting chants: "Death to the Jews," "Death to Zionism," "From the River to the Sea, Palestine Will Be Free." Keffiyehs abound: On heads, masking faces, framing shoulders. The Arab "street" is on the move—in Toronto, Montreal, Amherst, Washington, D.C., Berkeley, and in Oxford, Belfast, Paris, Amsterdam, and Brussels.

Western activists are busy "slumming," dressed as "persecuted" Arabs, even as Arabs are mob-dancing in the streets of Nablus, Ramallah, and Gaza—mobs whose leaders are armed with nuclear weapons, surface-to-air missiles, human homicide bombers, and rocket launchers.

What's new is that the supposedly "good people" have joined them.

March is not only Women's History Month, it is also the month in which Israeli Apartheid Week opens in 55 cities around the world. This is political theatre at its diabolical best. According to Dr. Catherine Chatterley, the founding director of the Canadian Institute for the Study of Antisemitism:

> The first [Israeli Apartheid Week] event was held at the University of Toronto in 2005. The following year, it included Montreal and Oxford. In 2007, it grew to eight cities; in 2008, to 24 cities; in 2009, to 38 cities; last year, to over 40 cities. This year, IAW will be held in over 55 cities worldwide. In July of 2005, 170 Palestinian civil-society organizations released an official call for Boycott, Divestment and Sanctions (better known as BDS) against Israel. The document clearly stated that the call was modelled on the example of the South African struggle against Apartheid.

Thus, Israeli Apartheid Week was born.

Israeli Apartheid Week takes place both on and off campus and lasts anywhere from four to eight days. This year at Berkeley, the political festivities began on March 1st on campus and featured Susan Abulhawa: "Telling the Palestinian Story." The programmers proclaim that "Palestinians are not always given the opportunity to share their experiences and their struggle."

This is a Big Lie since the pro-Palestinian point of view has flooded our culture on campus, in the media, on the internet, at the United Nations, in books, and at every human rights organization.

It is important to note that the Muslim Student Association is a key sponsor; it represents the Muslim Brotherhood. Canada's Dr. Chatterley believes that Israeli Apartheid

Week is the linchpin of a "global strategy to weaken Israel's connection to the West by delegitimizing Zionism." She is right.

How has Israeli Apartheid Week remained in existence for six years? The moneyed Saudi Lobby, the Arab League, the influence of Edward Said's work on the post-colonial western academy, the world-wide rise and influence of the Muslim Brotherhood, Hamas, Hezbollah and Khomeinism, and the anti-American and pro-"Palestinian" Western Left have all played a part in this grotesque tragedy.

The New Left, which came of age in the 1960s, refuses to give up the political "high" of fighting South African apartheid. That was their Good War, their best Broadway production, and they cannot bear to bring the curtain down.

Charles Jacobs, President of Americans for Peace and Tolerance, suggests that the ugly and out of control anti-Israel hatred on American campuses is due, in part, to the failure of American Jewish organizations to acknowledge and combat it. Jacobs writes:

> In 1990, James Zogby, president of the Arab American Institute, explained on Jordanian TV how the Arab Lobby can and will match Jewish political and organizational success in America. Zogby and his allies recognized that the campus and the media, unlike Capitol Hill, are two battle grounds that Arabists could win by allying themselves with the American left. Zogby focused on forming alliances with Marxist professors, die-hard socialist activists, African-American student groups, gay-lesbian groups and, most importantly, Jewish progressives.

Zogby's strategy, together with massive Arab funding, has worked. The world now believes that the most important and most persecuted group alive are the Palestinians, that the Israelis oppress them, and that Israel is an Apartheid nation state.

Professor Chatterley wants people to take responsibility for their own personal feelings of rage and frustration. Students must be encouraged to exercise self-control in multicultural public spaces. She wants to teach students to "unpack" the gross propaganda against Israel and she wants disagreements among informed truth-tellers to be civil and respectful.

As a scholar and former professor, I am not obliged to welcome Big Lies on campus merely because they may be protected by the First Amendment. I do not trust the "truths" of those who heckle, jeer, physically menace, and in so doing, silence and censor any speech with which they disagree. This decidedly uncivil behavior most resembles the Arab, Soviet, and Maoist Streets at their worst.

(3/8/11)

53 THE "PALESTINIANIZATION" OF LESBIAN ACTIVISM

*W*hen I was much younger, I took an idealistic view of gays and lesbians—invariably associating them with artists, writers, dancers, composers, playwrights, and civil rights activists. When I began working with lesbian and bisexual women as part of my feminist activism, I discovered that—like everyone else—lesbians were neither angels nor devils. Like men, many lesbian feminists had internalized sexism and homophobia and did not respect or trust other women. In some cases, like all women, they used their intimate groups to bully, isolate, and shun any lesbian feminist who was "out of line"—despite the common pretense that feminist groups are leaderless and free-thinking.

I discovered that lesbians, bisexuals and "queers" are often expected to toe a party line when it comes to the Middle East. I am talking about the Palestinianization of lesbian feminists, especially Jewish lesbian feminists, who are more concerned with the rights of a country that does not exist, "Palestine," than with the rights of real Muslim women who are forcibly face-veiled, married against their will, and murdered by their families in honor killings.

I have seen North American lesbian "queers" at university-based Israel Apartheid Week events in America and Canada, wearing keffiyehs, sporting buttons that say "I am a Palestinian," "I am a Jewish antiZionist" or "Jews For Justice in Palestine." Many wear military buzz cuts and boots, carry heavy backpacks and sport other insignia of the European-Arab Street and ACT UP-style protests. Were these women to dress this way in the West Bank or Gaza, they would be persecuted for their appearance.

According to a group called Jews Against the Occupation-NYC, "It's no coincidence that queers have been at the heart of Palestine solidarity groups for decades…The demonization and dehumanization of Palestinians under occupation resonates loudly for queers, as do other forms of racism and militarism."

These politically-correct lesbians do not see themselves as privileged, educated, and free. They imagine themselves to be outcasts, "occupied" by Western patriarchy. They long to be "Palestinian," a posture that allows them to share in the Palestinian's sacralized victim status. Perhaps they feel victimized by their own Jewish families, and by homophobia within Judaism, which has rejected them; in turn, they reject the Jewish state.

Ideologically, such Jewish lesbian feminists do not view Palestinian terrorists as "terrorists" but as freedom-fighters. They do not understand that, at many points in history (including this one), Islam has been the largest practitioner of both religious and gender "apartheid" known to humanity.

Lesbian feminist anti-Zionist groups ignore the fact that there are gay-pride parades in Israel and that "out" gay soldiers serve in the Israeli army. For years, Israel has been providing asylum for Palestinian homosexuals who have been tortured and near-murdered by their own people.

The loudest chants of "From the River to the Sea, Palestine will be free" are coming, not only from the Muslim Student Associations or from the Palestinians with loudspeakers, they are also coming from the mouths of American Jewish lesbian feminists whose very lives, certainly their political identities, are strangely bound up with Arab territorial claims and anti-Jewish exterminationism.

The Jewish lesbians among them are not "self-hating Jews." They are left-identified political opportunists thrilled by their own victimhood posturing—even if it means they must sacrifice the cause of women, Jews, Israel, and homosexuals in the process.

(3/22/11)

54 THE GOLDSTONE RECANTATION

On April 1, 2011, Friday night, the Jewish Sabbath, the *Washington Post* published a remarkable op-ed piece online by South African jurist Richard Goldstone. Goldstone recanted his own "Goldstone Report," a document that has been used against Israel in countless, damaging ways, a document which accuses Israel of possible "war crimes" and "crimes against humanity" in Gaza in response to the 10,000 rockets Hamas launched towards Israeli civilians in Sderot and southern Israel—a document which charges Israel with having "purposely targeted civilians in Gaza."

Goldstone now admits that these charges are false, based on too little or flawed information. He partly blames Israel for not "cooperating" with the venomously biased Human Rights Council, but in truth, Goldstone had access to much of the information that is now contained in Israel's careful investigation of what happened in Gaza.

Israel looked into the false allegations that it had "targeted civilians" and investigated its behavior thoroughly. Hamas did not oblige when charged with the same task. Finally, Goldstone notes that there are important differences between an open, transparent, lawful, ethical, and democratic Jewish state and an Islamist-terrorist organization such as Hamas.

I do not know why Goldstone has changed his mind, but once a lie has made the rounds, there is no stopping it, no way of taking it back. Like a rocket, once a Blood Libel is launched, it's done its work. If, a year or two later, one carefully documents that the entire incident (the false allegation that the Israelis murdered Mohammed al-Dura, the false allegation that the IDF committed a massacre in Jenin, the false allegation that Israelis were purposely shooting at civilians in Gaza) was nothing but Big Fat Black-hearted Lies, most people will have already moved on, their blood streams permanently altered, poisoned with Jew-hatred.

The United Nations, Muslim governments, and the world media have relied on the Goldstone Report to further delegitimize Israel.

I live in Manhattan. I read every Manhattan-based hard copy newspaper as well as 50 other newspapers articles online. Daily. Hard copy reveals certain things that online versions disappear. For example, let's consider how Sunday's *New York Times* (April 3, 2011) presents the Goldstone recantation.

The front page features a four column color photo that is captioned "Palestinians prayed near Israeli soldiers on Friday. They were protesting land confiscation in the village of Qusra, near Nablus." The photo shows us rows of peaceful civilians. Their heads are nearly touching the ground as they face a row of ten armed Israeli soldiers.

The column, which is immediately to the right of this page 1 photo, is titled: "In Israel, Time for Peace Offer May

Run Out. Growing UN Support for Palestinian State."

At the very bottom of this article, noted in bold black, we have the following title: "Gaza War Report Gets a Retraction." The Times gives four and a half lines on its first page to this major story. Four and a half lines—surrounded by peacefully praying Palestinians and a story about the continued pressure on Israel to give in and give up.

On the top of page A10, Ethan Bronner and Isabel Kershner's story is titled: "Head of U.N. Panel Regrets Saying Israel Intentionally Killed Gazans." There is a small black and white photo of Goldstone. This article takes up less than 1/3 of the page. It is immediately followed by an article titled "Strike Kills Gaza Fighters, Spurring Hamas Warning." Three Hamas operatives have been killed by Israel in an overnight airstrike. Their corpses are shown in their burial shrouds. We are meant to feel compassion for them—after all, they are dead. We do not see them launching rockets at innocent Israeli civilians. The size of this photo is about twelve times larger than Goldstone's photo.

This is how the Paper of Record, which has published countless articles about the Goldstone Report now positions, softens, hides, and slants the news.

The BBC has also just published news of the Goldstone recantation, but they link back to their previous articles that ran his allegations. Do they wish to remind their readers that, despite this recantation, Israel is still the state that one must remember to hate?

Interestingly, in recent years, Richard Goldstone published three op-ed pieces in the *New York Times*, all in 2009. This recantation appears in the pages of the *Washington Post*, not at the *New York Times*.

(4/4/11)

55 THE COMMUNIST UNIVERSITY OF NEW YORK HONORS ANTI-ZIONIST CELEBRITY PLAYWRIGHT TONY KUSHNER

On May 9, 2011, the City University of New York (CUNY) decided to honor playwright Tony Kushner. One trustee—a single trustee—opposed and tried to veto this decision. Pure pandemonium broke out. The *New York Times* published ten articles about this. Jeff Wiesenfeld, the sole trustee who objected to Kushner's being honored, was personally demonized in the media and received hate mail and death threats at home.

Kushner was nominated by faculty at John Jay College. Only one nominator, Professor Amy Greene, teaches theater. Dr. Michael Meeropol, the son of Ethel and Julius Rosenberg and a Visiting Professor of Economics, was the other professor who nominated Kushner. The committee of seven who rubberstamped this nomination teach criminal justice, politics, government, political science, sociology, and psychology.

For what, exactly, was Kushner being honored? Was it for his plays, his celebrity—or was it to honor his outspoken anti-Zionist views?

Kushner, long used to being heroized, was so shocked by the dissent of a single Trustee that he wrote a three-page letter to the Trustee Board, which accused them of "defaming" him by deciding not to award him an honorary degree. In the letter, Kushner explains that his view that Israel engaged in the "ethnic cleansing" of Palestinians in order to create a Jewish state is not an anti-Israeli or anti-Semitic view. He insists that the "brunt" of the "ongoing horror in the Middle East" has been "borne by the Palestinian people." He has been quoted as saying, "I have a problem with the idea of a Jewish state. It would have been better if it never happened."

Kushner also co-edited an anti-Zionist anthology, or as he might insist, an anthology that features Left Jews who are *Wrestling with Zion.*

To the best of my knowledge, he has not issued similar statements about "wrestling" with the crimes of Soviet Russia, Communist China, or Communist Cuba.

I am not opposed to CUNY faculty holding "communist" and/or "left-wing" views. I merely oppose the fact that this view trumps and silences all other views, and that few left-wing American intellectuals have acknowledged the horrendous crimes of Stalin and Mao. Few take responsibility for the crimes committed in the name of this ideology and its ideals. Instead, to absolve themselves of all culpability, they claim permanent victimhood and persecution, and focus obsessively on the crimes committed by Western capitalism and racism and fail to note these same crimes when non-Western civilizations of color, especially Islamic civilizations, commit them.

At first, Kushner vowed never to accept this award, but his supporters and admirers, those for whom "he died on the cross of celebrity," did not quit trying to resurrect his reputation and to destroy those who opposed his candidacy.

CUNY professors and students sent a letter to the Board of Trustees with the request that the names of the signatories not be made public in order to avoid their receiving death threats and hate mail. This letter said, in part:

> As alumni, professors and students of the City University of New York, we wish to comment regarding the character assassination that is now transpiring via email attack and media attacks on Trustee Jeffrey Wiesenfeld. We have also been made aware that professors who are politically pro-Israel are intimidated and prevented from speaking freely, out of fear of retribution when seeking reappointment, tenure and/or promotion. There is little doubt that there are valid bases for this fear… All this is reflected in the venom that is pouring out of the CUNY professoriate in the attempt to stifle Trustee Wiesenfeld for the simple exercise of his right and responsibility as a member of the Board of Trustees.

On May 15, 2011, Scholars for Peace in the Middle East also wrote to the Board of Trustees:

> We would like to express our distress at the politicization of the university revealed by your selection of Tony Kushner for an honorary degree.
> 1. We are distressed that you have chosen to give

your highest honor to someone who frequently makes incendiary and biased accusations against Israel, thereby feeding the fires of anti-semitism, hatred, and genocide incitement now prevalent in the Middle East. By accepting this politicized nomination, you are also giving the CUNY stage to a celebrity advocate of boycott, divestment and sanctions against Israel, through direct statements and through his role on the Board of "Jewish Voice for Peace." This is a position that all American universities have rejected.

2. We are further distressed that, based on political pressure from the press and a letter-writing campaign, your Executive Committee peremptorily overturned an earlier decision by your full Board to postpone Mr. Kushner's nomination for later discussion. Maintaining the board's initial decision would have demonstrated your dedication to inquiry into the many allegations and counter-allegations made about this matter. Sadly, your peremptory vote serves to suppress debate and symbolizes to students and the public that a distinguished university easily succumbs to political pressure.

The media did not cover this unprecedented letter sent by a group, which represents 55,000 professors, researchers, and students on 3,500 campuses around the world.

I challenged Kushner to consider writing a play about the Palestinians who are suffering because of their corrupt and totalitarian Islamic leaders.

I challenge CUNY to award honorary degrees to leading

anti-Islamist dissidents. I am not talking about the much-glamorized Tariq Ramadan, the grandson of the founder of the Muslim Brotherhood. I am talking about the man who "took him down" in an open debate in London. I am talking about genuine dissidents, such as Ibn Warraq (the London champion), who has penned a masterful critique of the work of Edward Said and who is a staunch defender of the West.

Kushner's support for a Palestinian "state," which is a code-word for the destruction of the Jewish state, is viewed as both his academic and "free speech" right and as the only politically correct opinion to hold.

The very conformist Western academy wishes to be seen as champions of liberty and tolerance for its support of totalitarian misogyny. Ironic and tragic. The left-wing CUNY faculty are exulting in their spurious "win." They expect a huge media turnout on June 3rd, graduation day, to further magnify and glorify their demonization of Israel.

This battle for the soul of the Western campus is part of the larger battle for Western civilization.

(May 2011)

56 EQUATING ANTI-SEMITISM WITH "ISLAMOPHOBIA"

Did you know that Jews and Muslims have a shared history in Europe? That Muslims have "deep roots" on the European continent and that Muslims are as imperiled by "Islamophobia" as Jews are by anti-Semitism?

Nothing could be further from the truth, and yet the first Gathering of European Muslim and Jewish Leaders issued a statement on May 9th and held a meeting in Brussels on May 30, 2011. The meeting was organized by two *American* Jewish groups, Rabbi Marc Schneier's Foundation for Ethnic Understanding and philanthropist Ronald Lauder's World Jewish Congress, and by the European Jewish Congress.

No Muslim organization seems to have shared in organizing the meeting, although two organizations and more than a dozen Muslim leaders attended and signed the joint declaration.

Why are the Jews doing the heavy lifting for a wealthy Muslim world? Why support such dangerously misguided concepts?

Why are Jews confusing "Islamophobia" with anti-Semitism? One understands that Muslims might want to assume the mantle of Jewish victimhood and make it their own, but why are Jews enabling them to do so? If the Muslims are coming in good faith, they would state some obvious truths, beginning with the Koranic roots of Jew- and infidel-hatred and the contemporary Islamist/genocidal intentions towards the Jewish state. A new kind of statement from Muslims would include their understanding of—and desire to break from—the historical Muslim persecution of Jews and infidels in Muslim-majority countries—and in Andalus, which Muslims conquered and occupied.

Anti-Semitism cannot, must not, be equated with "Islamophobia." European Muslims have nothing to fear from European Jews. European Jews have everything to fear from European Muslims.

According to the new declaration, "Jews and Muslims live side-by-side in every European country and our two communities are important components of Europe's religious, cultural and social tapestry." What contributions to European culture have Muslims made?

The declaration commits an outrage against history by equating the Jewish experience in Europe with the Muslim experience in Europe. Jews have been living as a persecuted minority on this continent for more than a thousand years. Muslims invaded and colonized parts of southern Europe, especially Spain. These are very different histories in Europe.

According to German scholar Clemens Heni, "Muslims did not at all live as long in Europe as Jews did. Muslims and Germans declared Jihad in November 1914, during the First World War. *This* is what the German-Muslim alliance in the 20th century is all about."

In Heni's view, the Muslim "history" in Europe is also about Muslim anti-Semitic alliances with German and Nazi anti-Semites.

With mock solemnity, the document proclaims, "We must never allow anti-Semitism...to become respectable in today's Europe"—as if anti-Semitism, in its modern guise of anti-Zionism, weren't already perfectly respectable in every corner of Europe.

Rabbis all over Europe have been telling their people to flee before it is too late. Many Jews have done so.

The alleged "Islamophobia" (or fear of Jihad) is not based on bigoted considerations of color, faith, or ethnicity; it is, rather, based on the increasing danger that Muslims pose to the stability and character of Europe.

Would these Muslim signatories agree to a declaration that critiques Iran, Saudi Arabia, and the Muslim Brotherhood in Egypt and in Gaza for their hatred of Israel, the Jewish state? If not, what is to be gained by standing in solidarity with such Muslims?

It is the midnight hour. What kinds of private deals and illusions are these leaders conjuring up for themselves?

(5/31/11)

57 ISLAM AND ANTI-SEMITISM AT YALE

*I*n June, 2011, Yale University shut down the Yale Initiative for the Interdisciplinary Study of Anti-Semitism (YIISA). The initiative, which has been housed at Yale since 2006, was given until July to clear out.

Yale has just rendered racism respectable, contributed to the academic isolation of scholars of contemporary anti-Semitism, and snuffed out truth-telling, genuine dissent, free speech, and academic freedom. This will be a permanent stain on Yale and on American academia.

The Palestinianization and Stalinization of the American professoriate coupled with the always hoped-for funding from the Arab world made this outcome inevitable.

Last year, Palestinians and their supporters bitterly and publicly complained to Yale about YIISA's conference on contemporary global anti-Semitism; the scholars, from five or more continents, dared to focus on the Islamic face of genocidal anti-Semitism.

The YIISA conference, in which I was privileged to

participate, was unique in focusing not only upon the politically correct view of anti-Semitism as a Christian, Western, and European phenomenon, but also on its historical, current, and lethal incarnation in the Islamic world. I was especially moved by Professor Alberto Nisman, the Argentinean prosecutor of Iran's terrorist plot against Argentina's Jews. The terrorist mastermind of this heinous plot escaped justice when President Ahmadinejad appointed him Iran's Minister of Defense.

The existence of YIISA gave my evolving work on Islamic gender and religious apartheid and on the contemporary betrayal of the Jews and the truth by Western intellectuals, a home, a point of gravity, a place where my work could be appreciated and critiqued—a place where I could meet other scholars. This Initiative is invaluable and does not exist anywhere else in the United States. It is a tragedy that Yale decided to shut it down.

Yale insists that the pre-existing study of dead Jews and of Jewish texts at Yale is sufficient proof that they are not anti-Semitic. Yale also says that the Initiative has not borne the kind of academic fruit to justify its continuation. However, according to Caroline Glick in the *Jerusalem Post*:

> Deputy Provost and Political Science Professor Frances Rosenbluth served on the faculty committee that reviewed YIISA's performance and concluded that the university should close the center. In recent years Rosenbluth appointed Judge Richard Goldstone and Iran-regime apologists Flynt and Hillary Mann Leverett to serve as senior fellows at Yale's Jackson Institute for Global Affairs. Last September the Leveretts brought their students to New York to

hold a seminar for them with Iranian President Mahmoud Ahmadinejad. Unlike the YIISA conference, the move did not stimulate any significant controversy at the university.

If objective and sophisticated documentation and analyses do not lead to the only politically correct conclusion, one which blames America, Europe, and Israel—but not Islam— for a history of colonialism, imperialism, and slavery; if one fails to heroize Palestinian terrorism and the so-called "Arab Spring," then, by definition, such work is not viewed as "academic." If one departs from the format of Big Lies and tries to tell the truth, one is castigated as a propagandist, reactionary, activist, and anti-academic.

Back in 2003, the *New York Times* did not review my book, *The New Anti-Semitism*. One of their own reporters, someone I did not know and whom I had never met, called me to say that she had wanted to do a review, but she had been turned down. I suggested that she forget about my book, but, since her specialty was higher education, that she focus on the chilling of free speech and academic freedom on American campuses when the subject involved Israel or Islam. I told this reporter that I had already received many emails from professors all across the country who were afraid to say what they knew to be true if their conclusions departed, however slightly, from the politically correct view on Israel. I got permission from at least 15 professors who were willing to speak to this reporter who began to work on the story.

You never read this article because, as I was told, the piece had been "killed at the highest level."

There is one other reason that Yale felt it could get away with shutting YIISA down. For nearly 50 years, Arab,

Saudi, and Palestinian money men have patiently, carefully, silently, funded the American professoriate and media. No other counterforce existed; no one chose to fund "the truth," or even "the other side." Over the years, I implored certain organizations to consider doing so. I failed.

No one thought that the War of Ideas on the American campus and in the American media was important enough to fight. When I say "no one," I mean no one. We are now paying for that mistake.

(6/13/11)

58 Unmasked: Judeophobia. A Film Review

*E*ven—especially—if you do not support Israel you should see Gloria Greenfield's *Unmasked: Judeophobia*. It is the visual antidote to a hatred that scapegoats Jews for the world's every sorrow.

I stand with Holocaust survivor Elie Wiesel, whose words open this compelling film: "I am afraid." Wiesel never expected to see the return of anti-Semitism in his lifetime—and with such a vengeance. Israel and America represent civilization at its imperfect but democratic best; both are universally "hated." As such "hatred" escalates and "globalizes," it invariably leads to pogroms, massacres, embassy and airplane hijackings, which in turn, are viewed as justified acts of "self-defense" against capitalist and colonial racist bloodsuckers.

Greenfield's film patiently, artfully exposes the increase in Jew-hatred ("Judeophobia"), and explains why it is a threat to Western civilization. *Unmasked* presents 50 of the most sober, principled thinkers of our time—I am honored and humbled to be among them—all of whom understand that it is crucial to tell the truth about the massive disinformation campaign against the Jews and the West, and that we must do so with courage and boldness. We believe that it is late, but never too late to do so.

Greenfield's experts understand that Jews are being blamed for the exact crimes committed by the Arabs and "Palestinians" against their own people and against the Jewish state. At this moment in history, Greenfield's talking heads are the witnesses for the defense. They explain that everything you have been told about the matter is false and dangerous to civilization.

One cannot stop watching the film. The amount of information packed into this fast-paced documentary is astounding.

For example, the film shows us medieval images of the Crucifixion, which visually remind us that until the Vatican "pardoned" the Jews in 1965, we were hated as Christ-killers. There are also the countless covers of that long-exposed forgery, *The Protocols of the Learned Elders of Zion* in German, Arabic, Persian, Urdu, and Hindi—alleged proof that Judaism or Zionism is a powerful world conspiracy.

We see Yasser Arafat's venerable ancestor, the Mufti of Jerusalem, shaking hands with Herr Hitler. We see brave pioneers in Israel who, only three years after "standing eyeball to eyeball with death in Auschwitz" (Rabbi Lord Jonathan Sacks's words in this film), won the 1948 war of independence against soldiers from seven Arab countries. We see Chaim Herzog, Israel's ambassador to the United Nations from 1975 to 1978, as he addresses the UN, describing it, presciently, as the "world center of anti-Semitism."

We see countless Nazi-era and contemporary Muslim cartoons in which Jews are portrayed as vulture-like child killers, big-nosed greedy bankers, disgusting octopuses, and disease-spreading vermin. This anti-Semitism is not learned from the West. It is indigenous to Islam. In fact, Muslims forced Jews to wear distinctive dress and insignia many centuries before the Nazi era.

What I first began writing and talking about a decade ago has here been brought to life, expanded, and dramatically enacted in this film.

The world has been saturated with images and films which portray Israeli "massacres" and child murders that never took place. Greenfield fights such visual lies on their own turf and in a medium that is treasured more than books currently are. In addition to the often unique footage and images, *Unmasked* also has an all-star cast of speakers who have devoted their lives and careers to Israel advocacy and/or to the study of anti-Semitism: Irwin Cotler, Alan Dershowitz, Manfred Gerstenfeld, Caroline Glick, Jeffrey Herf, Matthias Küntzel, Alvin Rosenfeld, Barry Rubin, Jonathan Sacks, Shimon Samuels, Natan Sharansky, Charles Small, Gerald Steinberg, Ruth Wisse, and Robert Wistrich, among others.

These people (and many more) are part of an Internet Defense Force in formation. If Israeli politicians really understood that the hottest war is the battle of ideas they would long ago have opened a Cabinet Ministry of Truth Telling amidst the Big Lies.

Why are the philanthropists not funding a Jewish Al Jazeera-like global network? Any further delay in this matter will prove tragic. We would not be covering Jewish subjects only nor would only Jews be allowed to work with us. The monied "princes" of Qatar are funding a very glossy Al

Jazeera in English that runs 24/7 with few commercials.

I have been monitoring Al Jazeera in English. It is very good. Now it has just "covered" the Gilad Shalit prisoner exchange. It did so from the "Palestinian" and Hamas point of view. All those Americans who are watching this station for its coverage of breaking news on every continent will gradually be persuaded that Israel is evil and that the "Palestinians" are justified.

The film closes with the words of Rabbi Lord Jonathan Sacks, who views the Jewish people as a "symbol of hope for every small country, for every persecuted people...Jews, having been through as close as you get to 'hell on earth,' have come through, have not looked back, have looked forward, have not nurtured feelings of resentment and revenge, have gone out and built the future. And if that is not a testament to the power of faith, I don't know what is."

(10/19/11)

59 THERE NEVER WAS A "PALESTINIAN" PEOPLE. READ HADRIANI RELANDI

For years, I have risked scorn, defamation, and even physical menace for telling the truth about the "Palestinian" Lie.

For millennia, the Middle East was Jewish, pagan, Roman, Greek, and Christian. Islam only arose in the 7th century CE and Muslims thereafter conquered and colonized the Middle East and Asia. Islamic genocide, imperialism, colonialism, forced conversions, slavery, anti-black racism, and both gender and religious apartheid characterized the Arab Muslim "takeover" of these regions.

Perhaps as early as 1920, perhaps as late as the 1930s—or even the late 1960s—a decision was made about how to fight a sovereign infidel Jewish presence in the Middle East. Arabs who were formerly south Syrians, Egyptians, and Jordanians, or who were wandering Bedu, increasingly claimed a historical and religious presence in the Judeo-

Christian Holy Land. It was a political and propaganda tactic, one which the Arab League United Nations, the world media, the professoriate, and the European Union has most ignobly aided and abetted.

Yesterday, former Speaker and Republican Presidential contender, Newt Gingrich stated that the Emperor Has No Clothes: "Remember there was no Palestine as a state. We've had an invented Palestinian people, who are in fact Arabs, and historically part of the Arab community. And they had a chance to go many places."

Jeremy Ben-Ami of J Street has now just issued a statement challenging Gingrich's point that there has never been a "Palestinian" people. According to Ben-Ami:

> Newt Gingrich's comments about the Palestinian people and the Israeli-Palestinian conflict are ill-informed, irresponsible and frightening. The former Speaker's assertion that the Palestinians are an "invented" people shows an appalling lack of understanding of the history of the Middle East in the last century following the break-up of the Ottoman Empire.

Former Speaker Gingrich is right, but in our times the truth cannot hold its own against Big Lie propaganda.

My attention was recently called to a book by the Dutch scholar Hadriani Relandi, which was published at the end of the 17th century. The book, *Palestina, ex monumentis veteribus illustrata,* documents Relandi's trip to the Holy Land. It is written in Latin. Relandi spoke Hebrew, Arabic, and ancient Greek, as well as many European languages. According to Avi Goldreich, Relandi surveyed 2,500 places where people who appear in the Bible, the Mishnah, and the Talmud once lived. Relandi mapped the Land of Israel and conducted a population survey and census of each community. He concluded that:

> Not one settlement in the Land of Israel has a name that is of Arabic origin. Most of the settlement names originate in the Hebrew, Greek, Latin or Roman languages. In fact, till today, except for Ramlah, not one Arabic settlement has an original Arabic name. Till today, most of the settlements names are of Hebrew or Greek origin, the names distorted to senseless Arabic names. There is no meaning in Arabic to names such as Acco (Acre), Haifa, Jaffa, Nablus, Gaza, or Jenin and towns named Ramallah, El Halil and El-Kuds (Jerusalem) lack historical roots or Arabic philology.

In 1696, the year Relandi toured the land, Ramallah, for instance, was called Bet'allah (From the Hebrew name Beit El) and Hebron was called Hebron (Hevron) as it was in the Bible.

UNESCO has just supported the "Palestinian" right to bar Jews from placing the Hebron Machpelah (cave) on Israel's Heritage Site list, the place where our Jewish ancestors are buried.

Relandi found that the majority of the land was utterly desolate. Where inhabitants existed, they were mainly Jews and Christians and they lived, primarily, in Jerusalem, Acco, Tzfat, Jaffa, Tiberius and Gaza:

> There were few Muslims, mostly nomad Bedouins. Nablus, known as Shechem, was

exceptional, where approximately 120 people, members of the Muslim Natche family and approximately 70 Shomronites, lived. In the Galilee capital, Nazareth, lived approximately 700 Christians and in Jerusalem approximately 5,000 people, mostly Jews and some Christians.

In Goldreich's view, Relandi's book "strengthens the connection, relevance, pertinence, kinship of the Land of Israel to the Jews and the absolute lack of belonging to the Arabs, who robbed the Latin name Palestina and took it as their own." Goldreich concludes:

Spain has a history of Arab rule, not Israel...No names of towns, no culture, no art, no history, and no evidence of Arabic rule; only huge robbery, pillaging and looting; stealing the Jews' holiest place, robbing the Jews of their Promised Land. Lately, under the auspices of post-modern Israelis—also hijacking and robbing us of our Jewish history.

Over the years, I have argued in favor of a "two-state solution." I have written about the pain and sorrow of the Other. And yet: the "two-state solution" might already exist. Jordan is the "Palestinian" state. As my friend and colleague, Dr. Mordechai Kedar has argued, a "two-state solution" is hardly realistic given tribal and clan rivalries. In his opinion, more stability might be gained with a nine or ten (city) state solution.

(12/12/11)

60 UP AGAINST A FAUX-ISTINIAN CULTURE OF HUMAN SACRIFICE

Day Six of Israel's decision to fight back, to stop the constant barrage of Hamas rockets, meant this: according to the IDF, in the first five days, over 500 rockets from Gaza rained down on Israeli civilians and the Iron Dome intercepted 287 such rockets. Additionally, they note that 45% of Israelis live within rocket range of Hamas's missiles and rockets. That number is equivalent to 140 million Americans.

I have been getting email and phone calls from friends in Tel Aviv and Jerusalem. The Tel Avivians and Jerusalemites are sober but slightly shocked to have woken up to a lesser, Sderot-like reality. Senior citizen friends cowered in stairways and hunkered down in "safe" rooms. Younger citizens rushed to shelters or hit the ground. No one was injured or worse. Everyone supports what the IDF is doing.

Would America or any other non-Muslim majority country live with such constant terror, such overwhelming vulnerability to attack?

Yet, demonstrations in favor of terrorism to exterminate the Jewish state have been taking place around the world.

People scream, they do not talk; screamers do not listen to reason, they march to kill.

In one instance, a Jewish Community Center on the Upper West Side of Manhattan ejected a young Israeli, Jacob Kimchy, when he interrupted the Big Lies being told by the likes of *Haaretz's* Gideon Levy, and *Jenin, Jenin* film director Mohammed Bakri. Kimchy said that his father had been murdered by Palestinian/Faux-istinian terrorists and what the panelists were saying was meant to defend terrorism against Israeli civilians.

Kimchy was thrown out.

While some Western democracies have finally supported Israel's right to defend herself, world leaders will soon want Israel, who is the true victim and who is fighting a war of self-defense, to lay down its surgically precise weaponry and resign itself to a life in which Israeli civilians are expected to live with the sound of 1,000 sirens and 1,000 rockets—or more—exploding every year.

The knee-jerk reflex of believing that Israel's destruction can stop the Muslim-on-Muslim and Muslim-on-infidel violence is undergoing a small "aha" moment. By now, a few more people understand Muslim-on-Muslim violence is not Israel's fault and that the sacrifice and terrorization of Israel will not bring peace to the roiling region. It is also increasingly obvious that Israel is the West's only stable and militarily sophisticated ally in the Middle East.

Dr. Anat Berko, a criminologist and Lt. Colonel in the IDF, has written two important books about the Faux-istinian culture that entraps vulnerable women and children into becoming human homicide bombs. Her recently released book, *The Smarter Bomb: Women and Children as Suicide Bombers,* depicts a death-eating culture in which women are honor murdered, not only by their families, but also by a culture that has brainwashed them to hate Jews, Israelis, and infidels (like their male counterparts)—and by a culture in which increasingly face-veiled women have absolutely no other pathway to glory, no other escape from truly wretched lives. Dr. Berko interviewed Palestinian female terrorists in Israeli jails who failed in their missions; many prefer life in an Israeli jail to their lives at home.

Dr. Wafa Sultan, the Syrian-born American psychiatrist, may have been the first Arab woman *in history* to tell an Arab religious man in public to be quiet, that it was now her turn to speak. She describes this in her searingly honest book, *A God Who Hates*, as a turning point in her life. This took place on Al Jazeera. Courtesy of MEMRI, her words went viral on the internet. Dr. Sultan shares one heartbreaking anecdote after another about the lives of women in Syria and in the Arab and Muslim world. Her book supports what Dr. Berko is saying.

This is what we are up against. Violent cultures that practice human sacrifice and apartheid are seen as both liberators and as oppressed, and non-violent cultures that believe in life, liberty, and human rights are viewed as villains and war-mongers.

Now, some truth-tellers are getting the word out. Videos, YouTube, Twitter, and the use of live action cameras—quickly uploaded to the internet—are beginning to compete with the usual Blood Libels.

It is too soon to tell whether this will create a lasting difference but in the thick of battle, one never knows how the war will turn out.

(11/19/12)

61 THE GRAND DECEPTION: A FILM REVIEW

*L*ast night, I saw the New York screening of counter-terrorism expert Steve Emerson's film *Jihad in America: The Grand Deception.*

It is a sobering film about the Muslim Brotherhood (MB) in our country, also known as the Council on American-Islamic Relations, the Islamic Society of North America, the Muslim Student Association, Students for Justice in Palestine, etc.; as Hamas in Gaza; Hezbollah in Lebanon, Syria, and Iran. The MB may be the template for al-Qaeda and for all such jihadist Sharia-based groups who dream of a global Caliphate.

The film depicts prominent Muslim leaders (such as Kamal Helbawy and Nihad Awad) talking about peace, tolerance, and justice—and then in Arabic, preaching "Death to the Jews" and "Death to the Infidels." Abdurahman Alamoudi had American friends in positions of political power in Washington DC, but is now spending 23 years in jail for raising funds for Hamas.

The anger of the on-camera Muslim speakers/preachers is frightening. The men sound like the Pakistani or Afghan Taliban, like highly traumatized people who may have been abused in childhood, whose arrogance, rage, and spite will never quit. There are quieter voices, often female jihadists, who calmly advise that jihadists need only use America's principles against us in the service of Jihad.

Afterwards, there was a panel, which Emerson moderated. A former MB member, Abdur-Rahman Mohammed, spoke. He said that he was in the room when the Muslim Brotherhood decided to employ the tactics of the gay movement. Allegations of homophobia seemed to work, why not allegations of Islamophobia? Mohammed said that it worked, people were intimidated, no one wanted to be called a racist. Thus, the grand deception was underway.

My colleague, Professor Richard Landes, talked about the "auto-stupefaction" of many Americans in power, "dupes," afraid to name the enemy we are fighting. Landes talked about "cognitive war" and how important it is in the context of an asymmetric war. He coined the phrase, a "demopath," to signify someone who uses the language of equality in order to paralyze us and to defeat real equality.

The film has a nearly comic/tragic ending with Congressional hearings in which both Attorney General Holder and the Assistant Secretary of Defense Paul Stockton refused to name "radical political Islamism" as even one of many factors that may have motivated the Fort Hood Jihad shooter.

Panelist Dr. Qanta Ahmed said that in Pakistan they call a "jihadist" a "jihadist." She cannot understand how America will defend itself against Jihad if we are too afraid to even name it for what it is. This film is the "first serious attempt to wrestle the narrative back to where it should be." Ahmed is a physician. She said, "If you can't identify and name a pathology, you cannot cure it."

(06/20/13)

62 UNICEF's Blood Libel Against Israel

UNICEF has just released a report which constitutes a blood libel against the state of Israel. The UN body claims that Israeli forces have mistreated Palestinian children and have "degraded" and "tortured" those in custody. The world media is repeating this, as is the Israeli Left media.

UNICEF has not released a similar report that focuses on the systematic use of Palestinian children as human shields by Palestinian jihadists; on the increase in honor killings of Palestinian daughters on the West Bank and in Gaza; or on the sophisticated indoctrination of Palestinian children by Palestinian adults into becoming human homicide bombs.

In the (more than 50) UNICEF reports on the "state of Palestine," blame is only placed on Israel for whatever harm comes to Palestinian children.

Palestinian terrorists in Israeli jails—even those with blood on their hands—receive better treatment than they would in Palestinian or Arab jails. Palestinian prisoners have many comforts, good medical care, prayer time, exercise time, access to books, newspapers, television, and to each other. Some of Israeli Criminologist Dr. Anat Berko's Palestinian jailed female terrorist interviewees report that their stay in an Israeli jail affords them a safer, less violent life than the one they had at home.

Last night, Israeli journalist, Ben-Dror Yemini, spoke at a parlor meeting arranged by Jacob Kimchy, the publisher of TLV (Tel Aviv) Faces, in the home of Dr. Barbara Chasen and Rafael Rubinstein. Yemini is a sweet and self-effacing man. He made small jokes ("journalists are people who know nothing about everything"), but he was very serious.

The industry of Lies against Israel is unbelievable, both the micro-lies and the mega-lies. When Ilan Pappé, an Israeli Jewish academic, accused Israel of wanting to "transfer populations" ("transfer" = ethnic cleansing), Pappé directly misquoted Israeli public policy, which, at the time, clearly stated that all Palestinian Arabs who were currently citizens of Israel may stay where they are—or may choose to leave, voluntarily, to join a Palestinian state.

Yemini published a piece titled "Ilan is a Liar."

Yemini said another Israeli journalist claimed that the "IDF ties Palestinians onto donkeys and then sends them into the wilderness to die." This Big Lie was picked up by the global media: "There is one problem. This never happened."

According to Yemini, "When Prime Minister Bibi Netanyahu spoke at the General Assembly of the United Nations he said that the Jewish state will protect the rights of all citizens. Columbia's Professor Joseph Massad wrote that 'Tel Aviv is the only Western city which has no Muslim inhabitant' and that 'Bibi has just called to expel 1.6 million Palestinian Israeli citizens.'"

The reversals of truth, the projection of Arab and

Palestinian behavior onto Jews and Israel is stunning. Yemini said that the Arab League's detailed plan was to "exterminate the Jews." And they are now falsely accusing the Jews of committing what they themselves have desired to do. According to Yemini:

> If you check the World Health Organization and World Bank statistics, you will find that infant mortality among the Palestinians has decreased dramatically; the people in Gaza are living more comfortably than the people in Turkey—in fact, the *Mavi Marmara* should have sailed *from* Gaza to Turkey! Palestine receives more foreign aid than any other group or country or group of refugees; and Israel's contribution to humanity (in terms of medical, technological, and scientific discoveries, etc.) outweighs the contribution of all Arab and Muslim states.

It is very late in the propaganda wars both against Israel and America. We must find ways of taking the offensive in terms of Truth Telling. The season of Big Lies has got to stop.

(6/20/13)

63 CHRISTMAS IN LONDONISTAN

The Brits have just built a large "security wall" at St. James's Church in Piccadilly and plan to use it to continue demonizing the Jewish state for the next twelve days beginning on Christmas day. It is an "art installation," political theater, very trendy.

Not shown, never mentioned, are the names or graves of Israeli civilians, including children and the elderly, who were blown up and butchered during the height of the Al-Aqsa Intifada; not mentioned are those who were disabled for life. It is forbidden to say that the "security wall" worked: the number of Israeli civilian casualties plunged because it existed.

Contrary to propaganda, Jesus was not a "Palestinian." He was a Jew; some say he was a rabbi, and that the Last Supper was a Pesach Seder. The attempt to appropriate Jesus as a victimized "Palestinian" by the very Muslims who are slaughtering Christians all over the Middle East and who have driven Arab Christians out of Bethlehem is disgusting and must continually be exposed.

Israel may not be a perfect nation but its Arab citizens, both Muslim and Christian, are the only Arabs in the Arab world who enjoy religious freedom, can vote and express themselves freely, and who have been peacefully elected to Parliament.

As Hamad Amar, a Druze citizen of Israel and the Speaker of Israel's Knesset has written in *The Hill*, an American Congressional blog:

> In our whole region consisting of over 350 million Arabs, there are only 1,658,000 Arabs who have complete political and religious freedom and have the right to vote in full democratic elections. It is no coincidence that all of these Arabs live as full and equal citizens in the one Jewish State.

Israel values human life; its enemies value death. To redeem Gilad Shalit, Israel released terrorists with blood on their hands to return as heroes and to resume their careers as terrorists. Jews value even one life this much.

I hope and pray that Jonathan Pollard will finally be set free while he and I are both still alive, and I hope that Israel does not have to pay too dear a price for his freedom.

Israel is compassionate and humanitarian. It has provided medical aid to Syrian refugees and to Lebanese in flight from Arafat's terrorism. Israel has sent medical and emergency teams all over the world wherever there has been a flood or an earthquake.

Oh, I could go on, but, for now, please allow me to wish all those Christians who support Israel, who love Israel, even more than some Jews do—the most wonderful holiday.

(12/24/13)

64 BURIED BY THE *TIMES*

*H*ere is how propaganda works: It gives pride of place to certain articles and omits or minimizes—buries—others; it presents opinion pieces as if they are objective news, and then supports such "news" with opinion pieces in the very same issue; it presents compelling but often misleading and wrongly captioned photos to accompany the biased news; and it does so every single day.

Sometimes this is done blatantly; more often it is a steady stream of low-level disinformation. Newspapers and websites will also inflate and sensationalize something minor and deny, omit or bury something that is quite major.

I have been covering media bias against Israel since the Al-Aqsa intifada began. By now, I must have written hundreds of articles on the demonization of Israel.

I do not do so on a regular basis, but every so often I am pulled in yet again.

For example, on December 16, 2013, the *New York Times* ran a 1,142-word story on the front page about a very small academic group (with only 5,000 members) that voted to boycott Israeli academics and cultural institutions, because, as their president said, "you have to start somewhere."

Not all 5,000 members voted. Only 1,252 members did, and among these voters, only 826 (16% of the total membership) voted to boycott Israel. Eight hundred and twenty six politically correct conformists and, yet, the "Paper of Record" found it worthy enough to anoint as front page news.

Perhaps it wished to encourage others to do likewise in the hope that they, too, would make the news in a prominent way.

What the Paper of Record subsequently failed to note was the overwhelming groundswell of distinguished academic and cultural disapproval of this vote which, I believe, may have changed the nature of the BDS movement and its infiltration of the academic world in America. On December 23rd, the *Washington Post* noted that:

> Schools including Johns Hopkins, Harvard, Yale, Cornell, Princeton, and Boston universities and the Universities of Pennsylvania, Connecticut, and Texas at Austin and others have slammed the boycott, issuing statements similar to one by Harvard President Drew Faust that said that academic boycotts "subvert the academic freedoms and values necessary to the free flow of ideas, which is the lifeblood of the worldwide community of scholars."

The *Post* also updated its original article and noted that Eliot Engel, ranking Congressional member of the Foreign Affairs Committee, wrote directly to the president of the American Studies Association to denounce the ASA boycott: the *Post* reprinted Engel's letter in full. It also reprinted the letters written by President of Boston University Robert A. Brown, President of the University of Connecticut Susan Herbst, and President of Harvard University Drew Faust.

On December 27, 2013, four days later, the Paper of Record hid the evolving, much larger story about this response to the boycott vote. They covered it on page A19, and at page bottom. They titled this story: "Prominent Scholars, Citing Importance of Academic Freedom, Denounce Israeli Boycott." It again quotes the representative of the ASA at length, and points out that two other small academic groups (the Association for Asian American Studies and the Native American and Indigenous Studies Association) have also voted to boycott Israeli academics and cultural institutions.

While the article notes that "four colleges and universities have withdrawn from the American Studies Association" and that "prominent university presidents and scholars" have denounced the boycott, it fails to describe that this boycott has evoked a tidal-wave response in which one major university president after the other has gone on record against academic boycotts. Guess what? The evolving story is not only on the bottom of page A19, it is also only 649 words, or about half the length of the original A1 article on this story.

The *Washington Post* article is 1,543 words, more than twice the length of the second *Times* piece, written by Tamar Lewin.

I read the *Times* magazine, book review, obituaries and wedding announcements. I read the paper from back to front, with the understanding that the news I am interested in is often found "buried" at the back.

I fail to understand why, on Israel, it remains so blatantly biased. Is it secretly funded by Saudi Arabia? Is it merely carrying on the owners' tradition of distancing themselves from being Jewish (through conversion), and thereafter, from the possible appearance of being seen as too Jewish or pro-Zionist? I simply cannot fathom it.

(12/29/13)

65 J STREET CHALLENGE: TRUTH TRUMPS LIES

In 2014, in his new film, *The Last of the Unjust*, Claude Lanzmann shares his 1975 interview with Viennese Rabbi Benjamin Murmelstein, the last and only surviving "Elder of the Jews" at Theresienstadt. Both Lanzmann (and I) are impressed with Murmelstein's wit, wisdom, learning, and survival skills. While Murmelstein submitted documents to Prosecutor Gideon Hausner, Murmelstein does not understand why the Israeli prosecution did not allow him to testify against Eichmann—a man Murmelstein characterizes as evil and monstrous, a man whom he personally witnessed shooting and hanging Jews and ordering others to do likewise. In Murmelstein's view, Arendt's adjective "banal" in no way applies to the man who systematically deceived, terrorized, and murdered Jews.

Although the Nazis gave him no choice—it was do their bidding or die—many have viewed Murmelstein as a collaborator and traitor. He actually could have escaped, but chose not to do so. Ultimately, Lanzmann is not persuaded that Murmelstein is a traitor, and that others really cannot judge men who are placed in such unbearable positions.

Based on the new film, *The J Street Challenge*, which premiered last night in Miami, Jeremy Ben-Ami may be a more morally problematic figure than were any of the Judenrat leaders during the Shoah. I say this because no one is threatening Ben-Ami with imminent death (each kapo and judenrat leader was death-threatened and in captivity). Ben-Ami lives in the United States and is a free man.

The J Street Challenge is short, powerful, and an absolute must-see. It has been released by Americans for Peace and Tolerance, the group founded by anti-slavery activist, Charles Jacobs. This film was produced, written, and directed by Avi Goldwasser and Ilya Feoktistov. Jacobs served as a "special consultant."

Ben-Ami has chosen not to focus on the escalating Jihadic attacks against the Jewish state and against infidels, nor has he condemned the global anti-Jewish and anti-Zionist riots and marches. Instead, he blames Israel for having provoked these attacks by "occupying" Palestinian Arab land; he calls for a "two-state solution, allies his organization with the BDS movement and with the Muslim Public Affairs Committee and other Muslim Brotherhood fronts in the United States." He insists that "Israel is no longer David but (has become) Goliath."

Ben-Ami is actively working with President Barack Obama to supplant and destroy AIPAC to become the President's leading "go-to" Jewish lobby. Here's an example of what kind of influence J Street has.

Recently, some of Ben-Ami's supporters signed "An Open Letter from NY Jews to Mayor de Blasio: AIPAC does not speak for us." The letter was meant to punish and shame

Mayor de Blasio for having dared to meet with and declare support for AIPAC, a group which does not represent "their" views. Among the signatories to this letter are Peter Beinart and Kathleen Peratis who support the J Street disinformation campaign and agenda.

According to *The J Street Challenge*, these signatories are part of a cabal that is being funded by George Soros and Genevieve Lynch, who is on the Board of the pro-Iranian National Iranian American Council.

With a heavy heart, I checked the J Street website and discovered that five additional signatories to this Open Letter (Rabbis Rachel Cowan, Sharon Kleinbaum, Ellen Lippmann, J. Rolando Matalon, and Burton Visotzky) are listed as J Street's Executive Rabbinic Council. Other signatories include feminists whom I know and have cared about: Barbara Dobkin, Eve Ensler, Erica Jong, Letty Cottin Pogrebin, Anne Roiphe, and Gloria Steinem.

While I respect free speech and freedom of conscience, and do not wish to silence anyone's views, some signatories know a great deal about Israel and care about it—and some know absolutely nothing and care even less.

As the film documents, J Street has become a very fashionable address, the kind of group you want to be networked into if you wish to get published, funded, and invited to the right parties. More important, if you are a young Jew, and want to be popular, not burdened by the need to defend an Israel that has been grossly distorted, you will follow Ben-Ami's call right down into extinction. He tells young and misinformed Jews that "their voice has been stolen from them…by a few large funders or a few loud voices who urge them to stay silent."

Ben-Ami wishes to dismantle organized Jewry entirely

and replace all structures with J Street, and J Street wants America to dictate to Israel the terms of Israel's surrender. Ben-Ami says "we make a mistake when we tell (our) children that they have to check their Jewish values at the door of Zionism"—as if Zionism is not a Jewish value or as if it opposes Jewish values.

The film exposes Ben-Ami for what he is. Eloquent experts are on camera, including Alan Dershowitz, Caroline Glick, Daniel Gordis, Charles Jacobs, Bret Stephens, and Ruth Wisse. When I asked Jacobs why they did this film, here's what he said:

> J Street goes unchallenged when it speaks on campuses and in the community because 1. AIPAC chooses (for now) not to answer them publicly, fearing it will give them a bigger platform, and 2. Federations and JCRC's do not want divisive public events. 3. Once having been accepted into the big (fundraising) tent, they are protected by the establishment: RULE: any Jew can (and may be encouraged) to criticize Jewish leaders in Israel, but it is taboo to criticize American Jewish leaders… Even if they are taking Jewish money by promising to protect us, but spending it on the liberal agenda.

The theater that premiered the film was sold out (400 people) in two days. Jacobs believes they will have to "come back here and do five more screenings."

(2/18/14)

66 HIJACKING FEMINISM TO ATTACK ISRAEL AT WOMEN'S STUDIES ASSOCIATION CONFERENCE

*T*he next National Women's Studies Association Annual Conference will take place in San Juan, Puerto Rico on November 13-16, 2014 and is aptly named "Feminist Transgressions." The conference itself *is* "transgressive" in that it minimizes the cause of women in order to focus, yet again, on the cause of Palestine, aka the destruction of Israel.

This is only the latest, among many other examples, of the way in which Women's Studies—a course of study I pioneered so long ago—has been Stalinized and Palestinianized.

The Association's line-up of professorial and celebrity talent is 100% politically correct; the speakers are mainly African-American, African-Hispanic, and African/Asian-Caribbean. While I may not agree with some of their views, I recognize that these speakers—my old friend bell hooks, Ana-Maurine Lara, Ana Irma Rivera Lassén, and Kamala Kempadoo—are genuinely feminist.

However, not so the plenary session speakers. The plenary session is titled "The Imperial Politics of Nation-States: U.S., Israel, and Palestine." The speakers include Brandeis graduate Angela Davis, the well-known communist, former associate of the Black Panther Party, and recipient of the Lenin Peace Prize. In 1970, Davis possessed the firearms that Jonathan Jackson, the brother of the imprisoned George Jackson, used (perhaps stole) in the kidnapping of a judge, prosecutor, jurors, and two or three African-American prisoners in open court. A police shoot-out ensued which led to the death of the judge and of three African-American men. Davis made the FBI's Most Wanted List, was jailed, tried, and found innocent by an all-white jury. Support for her was tremendous. She ran for Vice President of the American Communist Party.

Joining Davis is Dr. Islah Jad of Birzeit University. Dr. Jad may be a feminist, but she is mainly dedicated to the development of *Palestinian* women and *Palestinian* nationalism. She does not study or advocate for non-Arab or non-Muslim women. Further, her work does not seem to focus on honor killings, honor-related violence, forced marriage, forced veiling, polygamy, arranged marriage, feminist development under an Islamist totalitarian and apartheid regime—all burning issues on the West Bank and in Gaza. Some of her articles are titled "The Conundrums of Post-Oslo Palestine: Gendering Palestinian Citizenship" and "Islamist Women of Hamas: Between Nationalism and Feminism."

The third plenary speaker, Rebecca Vilkomerson, is the executive director of the infamous anti-Israel "peace" group, the Jewish Voice for Peace (JVP). This is a U.S.-based organization which views itself as the "Jewish wing" of the Palestinian Solidarity Movement. According to NGO Monitor, the JVP has "actively promoted the central dimensions of the political warfare strategy against Israel, which was adopted at the 2001 Durban NGO Forum." Advisory Board members of JVP include Daniel Boyarin, Judith Butler, Noam Chomsky, Eve Ensler, Melanie Kaye/Kantrowitz, Naomi Klein, Tony Kushner, Robert Meeropol, and Sarah Schulman. In 2013, even the Anti-Defamation League declared the JVP "one of the top ten anti-Israel groups."

These speakers and their organizations do not seem interested in women, per se, nor are they interested in gender apartheid as practiced in the Arab and Muslim world. They are not really interested in racism—not if anti-Semitism and anti-Zionism are properly understood as racism.

When feminist and anti-Islamist hero Ayaan Hirsi Ali had to leave Holland, not a single Women's Studies program offered her a perch. Only the conservative American Enterprise Institute did so. Most recently, the drive to disinvite Hirsi Ali at Brandeis was spearheaded by the Women's, Gender, and Sexuality Studies Program.

Many feminists claim they are pacifists and therefore condemn the United States for its violent invasions of other countries, including Afghanistan. Oddly, these same feminists do not oppose the murderous terrorism of the Palestinian liberation movement and Hamas, whom they view as "freedom fighters."

Feminist marchers have waved the Palestinian flag and worn Arab headdresses in various demonstrations. (Were they marching anywhere between Cairo and Kabul, they'd be wearing burqas, niqab, or hijab.) American feminists have condemned one nationalist struggle (the one being waged by Jews) and backed another (the one being waged by the Arab Palestinian people), and they have done so *as feminists*.

Academic feminists have not seemed reluctant to render passionate opinions on matters about which they have no special expertise.

Since 2000, every feminist listserv group that I've been on has been inundated with petitions against Israel and with anti-Zionist propaganda. The Internet atmosphere has become hostile toward anyone who questions this party line. It's as if the feminist world has become a wholly owned subsidiary of the PLO.

These very same feminists (so keenly aware of Palestinian suffering) have failed to condemn the terrorist attacks against Jewish civilians in Israel—not even when nearly half the dead and wounded are women and children. International feminists have not organized contingents of human shields to ride the buses in Tel Aviv and Jerusalem, or to live in endangered "politically correct" kibbutzim whose historic and current priority is peaceful coexistence with their Palestinian neighbors.

Like many academics, feminists are no longer independent-minded. They have also become the spawn of Edward Said's thinking about postcolonialism and Palestinian nationalism. Along with the rest of the herd, they are die-hard Lacanians and postmodernists, and one cannot understand a word that they write—except when they are clearly, cravenly, attacking Israel and Zionism.

'Tis a pity...

(6/6/14)

67 WHITE HOUSE'S "CONDOLENCES" FOR MURDERED ISRAELI TEENS ARE NOT ENOUGH

*M*y heart is broken, absolutely broken. Words never fail me, but at this moment mere words feel inadequate, even inappropriate. I am, of course, talking about the discovery of three dead bodies that once belonged to three beautiful Israeli souls: Gilad Shaar, Naftali Frenkel, and Eyal Yifrach.

This is a time for tears, but also a time for some very serious decisions. Prime Minister Benyamin Netanyahu has confirmed that "Hamas is responsible, and Hamas will pay." He added that the teenagers were "kidnapped and murdered in cold blood by wild beasts."

The Foreign Minister of France, Laurent Fabius, is "deeply shocked and upset" by the murder of these boys. He also expressed "horror" and indignation."

President Obama expressed his "deepest condolences" to

the family of the slain teenagers. He added, "I also urge all parties to refrain from steps that could further destabilize the situation." President Obama did not accuse Hamas of this despicable act nor did he say that our government would assist Israel in its search for security and justice. Obama has once again called for "restraint" and "stability." Does he mean that jihadists should refrain from jihad because it is "destabilizing" the entire Middle East or does he mean, more likely, that Israel should "refrain" from defending itself?

White House Press Secretary Josh Earnest also said, "We obviously condemn in the strongest possible terms violence that takes the lives of innocent civilians."

To what is Earnest referring? This could apply to anyone anywhere at any time. His lack of specificity is cruel and insulting. Why did Hamas operatives choose to kidnap these three boys? Why did they decide to kill them, apparently, almost immediately, and not use them to barter for Palestinian Arab terrorists in Israeli jails? Are these the actions of two low-level Hamas operatives hoping to be rewarded? Did the Hamas leadership decide they were not interested in hostage-taking especially since the boys could not be moved due to the massive IDF search for them? Or, is this a game-changer? No more bartering. Just Jew-killing.

The Muslim-on-Muslim violence that is taking down the Middle East is so fiery, so horrendous, that perhaps the death of these three precious boys will be minimized. Perhaps our passionate focus on them will be resented and mocked.

Jews will never forget these boys and their cruel fates. We will honor their martyrdom by our deeds of valor and courage.

Whenever an Israeli is killed, the Jew-haters quickly point out how many Arabs have been killed. However, they have mainly been killed by other Arabs and Muslims. This is accepted as a given. When an Israeli or a Jew fights back or seeks to rescue one of their own, that's when the world points a finger and starts its games of number counting and moral equivalencies.

May these dear, innocent boys rest in peace, may the lives they led be a blessing for us all, and may their families and all Israel be comforted among the mourners of Zion and Jerusalem.

(6/30/14)

68 AN AMERICAN-JEWISH HERO IN ISRAEL

I sit here savoring a treasure. It is a book about Jewish-American and Jewish-Palestinian heroism in the 1940s—a little known story and one I nearly didn't read.

The title is *The Jews' Secret Fleet: The Untold Story of North American Volunteers Who Smashed the British Blockade*. The author, Murray S. Greenfield, is the founder of Israel's Gefen Publishing House and of much else. Joseph M. Hochstein wrote it with him. Here's how the book came into my possession. Someone named Murray kept calling me. He said I should interview him, like I'd interviewed fellow activist David Gutmann, a"h ("Israel's Rebirth 'A Boring Story' to U.S. Jews"). Greenfield called at a particularly hard time and I could not meet with him—then he sent a messenger bearing his book. I then realized that this was a living hero of the Jewish people who wanted to meet me. Duty called. We met the very next day.

The ingenuity, boldness, idealism, and bravery of these "illegal" volunteer sailors and their Palestinian officers in HaMossad L'Aliyah Bet was beyond belief. It was a real David and Goliath story because they took on the cruel and mighty British fleet, and, despite losses, hardship, and unimaginable danger, they won, as the illegal boats and ships brought so many of the European Jews who survived the Holocaust into Palestine—well, mainly into British prison camps in Cyprus, but close enough. They drew world attention and, ultimately, sympathy by publicizing British heartlessness, the tragic plight of the post-concentration camp refugees, and the extraordinary derring-do of the volunteer sailors.

PC: How did this all come about?
Greenfield: It was very secretive. Only a few of us were Zionists, but everyone wanted to do the right thing. A guy, he didn't tell you his name, talked to you, very *shh-shh* and said, "We are getting the Jews out of Europe. You might get arrested or killed." I asked, "What's the pay?" There was no pay. They wanted people they could trust, who were doing this for the right reasons. I had to go.

What did you tell your parents?
I told my mother I was leaving to "do something for the Jewish people." She said, "In that case, you don't have to go to Hunter College!"

Could those boats really float?
They were hardly seaworthy, and definitely not made for an Atlantic crossing.

Who were the non-Jewish crewmembers on board your ship?
One Christian Polish man had worked in a Jewish bakery and he knew Yiddish. One Irish guy, McDonald, was on my ship. He was angry with the British. He left Harvard Law School. He painted the four-leaf clover on our ship.

What happened after Cyprus or Atlit?
I went right to Israel. An Israeli family adopted me. "This is your home," they said. I worked in the fields in Petach Tikvah. I never left. I just fell in. It was *bashert*.

Why did you write this book?
Decades had gone by and no historian had told this story. Sailors had died, materials had been destroyed and overlooked. Memories had faded. Historians all built upon early accounts that omitted this story. The *Encyclopedia Judaica* ignored the American role in its entry on "Illegal Immigration." The *Encyclopedia of Zionism and Israel* made no mention of American sailors.

Something Ben-Gurion said to me put me on this trail. I met him at his house on other business. I was working on bringing in investments from the United States and Canada to help build housing and provide mortgages. He asked me when I had first come to Israel. I told him on Aliyah Bet, as a volunteer sailor. He was dumbfounded. He looked confused. He did not know the story of Jewish Americans and Aliyah Bet! I realized I would have to tell the story. I found the sailors who were still alive. I spent years interviewing them and finding photographs, newspaper clippings, and archival material.

You published the first edition in 1987, and a 2010 edition with an introduction by Sir Martin Gilbert and a foreword by Paul Shulman, the First Commander of Israel's Navy. A documentary based on the book, *Waves of Freedom*, was released in 2008. Pretty impressive. But who helped you along the way? In the book, you note that Israeli historians and professors were either disinterested or even hostile.

Israelis understand Americans who give money to Israel. They have difficulty understanding Americans who choose to live in Israel, and still greater difficulty in understanding the Aliyah Bet volunteers's embracing a mission that held no glory but involved hard work and perhaps danger.

What did you do in Israel after Aliyah Bet and working the fields of Petach Tikvah?
I was interested in having North Americans invest in Israel. I tried to bring capital in to the Palestine Economic Corporation. Then I helped found the Association of Americans and Canadians in Israel and pioneered loans for housing and mortgages. This was hard work because investors were afraid that socialism would be more attractive.

I spent seven years as a volunteer working on behalf of the Ethiopian rescue mission. We would obtain fake scholarship promises, pay for an airline ticket to Rome, give them a visa to Israel, and fly them here. My late wife Chana [Lustig] and I founded an art gallery in Tel Aviv. We sold and exported Israeli art globally.

We got involved in the Terezin Ghetto Museum, because my wife saw that without her input, that museum would not be teaching visitors anything about the Jews. She created a program that did that. And she published a book, *Fragments of Memory*. And then I founded Gefen Publishing House, which has become the largest English-language publisher in Israel.

The question should have been: What *didn't* you do? You are truly a hero.
The real heroes are the survivors.

(7/4/14)

69 A Letter to My People

Dearest Friends and Colleagues:
I sit here, gazing at the wind-tossed Aegean, but my heart is in Zion—and it is breaking. I know that Israel must do exactly what it is doing, but I mourn the high price Jews have always had to pay to survive in this hate-filled world.

We have just lost young and not-so-young heroes, blessed heroes, who have already become part of the eternal pantheon of Jewish and Israeli soldiers who have fallen: honorably and forever.

All of us know Israeli soldiers and the parents and grandparents of Israeli soldiers. This war, like all such previous wars, has been agonizingly personal.

I have spent the days and nights of my vacation monitoring this hot war in Gaza, circulating articles where they might do the most good.

I believe that Hamas is, for the first time, diplomatically isolated; that Egypt, Jordan, and Saudi Arabia do not want a Shiite-Hezbollah or a Muslim Brotherhood victory in the region; that the media has been slightly more truthful about what is going on and therefore, more sympathetic to Israel's plight and narrative. Will this last? Will it last long enough to give some cover to Israeli troops who are trying to clean out the terrifying, nightmarish underground tunnels filled with weapons?

Israel is on the front line fighting against barbarism and international jihad. No great civilization is ever destroyed from the outside that has not first destroyed itself from within. Western countries have allowed hostile, devouring parasites to feed upon them and have justified both the hostility and the parasitism as justified, given the West's history of colonialism and racism.

The Western media and intelligentsia are rooting for the barbarians to win. They are *our* suicidal "bombers" by proxy since they are providing intellectual respectability to Hamas, ISIS, al-Qaeda, the Muslim Brotherhood.

What Israel is fighting—and dying for—is Western Enlightenment civilization and Judeo-Christian culture: individual rights, human rights, women's rights, freedom of conscience, freedom of expression and inquiry, the right to live in peace free of totalitarian and theocratic control.

At this time, I want to offer my most profound condolences to the families who have lost sons, daughters, brothers, sisters, fathers, mothers, spouses, cousins, friends, and colleagues. I stand with noble, surgically precise, and ethical Israel, which continues to spare as many civilians as possible while it is demonized for not doing so.

My people: We have been here a long time. We will ultimately prevail. I do not know the price we will have to pay this time.

(7/21/14)

70 CONDEMNATION OF ISRAEL PERSISTS EVEN AS UN OFFICIAL ADMITS HAMAS WAGES WAR FROM UN BUILDINGS

A senior UN official, UN Office for the Coordination of Humanitarian Affairs (OCHA) director John Ging, confirms what the IDF and other experts have been saying all along, but to little avail. In a television interview yesterday, Ging said that Hamas terrorists "are firing their rockets into Israel from the vicinity of UN facilities and residential areas."

This statement by a senior UN official confirms what the IDF has said repeatedly since the beginning of Operation Protective Edge, namely that Hamas uses Gaza's civilian population as a human shield. According to a transcript:

> JOHN GING: The militants, Hamas, and the other armed groups, they are firing also their weaponry, the rockets, into Israel from the

vicinity of these [UN] installations and housing and so on, so the combat is being conducted very much in a residential built up area.

CBC NEWS ANCHOR: The Israeli government has said repeatedly that Hamas is using human shields, they are using UN schools, hospitals—not only, by the way, to store weapons—I know 3 UN-run schools have been found with munitions stored in them, as weapons depots—but in the UN's experience, is Hamas or militant groups, Islamic Jihad, are they launching rockets nearby these shelters, these UN schools? Are they using it essentially as a shelter?

JOHN GING: Yes, the armed groups are firing their rockets into Israel from the vicinity of UN facilities and residential areas, absolutely.

As they say, this should function as a game changer. That is not the case. Even as I write, new petitions, signed by more Western academics and activists who condemn Israel, are in the pipeline; Jews are being attacked ("Death to the Jews") all across Europe and at demonstrations in North America. Media headlines, opinion pieces, and rants still focus on the number of human shield civilians that Hamas is sacrificing for reasons of propaganda in the belief that the pressure of world opinion will force Israel to stop before the mission of "de-militarizing Gaza" has been accomplished.

When Palestinian deaths occur, Israel is reflexively blamed—and then, when it becomes absolutely clear that Hamas rockets have killed their own human shields, or when Hamas did not allow their human shields to evacuate, the world media and human rights organizations simply move on. Their game is blaming Israelis, not in telling the truth.

On July 24, 2014, it was reported that 15 people were killed and many wounded due to the Israeli shelling of a UN School. UN Chief Ban Ki-Moon condemned the attacks. Israel had warned of this strike the previous night and told the Red Cross to evacuate civilians from the UNRWA shelter. Hamas refused to let the civilians leave. UNRWA spokesman Chris Gunness tweeted that Hamas rockets were also falling on the compound.

Ban Ki-Moon did not retract his statement or call an extraordinary meeting at the United Nations based on this information.

Yesterday, three young Israeli soldiers were killed when they entered a booby-trapped UN School. A booby-trapped school...and yet, the media refuses to understand what this means.

(7/31/14)

71 WEST BANK FEMINIST ACADEMICS CONDEMN ISRAEL (!) FOR PROMOTING RAPE, SEXISM, AND GENOCIDE

On July 31, 2014, the Institute of Women's Studies at Birzeit University put out "an urgent call" to condemn Israel, Israeli scholars, and the Israeli culture of "rape," "misogyny," "sexism," "genocide," and "ethnic cleansing."

The Institute also condemned one unnamed member of the Israeli Parliament who has allegedly called for "the killing of all Palestinian women;" another Israeli academic who has allegedly called for the "raping of Palestinian women;" and a Rabbi who has allegedly "call(ed) for mass murder of Palestinians while taking their foreskins as trophies."

Birzeit University is a Palestinian academic institution located in the West Bank. Currently, American and European listserv groups are circulating this filth, which is how it came into my possession last night.

The Birzeit academics, intoxicated by their own rhetoric and on quite a metaphoric high horse—perhaps with a real as well as metaphoric Hamas gun to their heads, too—do not mention Palestinian-style gender apartheid. Nor do they mention Hamas's culture of Jihad, human sacrifice, or Hamas's use of their own civilian human shields for propaganda purposes.

With the mention of "human trophies," it becomes clear that the Birzeit feminists are scapegoating Jewish Israelis for the considerable crimes of Islamic groups such as ISIS, Boko Haram, and Hamas, who actually do commit grisly, barbaric murders. They behead, crucify, castrate, rape-to-death, burn alive, and torture their victims in other unspeakable ways—and they mount heads on poles or play football with them. Palestinian Arabs lynch, and then smear themselves with the blood and gleefully hold up their blood-smeared palms and faces. Here I am thinking about the lynching of the two IDF reservists in Ramallah in 2000 by Palestinians. Palestinians dismembered them and danced for joy.

However, are these really the central concerns of Birzeit's Women's Studies Institute at this time? Where is their concern for the medical, food, and housing needs of the women and children who have been betrayed and abandoned by the Hamas leadership? Or, for the millions of women and children who have been forced into sex slavery, exiled, and slaughtered by the Muslim-on-Muslim violence that is currently raging in the Arab Middle East?

The Institute of Women's Studies at Birzeit calls upon "all scholars of the world, all women's organizations, all who fight for freedom and justice to take a clear stand against this racist state's continuous (colonial) war crimes." Do these Birzeit feminists and their global supporters understand that Islam has a long and bloody history of colonialism, imperialism, slavery, and conversion by the sword? Do they understand that if colonialism=sexism, then this is true for Muslim countries and cultures as well?

Further, this Institute is attacking a serious, feminist Israeli scholar (whom they dare not name, although they link to a potentially libelous article about him that was published on alternativenews.org.)

Dr. Mordechai Kedar, a leading Arabist and scholar of gender dynamics, never recommended that Palestinian women—or that any women—be raped. What he probably said—because he and I have discussed this—was more like this: In a shame and honor culture (Arab, Muslim, and tribal), for example, in Pakistan: if the Pakistani Secret Service has a suspected terrorist and a ticking bomb, the way that Pakistani Muslims get a Pakistani or Afghan Muslim suspect to talk is by bringing his mother and his sisters into the room, undressing them, and, if he is still silent, beginning to rape each one.

Kedar is not recommending this. He is on record opposing shame and honor barbarism, but, he is "telling it like it is."

However, Israel is never allowed to win. Remember the Israeli feminist M.A. dissertation that won a prize because she argued that Israelis are "racists" because the IDF does *not* rape Palestinian women in custody or in general?

I mourn the death of real feminism. I am outraged that Western feminists sound exactly like their Birzeit counterparts. I am heartbroken that Israeli feminists on the left share the Birzeit point of view.

'Tis the world turned upside down.

(8/7/2014)

72 THE LANCET SPECIALTY: ANTI-ZIONISM, NOT SCIENTIFIC MEDICINE

On July 23, 2014, *The Lancet* again engaged in a Blood Libel against Israel. Between July 28th and August 14th, they only published a handful of rebuttal letters—and many more in support of their anti-Israel "Open Letter." The editorial staff of *The Lancet* also published an editorial that justified its having published extraordinary lies as if they were scientifically accurate. It took them 16 days before they published a rebuttal letter by the President of the Israeli Medical Association.

Here's what happened.

In an article titled "An Open Letter for the People in Gaza," the violence against Israel perpetrated by the terrorist group Hamas and the Israeli Defense Force response to it is presented in inaccurate and defamatory ways. It was authored by Paola Manduca, Iain Chalmers, Derek Summerfield, Mads Gilbert, and Ang Swee Chai "on behalf of 24 signatories."

Manduca et al. write of Israel-perpetrated "massacres" and are "tempted to conclude" that "95%" of Israeli academics "are complicit in the massacre and destruction of Gaza." Manduca et al. write:

> We challenge the perversity of a propaganda that justifies the creation of an emergency to masquerade a massacre, a so-called "defensive aggression." In reality it is a ruthless assault of unlimited duration, extent, and intensity... We are appalled by the military onslaught on civilians in Gaza under the guise of punishing terrorists... Um Al Ramlawi who speaks for all in Gaza: "They are killing us all anyway—either a slow death by the siege, or a fast one by military attacks. We have nothing left to lose—we must fight for our rights, or die trying."

These *Lancet* authors do not mention the vast network of terror tunnels purposely dug beneath schools, mosques, hospitals, and private homes; no mention of Hamas's cold and ruthless decision to use their own people as human shields for propaganda purposes; not a word about the thousands of rockets that have rained down mainly on southern Israel for so many years. There is no analysis of the hate propaganda indoctrination against Jews and Israel that every Palestinian child receives and the glorification and payment to the family of "martyred" human homicide bombs, nor scarcely a thought about how much money was siphoned off by Hamas leaders for luxury lives, Swiss and Emirati bank accounts, and for the purchase of weapons and the building of a veritable underground city of cement-walled tunnels in which weapons and fighters are housed.

As Dr. Richard Cravatts, President of Scholars for Peace in the Middle East, and Dr. David Feifel, have noted, the *Lancet* authors do not come with "clean hands:"

> Paolo Manduca received funding from several anti-Israel NGOs including Interpal, which has been designated as a terrorist entity by the governments of the United States, Canada and Australia. US Federal authorities describe the organization as a global clearinghouse channeling money to Hamas and a BBC investigation came to the same conclusion. Interpal is a founding member of the so-called "Union of Good," an umbrella organization, which funds Islamic terrorists in Gaza. Its leader, Yussef al-Qaradawi, is a notorious jihadist who has publically lauded Hitler for "putting Jews in their place" and has said of the Israeli-Palestinian conflict: "We must plant the love of death and the love of martyrdom in the Islamic nation."

Lancet Editor Richard Horton himself has many ties to anti-Israel organizations.

This is not the first time that *The Lancet* has engaged in Blood Libels.

In 2010, *The Lancet* published a scurrilous pseudo-scientific attack upon Israel, which claimed that an increase in wife-beating "in the occupied territories" was due to the stress of "occupation." At the time, I helped some Israeli academics and physicians place their letters of protest in *The Lancet* and I also published a letter in their pages. The 2010 article was an intellectual joke but there was nothing funny about it.

The authors did not look at the normalized wife- and daughter-beating in Egypt, Jordan, Saudi Arabia or in any other Muslim Arab country that was not allegedly "occupied" by Israel. Nor did they note the normalized honor killing of girls and women in the region. They did not compare "intimate partner violence" in unoccupied Gaza with "intimate partner violence" in Sderot, Israel, where "civilians have endured 8,000 rocket attacks from Gaza." This so-called study did not note the increase in violence against women due to Hamas's fundamentalist misogyny.

The censorship of the truth and the presentation of highly biased articles are acting as a strong incitement to hate and possibly even genocide. But *The Lancet* is not alone in such censorship. I have been contacted by several journalists who also tried to write about the Manduca article in *The Lancet* but were rejected at their usual (liberal-left) websites.

We live at a moment in history when heroism is our only alternative. I wish people really understood that.

(8/4/14–8/5/14)

73 Gaza in Manhattan: Individual Jews Held Guilty and Attacked

Monday night, on the Upper East Side of New York City, a gang of anti-Semitic thugs attacked a peaceful but visibly Jewish man—he was wearing a skullcap. They also attacked his wife.

Two cars "flying Palestinian flags and multiple motorcycles" pulled up to the couple at 8:00 p.m. while it was still daylight. They began yelling "anti-Jewish statements." Then, they threw a water bottle that hit his wife, and when her husband came to her defense they "punched him in the head."

The suspects fled. No arrests have been made. The 27-year-old man refused medical attention at the scene.

This is my neighborhood, my home town. This incident took place about a mile away from where I live and work. So far, I have found only one brief article about this in the *New York Post*.

Are there more such incidents that are not being covered? Jews do not attack Muslims or Christians—or anyone for that matter—for wearing religiously identifiable clothing or jewelry. Only *some* Muslims appear to do that—some Muslims or pro-Muslim sympathizers.

Jews and Christians are not allowed to openly practice their religion in most Muslim countries, and yet Muslims in America and Europe expect to be able to practice their faith, often in very aggressive ways, in the West.

I remember Eric Larson's excellent book, *In the Garden of the Beasts: Love, Terror, and an American Family in Hitler's Berlin*. Larson describes how in 1933 Nazi thugs begin beating up Americans and Jews in the streets, quite openly. People saw. They walked on by. The American media and, more importantly, the American government did not want to publicize the beatings of Americans lest Germany use this as an excuse to default on loan repayments. The Jews? No one seemed to care.

This time it is not just happening in Berlin. This time, it is quite global. Such incidents have been happening for years in Australia, New Zealand, Europe, and North America. In August of this year, a Muslim mob in Uppsala, Sweden "set upon and severely beat a Jewish mother of four, for wearing a Jewish Star of David necklace."

In July of this year, in Australia, a gang of Arabic-speaking goons attacked Zachary Gomo in Caulfield because he was wearing a shirt with Hebrew lettering. Gomo was beaten, but he fought back; his attackers fled. Afterwards, Internet comments disturbed Gomo (who had served in the IDF) more than the attack itself. The comments said that wearing anything with Hebrew lettering was as provocative as wearing a Nazi armband or a swastika.

In March, in Paris, a Jewish teacher leaving a kosher restaurant had his nose broken by a group of assailants who also drew a swastika on his chest. In May in Paris, a Jewish woman with a baby was attacked at a bus station by a man who shouted "Dirty Jewess" at her. In June, in Paris, a Jewish teenager was attacked with an electric Taser by a group of teens. One of the teens was reportedly also carrying a club. The victim was wearing a yarmulke and tzitzit. Also in June in Paris, two teens were chased by a man with an ax, and another pair of teens was sprayed with tear gas because they were wearing skullcaps.

Jews everywhere are being held responsible for Israeli acts of self-defense, which have been touted in the media as aggressive and genocidal acts.

The decades of Big Lies in the media, inflammatory sermons in mosques, churches, and synagogues, which falsely present Israel and Jews as genocidal Nazis, have finally empowered the hatred among Arab Muslims and their sympathizers in the West to physically attack individual Jewish civilians as targets, symbols, and collaborators with the Israeli regime.

I will not hide my Jewish jewelry, and I plan to walk freely about my neighborhood. If anyone tries to mess with me, perhaps I will hit them with my cane, or better yet, smoothly remove my small, pink, pearl-handled revolver from my bag (filled with heavy tranquilizer pellets) and shoot to tranquilize.

No, I do not own a gun, but at times like these, I think I should.

(8/26/14)

74 BODY AND SOUL: THE STATE OF THE JEWISH NATION. A FILM REVIEW

*G*loria Z. Greenfield's third film, *Body and Soul: The State of the Jewish Nation*, is a cinematic and educational triumph. In only 65 minutes, the viewer comes to understand who the Jews are to the land of Israel and what the land of Israel is to Judaism and to history.

This film is not propaganda. There is no doctored footage. This is the truth made visual. The most wonderful maps, illustrated manuscripts, ancient coins, legal documents, highlighted newspaper articles, and film footage accompany a rapid succession of 36 soulful and scholarly experts.

The Jews are the indigenous people of the Holy Land. Their history began more than 3,000 years ago, and all their sacred journeys, both religious and geographic, have been towards the Promised Land, the Holy Land, Jerusalem. No occupier ever remained in Jewish Israel. They massacred, occupied, dispersed the Jews—and then disappeared.

Some Jews always managed to remain there, century after century; some Jews consistently returned to Israel, either on pilgrimage or to stay. The evidence for this is overwhelming.

This film is the antidote to a world that has been taught to believe that a false history is true, namely that the Philistines were the ancestors of the people recently designated as "Palestinians." "Palestine" was the name Rome used to punish the Jews who rebelled against them by linguistically wiping out what had long been known as Israel/Judah/The Holy Land and naming it after the Jews' classic enemy of biblical times, the Philistines.

The late-19th century pogroms in Russia, the ominous significance of the Dreyfus case in France, the Nazi-era Holocaust in Europe and in the Arab world, and the pre- and post-1948 pogroms in Arab lands all meant that the Jews needed a safe haven, a sovereign space. Jews prayed facing Jerusalem—King David's city; their daily prayers remembered Jerusalem, where both the first and second Temples once stood. Where else did the Jews come from? Where else did they belong?

The film gives us an excellent, graphic lesson in what the British did via their Mandate for Palestine (they appeased both sides but then fatefully sided with the Arabs against the Jews), an important account of the Soviet relationship with the Arab League and the incredibly invidious propaganda campaign they embarked upon, and the legal basis for the creation of the Jewish state and for its right to keep land conquered in wars of self-defense. An unexpected point of view is offered by historian Dr. Anita Shapira. She says:

> I think that the state of Israel was established despite the Holocaust, and not because of the

Holocaust; because the great reservoir of the Jewish people that (had) dreamed about the state of Israel, (who) were potentially the citizens of the future state—perished in the Holocaust. The Holocaust was important in the sense that it galvanized the American Jewish community around Zionism, around the idea of the Jewish state.

This is also true because America did not open its doors to the Jews who were in flight from certain extermination.

Today, the assault upon Israel is not merely military. According to MK. Dr. Einat Wilf, there is "an intellectual assault on Zionism which is unprecedented" in terms of its "ferocity."

Itamar Marcus, the founder of Palestinian Media Watch, reminds us that "in the 1990s, soon after the signing of the Oslo Accords, there was a conference of Palestinian historians where it was stated explicitly that one of the goals of the Palestinian historian is to write a Palestinian history that won't allow for the existence of any other people in the land." This is precisely what has happened.

Western intellectuals went along with this fake history because, as American military historian Victor Davis Hanson explains, once indoctrinated with a "mythic pseudo-history," the "elite culture" makes the "necessary" adjustments. He continues:

> So if I am a classical scholar or I am an ancient historian or I am a Byzantine historian I know that if I insert a particular thought or idea about Israel taking land or Israel being illegitimate, […] I understand there is going to be benefits

paid to me. I might get a professorship, I might get a medal, I might get a literary award.

Greenfield is a new breed of documentary artiste. Her films are available online and accessible to people everywhere. They are available for live streaming on Netflix, Amazon Instant Video, iTunes and YouTube/Orchard Movies. Her films are also subtitled in Arabic, French, German, Hebrew, Japanese, Russian, Portuguese, Italian, and Spanish.

Although she sells her films online, Greenfield has also pioneered traveling with them. She organizes openings, panels, and discussion groups after the film has been viewed. Her previous films have been screened countless times throughout North America, South America, Europe, Asia, and Africa.

One might say that Greenfield puts her own body and soul into this work and when she travels, she travels hard. Day after day, almost one day after the next, Greenfield accompanies the film across states and continents, traveling from coast to coast, often in back to back appearances. This intense pace is how she breathes.

All I can say is: Brava, Gloria!

(10/13/14)

75 OPERA V. TRUTH: THE DEATH OF KLINGHOFFER

I love opera. I was a regular contributor to NPR's program "At the Opera" for three years. I attend the opera as often as I can.

Metropolitan Opera General Manager Peter Gelb has a constitutional and artistic right to produce whatever he wants. Yet, his decision to stage *The Death of Klinghoffer* represents an abdication of moral responsibility and gravitas. Showcasing this opera is equivalent to a college president's inviting a member of ISIS, Hamas, or the Taliban to speak on campus because "all sides must be heard" since "all points of view are equally valid."

The Death of Klinghoffer demonizes Israel, which is what anti-Semitism is partly about today. It incorporates lethal Islamic (and now universal) pseudo-histories about Israel and Jews. It beatifies terrorism, both musically and in the libretto.

Composer John Adams, an admirer of Edward Said, has given the opening "Chorus of Exiled Palestinians" a beautiful, sacred musical "halo," à la Bach. The "Chorus of Exiled Jews," by contrast, is dogged, mechanical, relentless, hardly angelic.

The Metropolitan Opera production showed us an "Apartheid Wall" replete with graffiti. This security fence, which protected Israeli civilians from the almost non-stop human homicide bombing attacks that rose to near Holocaust-level proportions in 2002, did not exist in 1985 when the *Achille Lauro* was hijacked, nor did it exist in the late 1960s and early 1970s when the hijackers were growing up. Inserting it into the production was a politically trendy but completely ahistorical statement.

Likewise, the Metropolitan Opera production presented the Palestinian chorus as a Greek chorus: earth-bound, indigenous, permanent, eternal. The exiled Jewish chorus was dressed as European refugees, circa the 1940s, who had only recently arrived.

These production decisions, which present a false history, speak for themselves.

The libretto is not even-handed. The villains have more lines, and better lines. The terrorists command eleven arias—twelve, with the "Chorus of Exiled Palestinians." The Klinghoffers have two arias each, toward the end of the opera. Add the exiled Jewish chorus and you have five arias for the innocent victims versus twelve for their victimizers.

This opera treats six million murdered Jews of the Holocaust as morally equivalent to 700,000 Palestinian Arabs who left during Israel's founding. They were not murdered, not ethnically cleansed, but rather pushed to flee their homes by Arab leaders who told them they'd return as soon as the Jews had been slaughtered. Some Arabs stayed. Today, Israel has 1.7 million Arab Muslim and Christian citizens, about 20 percent of its population. Jews are willing to live with Muslims and Christians—it is the Arab Muslim leaders who want to ethnically cleanse Jews and other infidels from allegedly Muslim lands.

Klinghoffer does not note the 850,000 Arab, North African, and Central Asian *Jews* forced into exile between 1948 and 1972.

The lament of the exiled Palestinians is meant—but fails—to equal that of Verdi's celebrated chorus of exiled Jews in Babylon in *Nabucco* ("Va, pensiero, sull'ali dorate"). The Jews are longing for Jerusalem and for Solomon's destroyed First Temple. *Klinghoffer* equates the brief exile of Palestinians with that of exiled Jews who have been longing for Jerusalem for millennia—and this strengthens how the libretto renders the Holocaust of European Jews as morally equivalent to what the Palestinians refer to as the 1948 "Naqba" (Catastrophe).

Penny Woolcock, together with composer John Adams, directed the British movie version of this opera. In an on-camera interview Woolcock reveals a series of false moral equivalencies, which she delivers in an unnervingly soft, girlish, and school-marmish voice. She says, "You can't understand Israel without the Holocaust and you can't understand Palestinian suicide bombing without understanding the Naqba."

This is a lie, but by now almost everyone believes it is true. Those who identify as "Palestinians" do so by stealing the mantle of Jewish and black South African victimhood.

In the movie version of the opera, Woolcock shows us fictionalized black and white footage in which Israelis brutally force peaceful Palestinians out of their ancestral homes. The Israeli men brandish guns and are very violent.

We are not shown fictionalized or actual footage of the Arab Legion attacking Jews, which is what really happened, nor are we shown Israelis warning villages to evacuate, which also happened.

The historical black and white footage of skeletal Jewish corpses and of Jews being loaded into boxcars on their way to concentration camps is authentic but fleeting. Woolcock shows us a young Jewish man in a fictionalized black and white film. He is a presumed survivor of the Warsaw ghetto, and he turns up in her fictionalized movie as an angry and violent Israeli who menaces an elderly Arab woman, discards her possessions, and moves into her home.

The opera movie switches from World War II-era black and white fictionalized footage to contemporary, fictional Technicolor, which shows the Israeli Defense Forces harassing and punishing peaceful Palestinians; this is meant to explain and justify why young men become human homicide bombs.

The Palestinians sing, "My father's house was razed/ in nineteen-forty-eight/when the Israelis passed/Over our street." The Jews sing, "When I paid off the taxi, I had no money left." And Rambo, one of the terrorists, sings, "But wherever poor men/Are gathered they can/Find Jews getting fat...America/Is one big Jew."

The librettist, Alice Goodman, was born a Jew, converted to Christianity and became an Anglican Priest. More power to her. She seems to believe that the world will be redeemed, theologically, by the murder-crucifixion of a Jew.

This is a very Christian concept.

Only a dead and murdered Jew—"Leon Klinghoffer's body"—is allowed to sing an aria with some measure of grace (although I also found the lyrics somewhat incomprehensible).

I am struck by the theme of a Jew being thrown into the

sea. In Exodus, the Jewish slaves leave Egypt, and there is only the sea between them and an angry Pharaoh in hot pursuit. The entire nation would have drowned had not God parted the waters for them—but not for Pharaoh, who drowned in that same sea. Ever since the Jews established a sovereign state in the Holy Land, the Arabs have continually threatened to "drive the Jews into the sea."

In *Klinghoffer*'s case, this is exactly what the PLO terrorists do. Further, the librettist, but especially Penny Woolcock, visually and vocally surrounds Klinghoffer's corpse as it floats under water with radiant rays, the kind of rays that led Moses to wear a face veil, lest such proof of his intimacy with God terrify others; the kind of rays that halo Jesus Christ, the Christian Savior, and other Christian Saints. The great Michelangelo mistook Moses' radiance, or halo, for "horns," and his magnificent sculpture of Moses has horns, "carnaim." At one point, anti-Semites believed that Jews had horns.

Goodman's terrorists sing that they are "men of ideals," not "criminals," and that "this is an action for liberation."

Who were these so-called "men of ideals"? They were Palestinian Liberation Organization (PLO) operatives. On board the ship, Nazi-style, Entebbe-style, they tried to separate the Jews from the other passengers. Two elderly Austrians identified themselves as Jews and were beaten and manhandled. Please note: They were Jews—not Israelis. The remaining Jews, including the Klinghoffers and their friends, did not identify themselves as Jews. The terrorists forced the passengers to stand under the broiling Mediterranean sun for days. They forced trembling passengers to hold live grenades. They lied. They told the crew and passengers that there were 20 terrorists aboard and that they were going to blow up the ship. These terrorists did not allow Marilyn Klinghoffer to lie down—she was exhausted and in pain from colon cancer. In their limited English, they cursed America and praised Yasser Arafat.

Contrary to the opera (and to the movie version of the opera), the hijacking of the *Achille Lauro* was a 14-man Palestinian Liberation operation, and the orders came from the very top: Yasser Arafat and Abu Abbas. Their mission: the return of 50 Palestinian terrorists being held in Israeli jails, beginning with Samir Kuntar, the man who had murdered two young Israelis and two children in Nahariyah in 1979. Palestinians consider Kuntar a great hero; he was eventually exchanged in a prisoner swap. The passengers were to be held hostage until these killers/"freedom fighters" were returned. *No one was supposed to be murdered.*

But Arab Muslim terrorists are usually frustrated young men (those on the *Achille Lauro* ranged in age from 17 to 23), and they are always in search of father figures, whom they wish to please. Often, their handlers, who are serial killers by proxy, are the only father figures they have. However, such father-wounded sons are, by definition, bullies and cowards. They prey on the vulnerable and helpless.

Leon Klinghoffer had suffered several strokes, did not have full use of his hands, his legs were paralyzed, his speech slurred—and this is who Molqui murders and has thrown overboard with his wheelchair. One might suggest that Molqui cannot bear his own smoldering impotence and, for this, the Jew must die.

What happened to the terrorists who masterminded and carried out the hijacking of the *Achille Lauro*? Were they arrested, tried, convicted, and sentenced to many lifetimes in jail?

The answer is: not exactly. Eight planners and handlers simply walked out of Italy, claiming a diplomatic status they did not have. In a private interview with me, Michael Ledeen, President Reagan's negotiator, said that President Mubarak of Egypt told Italian Prime Minister Benito Craxi that if these men were stopped he (Mubarak) would be assassinated.

The PLO as well as Fatah, Palestine Liberation Front, Abu Nidal, Hamas, Islamic Jihad, etc. function like the Mafia. The *capo dei capi* rarely does jail time. Those who do jail time know that their families will be taken care of. When the Klinghoffer daughters sued Arafat, he insisted that he represented a "state" and could not be sued. The daughters won an out-of-court settlement with Arafat because an American judge discounted Arafat's claim that he represented a "state" and Arafat chose not to testify.

Those who had procured the arms received sentences that ranged from four to nine years. The on-board terrorists received sentences that ranged from four to 30 years with early releases. All were considered heroes across the Arab world.

The terrorists on board the *Achille Lauro* were born 15-20 years after the creation of the State of Israel and could have absolutely no personal memory of being exiled or dispersed. In the libretto, and especially in the movie version of the opera, we are moved by one of the terrorists who lost his mother in a camp in Lebanon. He has kept her photo on a chain around his neck his entire life.

The Holocaust and the "silent exodus" of Arab Jews also created Jewish orphans. They became physicians, scientists, teachers, farmers, poets, businessmen, bus drivers, and police officers, as well as first and second violinists. Very few of them became terrorists. In 1948, among those who did, their targets were British *officers*, not civilians. Since then, only a mere handful of religious extremists or mentally unbalanced individual Jews have targeted a Jewish head of state or Muslims peacefully at prayer. Moreover, they were immediately condemned by Israel.

As a feminist fan of opera, I wouldn't boycott an opera because the female heroes are betrayed, go mad, or are murdered. Gilda, Norma, Mimì, Cio-Cio San, Carmen, Lucia, Tosca, Lulu, Isolde, Marie (Berg's *Wozzeck*), Brünnhilde, Leonora, Azucena, Massenet's Manon, and Puccini's Manon Lescaut, all the Russians—die singing. As in life, our great operas are tragedies in which the heroes die.

But, in opera, where there are heroes, there are also villains.

The villain in Puccini's *Tosca* is unmistakable: He is Scarpia, the police chief of Rome who tortures political prisoners and attempts to rape the great singer, Floria Tosca. We don't get a backstory about Scarpia's dysfunctional childhood, nor do we sympathize or identify with him.

He is a heartless villain and the opera doesn't allow (let alone ask) us to pity or sympathize with him. We are meant to fear and despise him, perhaps even hate him.

Likewise, in Donizetti's *Lucia di Lammermoor*, Verdi's *Rigoletto*, and Puccini's *Madame Butterfly*, we are not meant to sympathize with Lucia's brother, Lord Enrico Ashton, or with Rigoletto's lecherous boss, the Duke of Mantua, or his paid assassin, Sparafucile, or with Cio-Cio San's Pinkerton. (And for those who immediately think of *Othello*: Yes, we sympathize with him, even though he honor kills his wife and thereafter immediately commits suicide. Othello is not the villain; Iago, who has goaded him into it, and who wants Othello's position, is the fiend.)

Klinghoffer begs us to sympathize with the villains—terrorists. This is something new.

Blood libels against Israel and the Jews, pseudo-histories—genocidal narratives—have permeated the media and the Western campuses. These falsehoods claim the privilege of free speech and academic freedom, and they have been welcomed by the intelligentsia. Here, these same ideas are making their debut amidst the trappings of high culture.

Choosing to stage *The Death of Klinghoffer* at the Met automatically confers upon it a prestige it does not deserve. The opera and this production betray the truth entirely and, in effect, join the low-brow ranks of propagandists against Jewish survival.

(10/19/14–10/24/14)

76 JE SUIS CHARLIE HEBDO AUSSI

I have been writing about the Intifada in France and in Europe—certainly in Israel, as well as the coming Intifada in North America—for a long time. Back in 2004/2005, I urged everyone to read Jean Raspail's 1973 brilliant, dystopian novel *The Camp of the Saints* immediately. Raspail envisioned a group of hostile "Others," in a flotilla, who land in France, are royally welcomed, and proceed to devastate and destroy France.

I again urge people to read this book now.

I and a small and much maligned group of scholars and journalists (Ayaan Hirsi Ali, Bruce Bawer, Bat-Ye'or, Paul Berman, Steven Emerson, Oriana Fallaci, Christopher Hitchens, Daniel Pipes, Ibn Warraq) have warned about, even predicted, a growing Intifada in the West as well as in Muslim countries. However, this Intifada is not visible to the Western intelligentsia. Even today, media and government leaders desperately prattle on about how Islam is a religion of peace—even after 9/11, 3/11, 7/7, the assassination of Dutch filmmaker Theo Van Gogh, the Shoe Bomber, the Fort Hood Shooter, the rise of ISIS, Boko Haram, Hamas—and now the Muslim massacre of journalists and cartoonists at *Charlie Hebdo*.

Some Western journalists write that the massacre was due to *Charlie Hebdo* having "provoked" the attack by insulting Islam. Yes, the satirical magazine insulted all religions and did not make an exception for Islam. Muslims expect that exception and will murder in order to get it. The West has mainly yielded.

Please recall: The Yale University Press chose not to publish the Danish Mohammed cartoons in a book about the cartoon controversy; American cartoonist Molly ("Draw Mohammed Day") Norris is still in hiding on the West Coast. The brave Danes and Swedes (Flemming Rose, Hans Erling Jensen, Kurt Westergaard, Lars Hedegaard, and many more) have been sued, nearly assassinated, and forced to either live in hiding or under police protection for "insulting" Islam.

Several journalists urge people not to confuse these Muslim terrorists with the majority of peaceful Muslims and worriedly note the rise of right-wing parties, especially in Europe—as if such parties are committing massacres. One columnist compared a negligible handful of Jewish extremists in Israel with Hamas, ISIS, Boko Haram, the Taliban, and al-Qaeda.

Those who are not heroes would, to paraphrase Stéphane Charbonnier, rather "live on their knees than risk dying on their feet." Since yesterday, few Western media venues have reposted the *Charlie Hebdo* cartoons.

The Western right to criticize, including our most sacred cows, is on the line. Free thought is on the line as is free speech, freedom of religion, freedom from religion, human rights, women's rights, gay rights—the entire Western Enlightenment enterprise is on the line.

Every newspaper and magazine will need the kind of police protection that only Israel has been forced to pioneer. Soon, every journalist might need a bodyguard—and her bodyguard might also need a bodyguard. And so on—at least until we stand, fight, and militarily decimate every last jihadist and pro-jihadist idea left standing. Nothing less will do.

I hope that an increasing number of people of all religions are now ready to consider that the West and Western values are actually worth defending.

Vive La France! Bravo to all those who peacefully assembled to say "We are *Charlie Hebdo*."

(1/8/15)

77 #Je Suis Juif (I am a Jew)

Yesterday, a colleague challenged me. She agreed that the murder of twelve French journalists was horrendous—barbaric—but she was bitter and was not going to be using the hashtag #JeSuis*Charlie*.

And why not?

Because, she said, no one had created hashtags or marches on behalf of any of the many Israeli Jewish civilians, women, children, the elderly, who were targeted and murdered by Islamic terrorists. No one had agreed to "ride the buses" the year that terrorists were blowing them up in Jerusalem.

I told her she had a point but I asked her to consider this: The Jews are often the first to model the future, the first to model how to respond to a situation. If the world callously looks away, if people believe that the sacrifice of the Jews will save non-Jews, if the world does not learn to identify with the plight of Jews, the world will reap a similar whirlwind.

Ironically, France was very friendly to Arafat and his family; the government behaved with enormous respect towards him and his murderous enterprise. This, and other grievous appeasements, has not spared France from a raging Intifada launched by its Muslim citizens.

I also told my colleague that the Jews have a sacred mission and that withdrawing entirely unto ourselves, refusing to understand our role in humanity's drama, is not entirely "Jewish."

Today, I think my colleague has a point. Today, I am waiting for people to launch the hashtag: #JeSuisJuif.

I am waiting for France to make the connection between "Israel," and "humanity," to comprehend that Israel is a symbol for the West, to understand that Arab Jews and Arab Christians were at the mercy of such Muslim barbarians for millennia, that the state of Israel "provoked" the age-old Islamic hatred of infidels, and that the jihad against the Jews has been going on since the beginning of the 20th century.

A sovereign Jewish state has "provoked" those Muslim terrorists who believe that the entire world should be Muslim and ruled by Sharia law. The Western world is now in their gun-sights.

In the last fourteen years, non-Israeli Jews, and French Jews, have been mocked, stalked, literally tortured, stabbed, raped, robbed, shot down, stoned, and blown up.

At least four, possibly five French-Jewish hostages, were killed by jihadists before the French police stormed the kosher supermarket. The jihadists were demanding freedom for the *Charlie Hebdo* jihadists.

Simultaneously, the police stormed the building in north Paris where the *Charlie Hebdo* jihadists were holding a hostage; they freed that hostage and killed the terrorists.

I am launching a #JeSuisJuif hashtag, not only in honor of these latest Jewish victims, but also in honor of all the

Jewish victims whose deaths have met with the hashtag world's indifference.

Today, I am a Jew, #JeSuisJuif.

(1/9/15)

78 WHAT THE WEST MUST DO IN ORDER TO SURVIVE

*I*f Europe does not do the following immediately, the birthplace of the Western enterprise will soon be conquered by barbarism.

First, the European Union must dissolve itself. Borders and passports must return. No one should be allowed to travel unhindered from one European country to another.

Second, each European country must pass legislation to deport all those who are on "no-fly" lists, all radical imams at radical mosques, together with their radicalized followers in mosques and in prisons, and all those who have traveled to Iraq, Syria, and Yemen for jihadi training.

Third, legislation must empower police and military forces to physically abolish the "no-go" zones—the hostile, separatist Muslim-only neighborhoods in which the European rule of law does not exist and that are ruled, instead, by vigilantism, terrorism, and a superstitious version of Sharia law.

Fourth, the most vigorous requirements must be put in

place for new immigrants and for the families of existing immigrants.

I truly wonder whether France will both pass and enforce such legislation.

As for America, the country that chose to send no important leader to rally against terrorism and in support of free speech in Paris:

We must immediately close our southern border. Here, I am not talking about Hispanic children or Hispanic would-be domestic workers. I am talking about the thousands of illegal immigrants who are coming into America via this route carrying Korans.

We must use language accurately. Jihad is not "workplace violence" or the acts of "mentally ill" and "lone" individuals. When a Muslim murders and massacres others, as the Fort Hood shooter did, yelling "Allahu Akbar"—this is an act of radical political Islam. The word "Islamic" (or "Islamist") must sanely be joined to the word "terrorism" in the lexicon of the FBI, CIA, and Office of Homeland Security.

For the civil libertarians and multi-cultural relativists among us: The West does not believe in collective punishment or in judging an individual based on collective stereotypes about that individual's race, religion, or culture. Not all Muslims are terrorists. But 95% of terrorism today is committed by Muslims who believe they are carrying out Koranic commandments. Until this changes, we must be on a war footing.

For those who forget: The first World Trade Center Bombers were Muslims; The U.S.S. Cole Bombers were Muslims; The 9/11 World Trade Center Attackers were Muslims; The Shoe Bomber was a Muslim; the Beltway Snipers were Muslims; the Fort Hood Shooter was a Muslim;

The Underwear Bomber was a Muslim; The Madrid Train Bombers were Muslims; The Bombay/Mumbai, India Attackers were Muslims; The Bali Nightclub Bombers were Muslims; The London Subway Bombers were Muslims; The Moscow Theater and Beslan School Attackers were Muslims; The Boston Marathon Bombers were Muslims; the Sydney, Australia Lindt Café Hostage Taker was a Muslim; The *Charlie Hebdo* and Kosher Supermarket Killers in Paris were Muslims, etc.

This list is short and does not include all the jihadi attacks against Jews and against Israelis for the last one hundred years—nor the jihadi attacks against all infidels (Christians, Hindus, Bahá'í, Zoroastrian, etc.), and against the "wrong" kind of Muslim since the 7th century AD.

Americans must understand that war has been declared against the infidel West by radical political Islamists and that the time to fight back is long overdue. Americans must demand that their government defend their country and their way of life.

We must defeat President Obama's plans, which are underway, to welcome thousands of Muslim immigrants who have not been vetted in terms of radical anti-American, radical anti-Jewish, and radical anti-Western prejudices.

Our lives depend upon doing so.

(1/13/15)

79 EVERYTHING HAS BEEN TURNED ON ITS HEAD

*L*ast night, I lectured at a synagogue in Westchester. Afterwards, a man came up "to shake my hand." He had asked me a question about Western survival, and I had answered him by paraphrasing my piece "What the West Must Do in Order to Survive." Then he told me:

> Our son was supposed to be at the finish line at the Boston Marathon. Luckily, something prevented him from going, but we spent the weeks afterwards calling up many of his Boston-area friends to see how they were. What will it take for Americans to wake up and to take jihad seriously? If 9/11 and Fort Hood and the Boston Marathon Bombing did not do it, I am afraid to think of what will.

A young college student told me: "If I say any of the things you have just said, my friends would call me crazy."

Said I: "So what? If you opt for popularity and conformity

you will never develop the strength to stand up to evil or to tell the truth. Remember: Evil always prevails when good people are afraid to stop it, lest they not only become pariahs but also lose their livelihoods and their lives."

I thought she was going to faint.

When I was asked something about President Obama, in passing, I said that "of course he is considered a Muslim by the Ummah. He is the son of a Muslim father and by definition this is all that counts. Obama might also be seen as an apostate because he embraced Christianity or at least attended a Black Nationalist Christian church in Chicago."

Again, some people heard me say something else, namely, that I think Obama is a *secret* Muslim and that this accounts for his pro-Islamic world policies and statements and his extraordinary "sensitivity" to Muslim feelings. Another college student said that if she said this to her friends they would say she was "crazy."

I said, "That's nothing. Wait until they call you a Zionist and start harassing you in your dorm."

What will it take for Westerners to wake up? A colleague who lives in Germany read my piece about Western survival and sent me the following email:

> Your suggestions about Europe have little chance of happening. Many don't (blame or) call it Islam. Many blame the Israeli conflict with Palestine as a major cause. Europe and its churches, intellectuals, etc., are more concerned about "islamophobia." Yesterday, 100,000 marched against islamophobia in Germany, but did not bother with the rally in central Berlin in September against anti-Semitism, despite the

fact that the rally was addressed by Merkel and President Gauck. They could only raise 4,000, mostly Jews, from all over Germany.

The political will and honesty are simply not there. Germans now see themselves as victims of Hitler, and Muslims also see themselves as victims. Palestinians are victims...Everything has been turned on its head.

One can see and hear "Jews to the gas" marchers in European streets. I don't think Europe can heal itself. It won't even define the problem correctly. In the meantime life goes on, with female slaves and 10-year-old girls in Nigeria used as suicide bombers by Muslim maniacs.

Yesterday, Chancellor Merkel proclaimed that "Islam is part of Germany." She said so at a Muslim rally that called for an even "more open and tolerant" Germany; the rally wanted to counter the anti-Islam protests that have recently taken place.

In France, many Muslim students would not comply with a moment of silence to honor the victims of the *Charlie Hebdo* massacre. (I must note that there was no moment of silence called for the Jewish victims in the kosher supermarket.) Instead, some students yelled out "Allahu Akbar." Others merely disrupted the silence. More importantly, at one school, 80% of the students refused to keep quiet and said that the *Charlie Hebdo* journalists deserved what they got. Students across France threatened teachers and confirmed their own desire to join ISIS; some said that they did not "understand" the need for honoring those who had dishonored the prophet Mohammed.

A French friend-of-a-friend, a Jewish-Catholic couple, wrote this:

We've both been pretty preoccupied with the heinous events of last week, especially the anti-Semitic aspect of all this. We're feeling like we need to be careful as to what we say and how we say it, because we will be labelled as racists. But we both have come to feel very anti-Islam. When you have so many terrorist acts, emanating from so many Muslim countries, then these people are no longer the exception. Of course I recognize that not all Muslims are anti-Semitic terrorists. But way too many are. We have a friend who is a public school teacher of 12-year-olds in Toulouse. The day after the first attack she discussed it with her class and her Muslim students defended the actions, saying the journalists deserved it because of their disrespect to Mohamed. Can you believe that?

Another French friend said this:

We were watching a French news panel last evening and there were two Muslim representatives. You should have heard what they said. They wonder why Jews are getting special treatment now, such as having police guard Jewish schools. Why don't Muslims get the same benefits, they questioned. And on it goes!

I'm not very optimistic about the future, certainly not here in Europe. I don't think any meaningful change will happen.

A college-era friend of mine in France wrote this:

One of our closest friends, Philippe HONORE

(a cartoonist) died in the first minutes. We are not only upset but even more ready to FIGHT! Yesterday, French Prime Minister, Manuel Valls, gave a passionate speech to the National Assembly in which he denounced the rise of anti-Semitism in France. Suddenly, he finds it unacceptable that the age-old chant "Death to the Jews" should be heard on the streets of France. He was careful to note that France is at war with "jihadism and terrorism...not against Islam and Muslims." Fifty three French people have been arrested for "anti-Semitism, hate speech, and glorifying terrorism."

I wonder: Will they keep them behind bars, deport them? What will France really do?

We do not know how many Europeans are really ready "to fight" or whether they can even prevail. No civilization can be destroyed entirely by external forces. The Western elites, intelligentsia, media, Western multi-cultural relativism, false narratives about Faux-istinians, and a general misuse of language, have all operated like a fifth column for at least sixty years.

Everyone believes that America and Europe are evil colonial and imperial powers—both racist and sexist. Israel is condemned as even more so. No one seems to understand the slightest thing about Muslim history in terms of its anti-black racism, conversion via the sword, hatred and persecution of the kuffar (infidel), its gender and religious apartheid, and its very long record of colonialism, imperialism, and genocide.

Anyone who points this out as a fact is immediately labelled an "Islamophobe," a racist, a conservative—a bloody

Zionist! Anyone who notes the surreal nature of Islamic barbarism operating today is also viewed suspiciously and nervously.

What will it take to turn this around before it is too late?

(1/15/15)

80 JIHAD BY CIVILIAN

*J*ihad has taken a new and ominous shape.
In the past, bombs were exploded—either human homicide bombs or car/truck bombs—rockets were launched. Unbelievably, planes were once flown into major Western targets.

Now, President Obama empowers the radical Islamic world further by refusing to join the words "terrorism" and "Islam" and by insisting that Islam is a religion of "peace." Obama continues to empower Iran to become a nuclear power and, most fatefully, empowers the recruitment efforts of the Islamic State.

He does so each time he refuses to say that the Free World or the Judeo-Christian West is at war with Islamic barbarism or with radical political Islam.

I once tried to monitor Palestinian and pro-Palestinian surging, potential lynch mobs in the Middle East, in Israel, and globally. The marches and demonstrations, both in the street and on campuses in the West, have become more aggressive, louder, more entitled over the years.

Now, the threat is a more individual one. Radicalized Islamist sleeper-cell individuals, or "lone wolf" jihadists, dressed in civilian clothing, are taking civilians hostage. They do not "look" like traditional soldiers—they dress like the people they hold hostage and like the people they massacre. We have seen this happen recently in Australia and in France.

Israel has long been used to this kind of challenge—that of facing warriors dressed as civilians who, in addition, hide behind innocent human shields; when they die in the combat which they began, the West counts them as "civilian" dead. The soldier disguised as a civilian, who is fighting a non-traditional war, is a phenomenon that the world at large has refused to understand as long as the victims are mainly Israelis.

Now, more ominously, individuals dressed as civilians are running their cars into crowds yelling "Allahu Akbar!"

They have butchered Jewish rabbis at prayer in West Jerusalem and, as of today, one individual jihadist has stabbed civilians on a bus and on the street. (Such wild stabbings have happened before in Israel.)

It is important to note that the attack took place in Tel Aviv, not in Hebron. As I have always said: The "settlement" that most offends the Arab world is Tel Aviv; the "settlement" that offends is a Jewish and Christian infidel presence in the Islamic world.

"Itbak al Yahud"—butcher or slaughter the Jew—is a very up close and barbaric method of homicide. We see the soldiers of the Islamic State beheading captives and broadcasting their gory deeds. This has attracted sociopaths, angry Muslims and angry people of color who have converted to Islam and who live in the West.

To the extent to which the Free World does not stop the

slaughter of the Jews, it will inevitably get to experience this form of "individualized" Jihad in their own countries.

(1/21/15)

81 PORTUGAL EXTENDS OLIVE BRANCH TO JEWS VIOLENTLY EXPELLED IN 1536

*P*ortugal, which expelled its Jews in 1536, is now poised to adopt a "return law" for the Jewish and non-Jewish descendants of Portugal's Sephardi Jews. This law was passed in 2013 and is expected to become "effective" by March 2015.

Portugal's Inquisition against the Jews—especially against those who had converted to Christianity—was brutal and long-lasting. Fiendish methods of torture were employed: racking, "relaxation," burning at the stake, rape, slave labor. All Jewish goods were confiscated. At least 40,000 Jews were tried, impoverished, tortured, murdered, or exiled.

Some Jews managed to flee. Some of these Jews had previously fled Spain during the Spanish Inquisition against the Jews and against Jewish converts to Christianity who were suspected of secretly practicing Judaism. A great hero—actually, a heroine—of the Jewish people, Dona Gracia Ha

Nasi (Beatrice de Luna Mendes), saved many of the Jews of Portugal.

Beatrice's family fled Spain in 1492 and was forcibly baptized in Portugal in 1497. Beatrice was born in 1510, and became enormously wealthy through marriage; in 1536, she fled Portugal for London, Antwerp, Venice, Ferrara, and finally to Constantinople. Dona Gracia funded the "underground" flight of Portuguese Jews, not only to Turkey but also to Salonika.

Victor Perera, a Guatemalan descendant of Portuguese Jews, has written a beautiful and painful family autobiography, *The Cross and The Pear Tree: A Sephardic Journey.* His ancestors fled Toledo, Spain, for Lisbon, Portugal, and thereafter went to Bordeaux and eventually to South America. Many converted; many remained "secretly Jewish."

Did Portugal rescue Jews during the European Holocaust?

It did, at least in a small way. According to *Sephardi Lives: A Documentary History, 1700-1950*, Portugal became

> a safe haven for thousands of Jewish refugees who arrived on temporary visas, making Lisbon one of the most important transit points for Jewish refugees fleeing Nazi-occupied Europe. Among those who sought refuge in Portugal were hundreds of Sephardi Jews who had been granted provisional Portuguese nationality in the first decades of the twentieth century due to their statue as "Oriental Jews of Portuguese Origin."

A single hero was responsible for this—bravely so, after France fell to Nazi German forces. His name was Aristides de Sousa Mendes, the Portuguese consul in Bordeaux. Against orders, he issued 2,862 visas between January 1 and June 22,

1940. For these "extraordinary humanitarian efforts, Sousa Mendes was sentenced, dismissed from office, and viciously condemned by Portuguese President Antonio de Oliveira Salazar."

In 1966 Israel's Yad Vashem recognized Sousa Mendes as Righteous Among the Nations.

Now, six centuries after Portugal first expelled its Jews, the country is ready to open its doors to the descendants of formerly Spanish-Portuguese Jews. This "law of return" has been described by its authors as "an act of atonement." Similar legislation is "underway in Spain, where it awaits a final vote in Congress."

This is ironic, pathetic, utterly tragic, rather late-in-the-day, generous, but potentially dangerous since this is being offered just as Europe's Jews are contemplating leaving Europe. Can Portugal be trusted? Are the *people* of Portugal and Spain pro-Jewish?

According to a 2013-2014 ADL Index, 56% of Portugal's 8,652,842 citizens believe that "Jews are more loyal to Israel than to the countries they live in;" 49% believe that "Jews still talk too much about what happened to them in the Holocaust;" 45% believe that "Jews have too much power in the business world;" and 43% believe that "Jews have too much power in international financial markets."

In other words, nearly 50% of Portugal's living citizens hold views that may be termed "anti-Semitic."

I hope that the descendants of Portugal's original Jews decide very carefully and wisely about whether or not to return to Portugal. Like France, Portugal may realize that *it* needs its Jews but do the Jews need Portugal?

(1/23/15)

82 NEW YORK TIMES LETHAL ANTI-ISRAEL JOURNALISM STRIKES AGAIN

*L*ike the White House, the *New York Times* is guilty of defamation and potentially of incitement to genocide; certainly, they are guilty of slanting the news about Israel in every way possible.

This time, the Paper of Propaganda, has published a 1,250 word piece that takes up three columns on page A4 and another three columns on page A9—and is accompanied by four photos as well.

Even as the Muslim and Arab worlds are on fire; even as Syria has displaced three million refugees; even as Islamic Sunni terrorists have massacred other Muslims, and have tortured Yazidi women and girls; even as Muslim terrorists are massacring civilians in the West—Jodi Rudoren has chosen to feature, in a high-profile way, the regrets of a handful of IDF soldiers who fought in the 1967 war of self-defense. Some claim they have been "censored" and that the "abuses" they committed have haunted them ever since.

Even as Muslim terrorists are beheading civilians and crucifying Christians, Rudoren quotes one Israeli soldier, who, "fresh from the [1967] front, bluntly recounts the orders from above. 'They never said, 'Leave no one alive,' but they said, 'Show no mercy,'" he explains. 'The brigade commander said to kill as many as possible.'" She quotes another: "All of us…we're not murderers. In the war, we all became murderers."

Rudoren has chosen this moment in history to review a new film by a young, Left filmmaker, Mor Loushy, titled *Censored Voice*. It has just premiered at the Sundance Film Festival.

The film echoes the political views of the Israeli and American Left: The soldiers feared that after 1967 the "Arab hatred towards us will be much more serious and profound." One soldier, possibly traumatized by battle in 1967, "likened [the IDF actions] to the Nazi treatment of European Jews."

That soldier did not know his history and Rudoren's piece is only based upon what only a few Israeli soldiers have to say about a war fought in self-defense against soldiers from *seven* Arab countries nearly 50 years ago.

I am reminded of how reverential an Upper West Side crowd was towards another Israeli leftist film, *The Gatekeepers*. This 2013 film had former Shin Bet directors on record regretting Israeli policy. Interestingly, four of these six former directors were the men who had gone on record castigating Sharon's "settlement" policy. Sharon caved and pulled out of Gaza, which resulted in Hamastan next door.

Both films (I have not seen the Loushy film) seem to be holding Israel to the highest standards of moral purity—and failing to hold the barbarians to any standard at all.

I agree with Yossi Klein Halevi, the lone sane voice whom

Rudoren quotes. Halevi wrote a book about the Six Day War: *Like Dreamers: The Story of the Israeli Paratroopers Who Reunited Jerusalem and Divided a Nation.* He says: "People abroad who don't remember the way we do the circumstances of the Six-Day War will turn this into one more indictment of Israel. If there were isolated acts of abuse by our soldiers, that should not become the narrative about what the Six-Day War was about. Many of us here are, frankly, sick and tired of the blame-Israel-first narrative."

(1/26/15)

83 FRANCE IMPLORES JEWS NOT TO LEAVE, OFFERS MILITARY PROTECTION

*E*arlier this week, before leaving for Auschwitz to commemorate the 70th anniversary of the Soviet liberation of the Nazi German extermination camp, President Francois Hollande appealed to French Jews, saying that "You, French people of the Jewish faith, France is your country, your place is here, in your home."

Earlier in January, in an interview in *The Atlantic*, French Prime Minister Manuel Valls said that "If 100,000 people of Spanish origin were to leave, I would never say that France is not France anymore. But if 100,000 Jews leave, France will no longer be France. The French Republic will be judged a failure."

What have we here? Is the country of Dreyfus—the country of Vichy and Drancy, Nobel Peace Prize winner Yasser Arafat's home away from home, the country in which "Death to the Jews" has been yelled by mobs in the 19th, 20th, and 21st centuries—actually waking up?

As my colleague Dr. Richard Landes has noted recently, in the *Los Angeles Review of Books*, somewhat bitterly: These very vocal French leaders and the French media have been missing in action for the last fourteen years when French Jewish-only blood was spilled: In Marseilles, Toulouse, and Paris. Anyone who cried out "anti-Semitism" or Intifada was considered an alarmist and an annoyance. Philippe Karsenty was sued by France's Channel 2 for his righteous challenge regarding its broadcast of the Al-Dura Blood Libel.

Honorable Monsieurs: A French (and European) Intifada against the Jews has been raging, not only in Israel but in Europe (especially in France), from the autumn of the 21st century. Did you really think your non-Jews would be spared?

France may have reaped a whirlwind of its own making as an oil-hungry nation who, under De Gaulle, got the oil breaks only if they welcomed Muslim immigrants, their families, and their "customs."

Europe did not want to do the hard work of vetting, deporting, or educating those Muslim immigrants who envied, feared, despised, and were intolerant toward the entire Western Enterprise. Instead, it adopted a policy of "multi-cultural relativism," which allowed such immigrants to create rural mini Algerias, Turkeys, Iraqs, Afghanistans, and Pakistans right in the heart of Europe. This was supposed to prove that an unredeemed Europe was anti-racist.

Tell that to the Muslim girls and women who were and are still are being forcibly married and veiled against their will—or honor killed for resisting.

France, Holland, Germany, England, Italy, and Scandinavia refused to understand that such immigrant workers would have to be carefully assimilated or they might very well form parallel, potentially hostile, anti-Western communities—which they proceeded to do. No one foresaw that second and third generation Muslim immigrants might become radicalized and turn to jihad both abroad and at home in Europe.

French author Jean Raspail envisioned all this. In 1973, Raspail published an extraordinary and prescient novel, *The Camp of the Saints*, in which he imagined a flotilla of millions of brown-skinned immigrants traveling from the Ganges to France. An all-powerful, multi-culturally correct intelligentsia that has taught Europe that it must atone for its racist, colonial guilt welcomes the invasion. France (European culture) is destroyed. The novel is raw, thrilling, overwhelming, ironic, cruel, bitter, and every bit as brilliant as George Orwell's *1984*. At first, Raspail was attacked as a racist. Within a decade, European government leaders were all reading his work. Now what Raspail feared has seemingly come to pass.

Oriana Fallaci also called this out early in the 21st century—and was condemned as a racist, sued by a convert to Islam in Italy for "blasphemy," put on trial in Paris for "inciting racial hatred in a book which has denigrating passages about Islam," and finally forced to flee Europe only to spend her last years, quite ill, away from her beloved Italy.

In a long piece at *The Atlantic*, Shadi Hamid, a Fellow of the Project on U.S. Relations with the Islamic World at the Brookings Institution (and a former and perhaps current member of the Muslim Brotherhood), has just suggested the unthinkable. Paraphrasing Yale political theorist Andrew March, Hamid writes that it does not take too much "moral courage" to announce that one is "against the killing of apostates, mutilating genitals, and kidnapping schoolgirls." Wait for it. Hamid writes, "What presumably would take more courage, at least in France, is for a major political party to call for a rethinking of *laïcité*, and for broadening, rather than narrowing, French national identity."

Polygamy, child brides, the burqa, and the stoning of apostates and adulteresses—here it comes.

Over the years, I have suggested that Europe may have reaped a terrible, karmic destiny: It slaughtered the non-violent, highly assimilated Semites (the Jews), and in return has gotten our violent, Semitic cousins from North Africa, the Arab Middle East, and from central and southeast Asia. Europe continued their own anti-Semitism by siding with the Arab Street/the Intifada against the Jews; they also hoped that their pro-Palestinian and anti-Zionist views would spare them a general anti-infidel Intifada in Europe.

Only because non-Jews (*Charlie Hebdo* journalists and cartoonists) were massacred for what they *did*, has France noticed that four French Jews were, in a connected action, massacred for who they *are*.

There are currently 475,000 – 550,000 Jews living in France. Between 1948 and 2013, 81,885 left France, most often to Israel. Between January and August of 2014, nearly 5,000 French Jews left for Israel.

An American-Israeli friend tells me that "One can walk in Tel Aviv, not just in Netanya, and hear only French being spoken.

A French-Jewish man said, "Why should I have to leave France? It is my country. Let the trouble-makers leave."

A French-Christian man who was close friends with one of the *Charlie Hebdo* victims told me: "We are all equal citizens of France and of the world and I am sad to see thousands of Jews leave. What's important is what we DO now, how we get the bastards who did this. The situation is tough for all of us here. The jihadists are OUR enemy too."

I am not sure that wealthy French Jews will willingly leave comfortable lives for an impoverished or uncertain future in Israel. Many wealthy German Jews lingered until it was too late to get out. Prime Minister Netanyahu is to be congratulated, not condemned, for welcoming French Jews "to the land of (their) forefathers." Neither should Netanyahu be condemned for his willingness to speak to Congress about Israeli security, the Israel-American alliance, and the extraordinary danger of a nuclear Iran.

All of us—civilians, citizens of the world, Christians, Jews, Muslims, Hindus, Buddhists, atheists—all share this danger.

(1/28/15)

84 OBAMA'S BOYS CAMPAIGN FROM TEL AVIV – TED CRUZ RESPONDS

*T*he White House is "dismayed," "displeased," and "angry" over Prime Minister Netanyahu's upcoming address to Congress.

The White House's "Dismay over Netanyahu Visit Extends to (Israeli) Ambassador." This is the title of a January 29th piece in the *New York Times*. Accepting Speaker Boehner's invitation is seen as proof of "a further decay in relations between Republicans and the White House;" the White House has called the (Republican Congressional) invitation "a breach of diplomatic protocol," and has announced that President Obama will not meet with PM Netanyahu as a "matter of policy": The White House does not meet with world leaders close to their election so as not to interfere in a foreign election.

Although you will probably not read about this in the mass media (the *New York Times*, etc.), Obama's 2012 campaign field director was selected to head a "five man Obama team" to run a campaign, Chicago-style, Alinsky-style, Obama-style, on the ground, in Israel. Grassroots, young people are already urging others to drink the Kool-Aid of "change," and are looking for more and more volunteers to go from apartment to apartment.

This Obama-initiated campaign has been reported by *Breitbart, Bizpac Review, PJ Media, Truth Revolt,* and *Haaretz* (but only in Hebrew, not in their English edition). The estimable Caroline Glick pointed this out in a tweet and *Independent Media Review and Analysis* translated it into English. Glick is quoted by Thomas Rose in *Breitbart*:

> Obama won't meet Benjamin Netanyahu in Washington when he addresses the Joint House of Congress in March because of Netanyahu's visit's proximity to the Israeli elections. And Obama, of course, believes in protocol and propriety which is why he won't get involved. He is just sending his 2012 field campaign manager to Israel to run a campaign to defeat Netanyahu.

No interference at all.

Journalist Roi Arad, in *Haaretz,* happily announced that the foreign funded organization "One Voice" is bankrolling the V15 campaign to defeat Binyamin Netanyahu in the 2015 elections. Jeremy Bird, the Obama campaign's national field director is running this campaign from an office in Tel Aviv that takes up the entire ground floor of the building. V15 is not supporting a specific party. They are for anyone, "just not Bibi." Therefore, the foreign funding pouring into the campaign may not be subjected to Israel's campaign finance laws.

Obama may not know anything about the economy, foreign policy, military strategy, health care, or universal human rights, but, as *BizPac* painfully points out, "if Obama has a singular talent, it's this: He knows what it takes to win an election."

Imagine what this means: Obama is trying to unseat a democratically elected President of America's most stable and militarily prepared ally in the Middle East.

Today's *New York Times* describes Israeli Ambassador, Ron Dermer, as "a political operative, not really an Ambassador." This is what Daniel Kurtzer, a former American Ambassador to Israel says—and Kurtzer goes even further. He would not be surprised if Dermer were to be declared "persona non grata" or at least "reprimanded or removed."

And why? Because he is thought to have engineered House Speaker John A. Boehner's invitation to Netanyahu to address Congress about many things, especially that of Iranian nuclear power.

Obama wants to give Iran all the time it may need to develop nuclear power by refusing to strengthen sanctions and by delaying crucial deadlines. He does not want Americans to hear any other view at this time.

Today, U.S. Senator Ted Cruz, R-Texas, and Congressman Lee Zeldin, R-NY-1, sent a letter to Secretary of State John Kerry asking for information regarding media reports that U.S. taxpayer dollars are being used to fund efforts to influence upcoming elections in Israel.

The partial text of the letter is below.

January 29, 2015
Dear Mr. Secretary:

We write to express strong concerns over the

recent media reports that a U.S. taxpayer funded 501(c) non-profit organization called OneVoice is actively working with a campaign operation called V15 or "Victory 2015" in an effort to influence the outcome of the elections in Israel on March 17, 2015.

On January 26, 2015, the Israeli newspaper *Haaretz* reported on the close coordination between these two entities. The reporter described his visit to the campaign operation in Tel Aviv, Israel, and the significant role Jeremy Bird, President Obama's former deputy national field director (2008) and national field director (2012), is playing with V15.

V15 organizers instead of calling the operation "Anyone but Bibi," merely phrase it slightly differently: "We say 'replace the government,' it's not directed at specific individuals. There have been many years of right-wing governments during which little happened, it's time to change course and give people hope... We will go to homes and we will win...The work with the research team that Bird brought has really ignited sparks..."

Given the public statements by a number of Obama administration officials, including the President, that it would be "inappropriate" for the government of the United States to exercise any influence over elections in a foreign country including Israel, we believe this issue demands your urgent attention. There appears to be a danger that U.S. taxpayer funds are being used to directly shape the outcome of the upcoming Israeli election—and specifically to campaign against Prime Minister Netanyahu—something all would agree would be highly inappropriate.

We request a thorough investigation by the State Department's Inspector General within the next 15 days.

Sincerely,
Sen. Ted Cruz and Rep. Lee Zeldin
Members of Congress

(1/30/15)

85 SADISTIC DEATH PORNOGRAPHY COMING TO A THEATER NEAR YOU

This is a year of sadistic death pornography. For the last eight months, the death artists of ISIS have enslaved women and children, beheaded Western journalists, tossed gay men out of buildings, and burned Muslims and infidels alive. These gruesome deeds were faithfully, lovingly, preserved via video and released to the world.

The West, and civilized people everywhere, seem unprepared, even shocked, by all this. But why?

The entire 21st century has been characterized by an alarming and exponential rise in anti-Semitism, the beheading of Western journalists, planes being flown into buildings, ships and trains being blown up, Embassies being torched, hotels being taken hostage, children being kidnapped into slavery or used as human shields; there has been a rise in genocides, massacres, grisly crucifixions, human homicide bombs—and all the perpetrators have been Muslims who insisted that they were engaged in holy jihad against an infidel world (or against the wrong kind of Muslim) whose values are anti-Islamic.

King Abdullah of Jordan, like President Obama, insists that ISIS has nothing to do with Islam; that they are a criminal gang of psychopaths. I am sure they are, but they are being empowered by what they view as a religious mandate.

Some say that European Nazis did not represent the values of post-Enlightenment Europe and that Stalin did not represent the values of Marxism.

Whatever the case, the fact that so many good people failed to stop them at the outset condemned hundreds of millions of innocent people to brutal, untimely deaths.

This can happen again. It *is* happening again.

People can feel it in their bones. There are so many Hollywood movies set in a post-nuclear Holocaust future; usually, there are a handful of survivors amidst bleak and smoking ruins.

Whoever and whatever these masked men of ISIS are—religious zealots, psychopaths, demagogues, barbarians, death-eaters—they must be defeated, definitively, and starting now.

President Obama, the so-called head of the free world will not do it.

The atrocities of ISIS, meant to shock (and shock they do), are only a diversion from and a prelude to what can happen once an equally barbaric Iran obtains nuclear power—apparently, something that President Obama welcomes.

Once again, Jewish Israel is at the center of this storm. The survival of the entire world may depend upon whether Prime Minister Netanyahu can persuade the American people to stop their President who is counting on a fully nuclear Iran to stabilize central Asia and the Arab Middle East.

He has kept most of his negotiations hidden and out of sight. Please read Michael Doran's piece about *Obama's Secret Iran Strategy*.

May God be with Prime Minister Netanyahu and with us all as this world spins ever more wildly out of control.

(2/4/15)

86 NETANYAHU'S SPEECH UNITES CONGRESS—AND DIMINISHES OBAMA

*P*rime Minister Benjamin Netanyahu delivered a passionate, inspiring, thoughtful, and "game changing" speech before the American Congress which lasted for about 45 minutes, during which time he was applauded 43 times, often for 15 seconds at a time. His words elicited many standing ovations.

The only other foreign leader to have spoken to Congress three times was Winston Churchill, the British Prime Minister. In honor of that, Speaker of the House, John Boehner plans to present Netanyahu with a bust of Churchill.

Netanyahu received wild applause when he said: "The world should demand that Iran do three things. First, stop its aggression against its neighbors in the Middle East. Second, stop supporting terrorism around the world. And third, stop threatening to annihilate my country, Israel, the one and only Jewish state."

Israel's Prime Minister again received rather thunderous applause and a standing ovation when he noted that Holocaust survivor Elie Wiesel was in the audience—and when he said: "My friend, standing up to Iran is not easy. Standing up to dark and murderous regimes never is. Elie, your life and work inspires to give meaning to the words, 'never again!' And I wish I could promise you, Elie, that the lessons of history have been learned. I can only urge the leaders of the world not to repeat the mistakes of the past."

At this point Congress outdid itself in term of applause and a standing ovation.

PM Netanyahu was greeted with a thunderous ovation when he first arrived and again after he was introduced. He recognized Senate Democratic leader Harry Reid, who had suffered an exercise-related accident. Netanyahu said "You can't keep a good man down." He carefully and jovially greeted both Democrats and Republicans.

The House was packed. The absence of all those who chose to stay away was barely noticed. In fact, the demand for seats in the gallery were overwhelming.

PM Netanyahu praised America's support for Israel, including President Obama's support, both in terms of military aid and the Iron Dome. He referred to aid that cannot be discussed.

"Thank you America for everything you have done for Israel."

And then, Netanyahu brought in the upcoming Jewish holiday of Purim, which begins tomorrow night, and which commemorates a time long ago when another Persian state wanted to annihilate the Jews.

"Again, another Persian potentate wants to destroy us. Khamenei tweets in English that Israel must be destroyed."

But Netanyahu understands that the threat is bigger than one leveled only against the Jews. Iran threatens the entire Middle East, America, and the world as it gobbles up country after country. He reminded the assembled that Iran's leaders and their Revolutionary Guard cry "Death to America;" that "Iran and ISIS are competing for the crown of militant Islam;" that "both want to impose a militant Islamic empire." "In this deadly game of thrones there is no place for America or Israel, no peace for Christians, Jews, or Muslims who don't share the Islamist medieval creed, no rights for women, no freedom for anyone."

"When it comes to Iran and ISIS the enemy of your enemy—is your enemy!"

Netanyahu explained that the deal President Obama was working on will only pave the way to a nuclear Iran, that it will never stop it. This "bad deal" will guarantee that Iran develops nuclear weapons."

It was clear that the Senators and Congressmen who were listening to Netanyahu's speech agreed with every word he said.

In my opinion, PM Netanyahu won the moment and President Obama's absence and hostile attempts to minimize or demonize Netanyahu's upcoming speech as "partisan" failed.

We must contrast Netanyahu's graciousness and respectful tone toward Obama with Obama's peevish, hostile, and petty nastiness towards Netanyahu. Clearly, Netanyahu, not Obama, is the world-class statesman.

Bravo Bibi!

(3/3/15)